ALL THE VERY BEST!

ALL THE VERY BEST!

THE AUTOBIOGRAPHY

Vin Garbutt

mcgeary media

Published by McGeary Media
www.mcgearymedia.co.uk
07967 023083

Cover photo by Kev Howard

Cover design by Lovell Graphic Design

Layout by Kinship

ACKNOWLEDGEMENTS

Vin and Pat with Michael and Lyndsey McGeary

I was eight years old when I first heard Vin sing. One of my older sisters had brought home a copy of his first live LP, *The Young Tin Whistle Pest.* My siblings and I listened to it so often as we grew up that we could recite every word of the stories and patter between the songs, in the way other kids reeled off Monty Python sketches. Punchlines such as, 'To cut a long story short, they hung him...' and 'He'd only sent her out for a loaf!' remained part of our family folklore long after we had forgotten the rest of the tale!

I became a confirmed fan as I grew older and saw Vin live whenever I could. I once hitch-hiked back from university to see Vin play at the Albert pub in Middlesbrough. It was sold out but Pat kindly let us in when I told her how far we'd come. My younger sister asked Vin to sing our favourite song.

'The requests are coming in thick and fast,' he said. 'And that's the thickest one yet!'

I wrote so many stories about Vin during my time as an *Evening Gazette* reporter that one colleague dubbed me the paper's 'Vin Garbutt correspondent'.

When I left my job and decided to go it alone as a ghostwriter, my first port of call was the Garbutts' home in Hummersea, where I outlined my idea for a book about Vin's life. Fortunately, Vin and Pat loved the idea, and I had the pleasure of working closely with one of my musical heroes for four very special years.

I sent the first draft of the book to Vin on Sunday June 4 2017, but sadly, he never saw the email. I hope Vin would be proud of the result of our efforts.

My thanks go to writer and Vin fan Paul Vallely, who very kindly read the first draft and offered helpful feedback. Thanks also to Vin's film biographer Craig Hornby, for his expertise and guidance, to my friend and proof-reader, Danny Skipper, and my sisters, Mary Lombard, for offering many helpful suggestions, and Anne McGeary Carvell, for her skilful editing and meticulous attention to detail. Thank you to Dom Finn, for permission to use extracts from her interview with Vin. Thanks also to my wife, Lyndsey, for her patience and support. A special thank you to Vin's fans, who contributed photos and memories that were included in the book, as well as those we couldn't fit in. Finally, thanks so much to Pat and Vin's family for their invaluable input and for so generously sharing their beloved husband, father and brother with the rest of us.

Michael McGeary

FOREWORD

By Pat Garbutt

Vin was so enthusiastic about this project. It really appealed to him to have a record of the extraordinary experiences he had during his lifetime. He lived to walk out onto the stage and give his all to a bunch of music-loving strangers. His journeys from his front door to the stage door were often weird and wonderful and long – oh, so long! He travelled by public transport, a tough choice but a great way to meet people. They inspired him, cared for him and supported his career.

Vin often vocalised that he had, 'the best job in the world' and that job took him all over the globe. It's all here from start to finish. The highs and lows of carving out a career that in the beginning could not have appeared more unlikely or hazardous.

In his writing, I get a sense of disbelief that it all actually happened and that he achieved so much. But he did, he reached the top, and everybody loved him.

He was unique, an absolute one-off and we were all so lucky to have had Vin in our lives whether it was for five minutes or, like me, forty-eight years.

'For a human character to reveal truly exceptional qualities, one must have the good fortune to be able to observe its performance over many years. If this performance is devoid of all egoism, if its guiding motive is unparalleled generosity, if ... it has left its visible mark upon the earth, then there can be no mistake.'

Jean Giono, *The Man Who Planted Trees*

CONTENTS

VIN: A TRIBUTE

By Paddy McEvoy

Delivered as part of the celebration of Vin's life at St Mary's Cathedral, Middlesbrough, June 16 2017

Our dear friend Vin Garbutt was Slaggy Island put to music
Vin was the open-throated blast of the East Wind
Vin was the guttural vernacular of South Bank
Vin was the beating heart of Roseberry Topping
Vin was a leaping salmon of knowledge in a clear, crystal Tees
Vin was a lightning conductor, ever-raging against man's inhumanity to man
Vin the Healer, the one-to-one communicator, was a practitioner in the art of soul-to-soul resuscitation
Vin was the thrilling, trilling, whistling, soaring notes of the lark, who has now saluted the sky, whistle in hand
Vin was an instrument chosen by the gods as their mouthpiece
Vin sang his heart out, that great heart that beat out the rhythms of our time
Vin's light-hearted gravitas helped us laugh through our tears
Vin, the Teesside Troubadour, the Bard of Eston, the jingle-jangle minstrel, the pied piper of the Raphael curls, led his global entourage to a good place
Vin has left us, somewhere on the road to Youghal, with a smile in our grieving hearts
Vin was the unvarnished visionary voice of the vulnerable and the voiceless
Vin's belly laugh is now cheering up a downcast deity

Vin was a life force who lightened the load of all those whose lives he touched
Vin, the Tommy Cooper of the folk world, made us laugh, and marvel at how a gift of such consummate professionalism could be wrapped up in such a parcel of eejitry. Just… like that.

Vin's life stood four-square on the foundations of his love for his adored wife Pat, who was the scaffolding around his existence, and of his beloved children and grandchildren; of his deep and sincere faith, which inspired his passion for justice of all kinds, both the human and the environmental; of his ardent love for music and language; and the fact that everything he took on board was grist to his creative mill.

Vin Garbutt, old friend, legend who has now entered the pantheon, storyteller, songsmith, *seanchai*, raconteur of the innocently hilarious, raised us up with his absurd patter and then put us down again in a more enlightened place, shedding tears of joy at our predicament.

He was the maestro of the high-wire, corny, belaboured, clunking pun – Norman Wisdom, Hamish the Tambourine man; But come ye back...; Tuaregs; Parbold eggs; Buttermere toast; and top of the list... Rudyard Kipling… As Vin's old friend Pete Betts would have put it, 'They won't make 'em like Vin any more.'

But our dear friend has stepped off life's carousel a few stops too early, in mid-jest, leaving us groping for the punchline...

Farewell Vincent, dear friend
May your valiant, noble soul be at God's right hand.

Slan leat a Uinseann a chara dhil
Ar dheislamh De go raibh do anam croga uasal.

'Love can be said in a word, but there should be no doubt of it in your actions.'

Vin Garbutt

I've got the best job in the world – and I just fell into it. I left my secure employment at ICI in 1969 to go busking in Spain and I've been paid to travel the world and sing to people ever since. I haven't worked with cut-throat, showbiz types only doing it for the money. No, I've been lucky enough to work with fantastic people who for the most part run folk clubs as a hobby and who throw open their doors and welcome me into their homes. It's been a tremendous privilege and I consider myself incredibly fortunate. This is the story of my life…

Vin sitting up in his pram

Young Vin with his dad, on holiday at Stanghow

Vin is second from the left in this seaside snap

BUCKETS OF LOVE

'When I was young, in your streets I did laugh and play
In Coral, Connaught, Pearl Street too;
Your walls protected me from the wind and the rain.'

Vin Garbutt, *Slaggy Island Farewell*

I was born in a bucket. Like most Middlesbrough houses just after the war, our toilet in Coral Street, South Bank, was outside at the end of the yard. Mam popped out to the loo and went into labour while she was down there. Dad heard the screams and rushed out to fetch the midwife. That was his story, anyway – I've always had a sneaking feeling he was just getting out of the way. When I dropped with a thud into the white enamel pail, Mam thought that was the end of me.

'Me baby! I've killed me baby!' she wailed.

I was unscathed, to the best of my knowledge, although some people would say I've never been quite the full shilling. It was November 20th 1947. None of the neighbours heard the commotion at number eighteen because they were all glued to the radio, listening to Princess Elizabeth's wedding to Prince Philip at Westminster Abbey. While the rest of the nation followed the future Queen's progress up the aisle, there I was being dumped unceremoniously into a bucket.

Why Mam chose the name Vincent for me I'm not sure, but just before my baptism at St Peter's Roman Catholic Church in South Bank, my Nanna Kelly said it was only half a name.

'You can't have Vincent without Paul,' she said.

So I was named Vincent Paul Garbutt, after St Vincent de Paul, the French priest who went into the Church because he thought it would provide a cosy living and ended up dedicating his life to serving the poor. Whether Dad had any say in it I was never told, although being a Methodist he was fairly easy-going and probably just let the in-laws get on with it. Dad's siblings all had traditional English names like Alfred, Ena, Florence, Constance, Beatrice and William. But the names in Mam's family reflected their Irish Catholic ancestry – Michael, John, James, Bernard, who was known as Uncle Barney, and Mary.

Vin's parents, Alf and Tess, pictured in 1993

Vin and his mam in 2007

When I was old enough I went to York Street Nursery School, which was in the shadow of the works and a fine place for delicate little lungs to be drawing their early breaths. Every afternoon we all had a nap on bunk beds – at least us kids did anyway, I've no idea what the staff got up to. One afternoon I lay in the bed needing a wee and didn't dare tell anyone. To this day I can remember the warm, wet feeling of relief running down my legs when I gave in and let go.

Despite my unpromising start in life I enjoyed a wonderful childhood. We had a loving family and although we weren't well off, we never wanted for anything. I was the third of four children – there's Michael, Mary, me, and then a nine-year gap to the youngest, our Ellen. Mam didn't go out to work, she had enough on her plate looking after us kids and the house. Dad was an electrician's mate at the sprawling Dorman Long steelworks that was partly responsible for the plumes of smoke that trailed across the South Bank sky, day and night. He was one of life's gentlemen. My earliest memory is of him waking up at the crack of dawn and traipsing sleepily down the stairs before his six-till-two shift, with me following after him. Then he'd give me a slice of what he called 'cakey'. It was just ordinary thick, white bread cut from a proper loaf and smeared with real butter, but it was delicious. The memory is so evocative that even now when I eat bread and butter it brings warm memories flooding back of standing on the doorstep with a slice of cakey in my hand, seeing Dad off to work.

As I was growing from a toddler into a little boy, King George VI was becoming older and more infirm. I don't recall hearing about his death in the winter of 1952, but I do remember Queen Elizabeth II's Coronation the following summer, when I was only four years old. Every street in South Bank held a party, with red, white and blue bunting draped between the houses and trestle tables in the middle of the roads. There was a festive atmosphere and we all wore fancy dress. I put on my little cowboy suit and felt like Roy Rogers, the King of the Cowboys. We all won first prize because it was such a special occasion and all the grown-ups were feeling generous.

I remember the day our Ellen was born. It was February 19th 1956 and there was thick snow on the ground. I was playing out on a sledge Dad had made for us, when my cousin Tessie Dales came walking towards me down the street.

'You've got a new baby sister,' she said.

I heard the words but didn't take in what they meant, so I stayed out playing in the snow until it was time for bed.

South Bank was dead friendly in those days. It was nicknamed Slaggy Island because of the slag tips all around, big piles of waste from the iron industry. The nickname gave me the title for one of my early songs. Nobody had cars, of course, and there was hardly any traffic of any kind. At least once a week a man came round with a horse and cart and we rode around the streets for the fare of a few small coins. My Uncle Ray owned a greengrocer's shop and I loved tagging along with him to the fruit and veg warehouse in his lorry and helping carry a few carrots and beetroots into the shop while he lugged the big sacks of spuds in.

Each street had its own bonfire on Guy Fawkes Night. Ours was on Middlesbrough Road, where a bombed-out house made the perfect site. Our gang went 'bommie raiding' to pinch the materials other gangs had gathered together ready for the big night. We weren't the best fighters, so we made up for it by being sneaky and making sure we weren't caught. We'd return triumphantly carrying a few stolen branches or sticks of old furniture, whistling *Colonel Bogey's March* together like a little ragtag army on their way to war.

We sometimes had family holidays in Scarborough or Blackpool but my warmest memories are the times we stayed at Dad's mate's wooden chalet at Stanghow, out on the Moor Road. Although it was only a few miles away it was the countryside to us South Bank kids and even now when I smell cows and rabbits, I'm back there again in my mind. I would never have believed that I would one day buy a house nearby and live in it for over thirty years. It must have been a tight squeeze inside that chalet because as well as the six of us, Uncle Ray and Aunty Mary came with their kids. I can still picture us climbing out of the windows in the evenings when we were supposed to be in bed. In the daytime we roamed free-range on the moors collecting frogs or bilberries, with no adults to tell us what we should and shouldn't do.

There was huge excitement every summer when Crows Fair came to the common at the end of our road. One year I fell in love with the girl on the hot dog stand. Life could have been so different if she'd accepted my advances and let me run away with her. I could have had my ear pierced and spun people round on the waltzers for the rest of my days. Instead I had to wait until I was nine years old to leave South Bank behind.

First we moved just a few hundred yards away to Spencer Road in Teesville East and then later to Ambrose Road, a mile away on the Normanby side of Eston. I'm not saying we're parochial on Teesside but there was a big stone road sign at Crossbeck Convent that marked the border between Normanby and Eston. The different distances marked on the front and back suggested it was half a mile from one side of the stone to the other!

Mike and Mary went to St Peter's Infants and Juniors, but just before I started school St James' Juniors opened on the corner of the Trunk Road and Normanby Road. I

The Garbutt family together in 1986 – Mike, Alf, Ellen, Tess, Vin and Mary

went there until I sat the eleven-plus – and failed it miserably. Nearly everyone else passed. The headteacher, Sister Mary Dennis, whacked them through it. She was a tiny nun who slid along the corridors in little shuffling steps but could move surprisingly quickly when she wanted to. In fact she was faster than a real penguin. She had a lovely smile, although you wouldn't know that if you went to my school. It was only years later when she came to our house visiting Mam that I saw it for the first time. We kids hated her because she whacked us and I still have a scar on my forefinger as a memento of one beating she gave me with a stick. But Mam loved her and said she had a heart of gold.

Even Sister Mary Dennis's whackings couldn't help me, though. I was always a little bit slow with my thought processes anyway, but any hope I had of passing disappeared on the exam day when the ink from my old-fashioned fountain pen leaked. I still remember one of the few questions I got right – 'What is the shaven patch on the top of a monk's head called?' I knew that one and enthusiastically scribbled down 'tonsure'. No sooner was the word on the paper than I was staring in horror at the blue ink flooding indiscriminately over that and all my other answers, right and wrong alike. I gave in and accepted my fate after that.

Failing the eleven-plus wasn't such a disaster. All my life I'd walked everywhere I needed to be – to school, church and the doctors – and I was daunted by the prospect of travelling all the way to St Mary's College in Middlesbrough every day. The very thought of being that far from home was terrifying. I don't suppose Mam and Dad expected any of us to pass the eleven-plus anyway. That was something doctors' and teachers' kids did. So off I went instead to St Peter's Senior School in South Bank, where

Middlesbrough Football Club's greatest ever player, the Golden Boy, Wilf Mannion, had been a pupil twenty-five years earlier.

Pete Betts, who later became my big mate, was always getting into scraps and our Mike paid him a couple of bob to thump me and try to toughen me up. Mike was what I'd call a 'nark', always teasing everyone. He gave our Mary a hard time, narking her so much that she'd try to scratch and kick him. He just laughed while she was going berserk, which only infuriated her more.

I didn't escape Mike's teasing either. Once he was after me for some reason and chased me all over the house. I managed to give him the slip and scarpered upstairs, taking two glass milk bottles with me. I filled the bottles with water and went to the toilet for a wee, leaving the door just slightly ajar. I heard him sneaking upstairs to get me and when I finished weeing I poured the first bottle slowly down the toilet to make him think I was still going strong. When that was empty, I started pouring the second one out. At that point Mike pushed the door open with an amazed look on his face, in awe of my seemingly bottomless bladder. We both fell about laughing and I narrowly avoided a beating. Maybe that was when I first learned that making people laugh could be useful.

Now and again I got my own back on our Mike. When I was fifteen I found a baby rook in the woods. Instead of leaving it there as I should have, I christened him Fagin and brought him home to keep as a pet. He sat on my right shoulder and would fly up and perch himself on the aerials of the houses in our street. He became a local celebrity and the neighbours all called him by his name. One night Mike brought his first girlfriend home. Mam was out, so I sneaked Fagin into the house and let him have the run of the place. To Mike's eternal embarrassment Fagin pooed all over the settee, right there in front of his young love. The girl can't have been too shocked, mind. She still married him. But Fagin couldn't forgive himself. Shortly afterwards he spread his wings and flew off to join the thousands of other rooks living in the trees outside Crossbeck Convent. I suppose Fagin was never mine to own, after all.

The Mystics

The Mystics with Kathy Kirby on the night they played on the same bill in South Bank – Vin is second from the right

MY MUSICAL AWAKENING

'Love, share and practice folk music.'

Vin Garbutt

Like everyone else growing up in the 1960s, I listened to mainstream pop bands including The Beatles, The Hollies and The Rolling Stones. I forgave Pete Betts for all those childhood fights and we formed a pop group together called The Mystics. We played gigs all over Teesside and even supported Kathy Kirby, then the highest-paid female singer in the country, at the Oak Leaf in South Bank. I sang and played rhythm guitar and we did all the popular chart hits of the day and enjoyed every minute of it.

By this time I'd also started singing in some of the numerous folk clubs that sprang up all over Teesside in the early 1960s. The place to be was the Rifle pub on Denmark Street, just off Middlesbrough's famous Cannon Street. It was an area tightly packed with two-up, two-down Victorian terraced houses that were on their last legs before being bulldozed and replaced by car showrooms and furniture warehouses. I listened in awe to songs about oppressed slaves, tales of hobos stowing away on freight trains during the Depression and of heartbroken travellers missing their true loves in faraway lands.

Then there were the Irish ballads. I sat entranced as I heard about impoverished peasants being evicted from their homes, mass emigration to England and the United States and the thousands of Irish men, women and children who starved to death in the potato famine of the mid-1800s. South Bank was full of families with English accents and Irish names. Mam knew fragments of Irish ballads, mainly rebel songs like *Bold Robert Emmet*, *The Croppy Boy* and *Kelly the Boy from Killane* – her maiden name was Kelly so she made sure I knew that one. Our Kellys came from County Mayo on Ireland's Atlantic coast, one of the counties worst affected by the potato blight that led to the famine.

Great singers like Stan Gee and Ron Angel regularly played in the Rifle and at Stockton Folk Club in the Stork and Castle pub, where the popular Teesside Fettlers band were based. Experiencing all those live performances had a big effect on me and something began to stir deep inside. Being introduced to the music of Graeme Miles was another key moment in my musical awakening. Although born in Greenwich, his

Vin at home on the Eston Hills – did he draw ICI in the background?

family moved to Billingham when he was six months old after his dad got a job up at ICI. He wrote songs about subjects I could relate to – the steelworks and the chemical plants, the Teesside landscape and the pollution all around us. It was all part of this strong connection I had discovered between the past and the present day, a living tradition that's still going strong. I began to realise they weren't just stories made up to fit a tune, as most pop songs were. Folk music was a different kettle of fish. Although I enjoyed singing rock and pop songs, I couldn't tell you what the lyrics were about. There was nothing deep or meaningful about them, it was just about matching nice words with catchy melodies. When I heard these wonderful folk songs that were sometimes modern or could be a hundred or even two hundred years old, my view of music changed. I fell completely in love with them and started asking myself where they came from. Gradually it dawned on me that people have been writing them forever. They were part of a living tradition, a continuous thread of songwriting about generations and generations of real people. They weren't just written for commercial purposes, to make a few quid from having a hit record. They were part of my own history.

The folk scene was still fairly underground in England back then, but in America and across the water in Ireland it was a different story. Bob Dylan, Peter, Paul and Mary, Phil Ochs and Simon and Garfunkel were all achieving mainstream success in the States and becoming major stars. The Irish have always been passionate about their musical heritage and over there The Clancy Brothers, The Chieftains and The Dubliners were hugely popular and there was a thriving market for folk music. It was on radio and television all the time and because the media feeds off itself, we also heard those bands in England. There were piles of their LPs on sale in the shops, but virtually nothing from the homegrown folk scene had been heard on the radio or TV since Ewan MacColl's Radio Ballads programmes, before my time in the fifties and early sixties.

Eventually I sussed out what was going on. It was all about business. If the music industry thought there was money to be made, they fed folk songs to the media, who then filtered them and decided whether they were good enough for the rest of us to hear. If they didn't see a profit in it then we never even got to hear the music and make up our own minds.

But the American and Irish revival blew across and caught people's imaginations over here. Ordinary blokes like me were inspired to pick up a guitar and have a go at singing *Blowing in the Wind* or *The Irish Rover* in the folk clubs. Not long after my introduction to folk at the Rifle, Eston Folk Club started up closer to home, at the Cleveland Bay on Jubilee Road. Soon it became my regular haunt as folk became my music.

John McCoy was a legendary figure on Middlesbrough's thriving music scene. As well as being lead singer of several blues bands, including the Real McCoy, he ran memorable venues that attracted some of the biggest names in rock history. There was the Outlook, where The Rolling Stones played their first gig outside of London and where I saw an excellent Merseybeat band called The Fourmost. One night I'd been playing in the folk club upstairs in another of his venues, Mr McCoys, and John agreed to let me into the gig downstairs. There I watched in awe as a fourteen-year-old musical genius bewitched the audience. His name? Little Stevie Wonder.

By the age of eighteen I'd progressed from the folk club singarounds to picking up my own local bookings at Anchor House in Middlesbrough town centre and up into the folk clubs of County Durham. If it wasn't for my ICI apprenticeship I would have gone for it and tried to turn professional then, but I thought I might as well have a trade under my belt first.

I'd wanted to go to art college when I left St Peter's School in 1962, but Dad didn't think there would be too many jobs for fine artists in Middlesbrough and I suppose he had a point. Instead I enrolled on a six-month commercial course at Redcar Technical College and learned typing and bookkeeping.

I fancied going into journalism and learned Pitman shorthand, but Dad had other plans for me. He lined me up an interview at ICI, the chemical works that dominated Teesside's skyline and employed half the town. It was easy to find work, especially if you had relatives working there already. My first choice was an apprenticeship as an instrument artificer because Dad said it was a good job. If I didn't manage that I thought being an electrician would be interesting. If neither of those came off, my third choice was to be a fitter. But it seemed that whatever ideas I had there was something else waiting for me, and I was offered an apprenticeship as a turner instead.

'Thank you,' I said to the foreman as I stood up and shook his hand at the end of the interview, delighted to have been offered a job. Then just before I left the room I turned back sheepishly.

'What does a turner do?' I asked.

The first thing I learned on the Monday I started was that a turner worked on a lathe. The second had become clear by about half-past ten – I wasn't very good at it. Maths was a big part of the job and it wasn't my strong suit. The work was all done manually back then. When you cut a screw thread you used its diameter to work out which cogs to put on the end of the lathe. I was hopeless. The ace turners worked so fast that they picked up all their own bonuses plus extra chits they couldn't use, so I was often given them at the end of the week. I don't think I ever worked fast enough to earn one legitimately for myself throughout my short career.

> I worked with Vin at ICI and socialised with the same group of friends, Phil Bryan and Jan, Alan Woodhouse and Meryl, Colin 'Bimma' Simpson, Colin 'Fruity' Rowntree and a bunch of others. Vin occasionally entertained us during dinner or tea breaks in the locker room, when he would play the guitar or stick two recorders up his nostrils (nose pipes, he called them) or try to teach us about harmonising utilising the end of *She Loves You*.
> **Owen Davies**

I didn't learn another pop song after 1968, even though I still enjoyed listening to them. Instead of strumming along with the tunes they were playing on the radio, I started writing songs of my own. I didn't record the first few I came up with, which were set to familiar tunes like *McNamara's Band* rather than my own melodies. One was called *The Dirty Purple Working Shirt*, sung in a broad Boro accent to sound more like *The Dairty Pairple Wairking Shairt*. I can still remember some of the words…

It happened in 1968 in the middle of July
They were having a singing contest and I thought that I would try
I went down to the Eisteddfod in all me grease and dairt
dedadedadedadeda in me dairty wairking shairt…

It was inspired by an incident when I nicked off my shift at ICI to go to the Billingham International Folklore Festival, which was a major event in Teesside at the time, drawing performers from all over the world. When I arrived I was horrified to walk straight into my foreman. I felt sick, fearing I'd be given the sack. Then I realised that wasn't going to happen – because he was supposed to be at work as well! We both kept on walking and neither of us ever said another word about it.

Another song, *The Wilton Strike,* was also based on real events. The whole site came out on strike after works' convenor Paddy Tombs was sacked for swearing at a manager. Some sensible older folk told me Paddy deserved to be given his cards because he was out of order. But that didn't seem to matter – it was one out, all out. The song was about striking for a cause you knew nothing of. I was on strike when I wrote it and didn't have the faintest idea why I wasn't at work as usual.

My first proper song was *Valley of Tees* and I still sing it today. It's about the stark contrast of a grimy industrial town being surrounded by beautiful countryside such as Farndale and the North York Moors. It was subconsciously inspired by Graeme Miles' *Ring of Iron* and is the same song in some ways, with its own tune but taking a slightly different angle on an identical theme. In singing and writing songs I had found my true vocation. It was just as well. Out of the thousands of turners who went through ICI's gates over the years, I must have been the worst one they ever had. Fortunately, both for ICI and for me, I didn't stick around for too long.

Vin with his relative Michael Gallagher and Michael's daughter, Angela, during one of those 1960s' visits

THE IRISH CONNECTION

'One sunny summer morning, I rambled from my home,
Down by the side of a silvery stream, I carelessly did roam.'

Traditional, *The Glens of Sweet Mayo*

Ireland is in my bones. Hooked by the traditional music I heard at home from Mam and later in the folk clubs, I started making trips when I was still in my teens to tap into the tradition for myself. Before I went, everything my family knew about the Irish connection came from the Christmas cards that passed between Mam and whichever surviving female member of the family on the other side of the Irish Sea returned news of births, deaths and marriages to us. As time went by, that person would die and the next one in line inherited the job of keeping in touch with Tessie over in England. Mam never met any of them. She was born in Middlesbrough and stayed here all her life.

I fell in love with the country as I hitch-hiked through *The Glens of Sweet Mayo*, which I later sang about. I searched for songs and tunes and discovered the places my family came from. I'm the only one of my generation to have gone over to track down our relatives and it was a special experience. They always made a big fuss of me and I loved meeting them.

On one of my first trips, with my pal Mick Sheehan, we visited distant relatives in Crossmolina, County Mayo. The Gallaghers lived in a modern bungalow built through a government scheme to move people into more habitable houses, but the old family thatch was still standing next door. We all went to the local pub and on the way home they told us they were stopping to pick up Katy Daly. I remember thinking, 'You'll never squeeze anyone else in this car – it's already rammed!' We stopped at a lay-by and the driver shone the headlights towards the hedgerow. Then one of my cousins jumped out and ran into the bushes, before returning with three bottles of *poitín* in his arms. It transpired that Katy Daly is the local codename for moonshine and has even made its way into a song, *Come Down from the Mountain, Katy Daly*. Back at the house we ate thick slices from a big leg of ham that was hanging up, accompanied by shots of *poitín* that burned the back of my throat as it trickled down. The family also made their own *poitín* in a little shed at the end of the garden.

Vin entertaining the locals at the Bog of Allen, County Kildare

'Don't you worry about the Garda coming and finding it?' I asked.
'Ah, not really,' they said. 'They always call and tell us they're on their way.'
We slept on the floor and there were some extremely sore heads the next morning.

Mick Sheehan's recollection of the trip…

> A friend of ours, Tony Blades, was a car salesman and could borrow a car so we came up with the idea of going over to Ireland for the Rose of Tralee Festival together. We decided to set off after the Saturday night Liffey Folk Club I ran in Darlington. So me, Vin, Tony and Kev McLean all piled into Tony's old air-cooled NSU late at night and drove to Stranraer and went across on the ferry. It was all right leaving Darlington full of beer, but by two o'clock in the morning we all felt dreadful. And by the time we stopped off to visit Vin's relatives in Mayo the next day we were dead on our feet. But they were delighted to see us and put a big hoolie on that night. I remember Katy Daly well. There were about ten of us in the car and the last thing I needed that night was to drink raw alcohol! We woke up early the next morning and one of Vin's cousins said, 'This is just the thing you need to set you up for the day – home-cured bacon!' Now Irish home-cured bacon has about two inches of fat on top with a thin layer of lean meat running through it. They put thick slices into the pan and it was hardly cooked. I just couldn't eat it and made my apologies, but Vin sat down and polished it off and then asked for more. I thought, 'Vin, if I didn't admire you before, I do now – what a constitution!'

When we reached Tralee we played in a few pubs, had a good time and met some interesting people. I'd never heard Travellers sing before and was impressed by the incredible way they throw their voices and command a crowded, noisy pub. The Travellers all had scars on their faces and their knuckles and eventually some fighting broke out and me and Vin and everyone else ran for the door.

There were no camping sites, so we just parked up in a field outside Tralee along with many others. Two of us slept in the car and two in the tent – one night I ended up sleeping underneath the car, I don't know how that happened! This makes me smile today – one morning when the bacon and the drink were kicking in, Vin said: 'I've got to have something green – I don't care what it is, as long as it's green!'

After a couple of days our money ran out and we drove back across Ireland without stopping. Having finally got to put my head on something comfortable I crashed out and slept for something like fifteen hours until we boarded the ferry at Dublin.

Mick Sheehan

The following year I went over for the famous Puck Fair in County Kerry with my mate Billy Bateman and we stopped off for a few nights in Dublin on our way. It was before the last IRA campaign started up but some republicans had recently blown up Nelson's Pillar in the centre of the city to mark the fiftieth anniversary of the 1916 Easter Rising. There were lads on street corners selling lumps of rock they claimed were various parts of poor Horatio's anatomy. One night we couldn't find anywhere to sleep. As darkness fell we gave up looking and pitched our tent on some grass.

We slept like logs after walking all day and then drinking a few pints of Guinness in the evening. But the next morning we awoke to the rumbling of traffic all around us. I stuck my head out of the tent and discovered we'd camped on the central reservation in the middle of Dublin's only dual carriageway! We attracted plenty of attention with our unusual sleeping quarters in a leafy part of the city, but we can't have looked too much like vagabonds. A sash window was hoisted open in one of the houses in a smart Georgian terrace overlooking us and a kindly gentleman leaned out and waved a teapot at us. We went up and drank mugs of tea and munched thick slices of hot, buttered toast with a total stranger. It was heaven.

Puck Fair was wonderful. It's named after King Puck, a bronze statue of a billy goat that stands on a huge tower in the middle of Killorglin. A real goat is brought down from the mountains and made king for the three days of the festival. When we arrived I was confused by a sign I saw in a bar window – 'Bar exemption until three o'clock in the morning.'

'Do you mean bar extension?' I asked.

'No,' replied the barmaid, not looking up from the glass she was drying. 'We're exempt from closing until three o'clock.'

'That'll do for me!'

A later visit to Ireland, in the early 1970s, with relatives including Michael and Louie Gallagher and their daughter, Angela

There was a session in full swing and I was delighted to join in. Some tremendous musicians were playing, including Patrick 'The Pecker' Dunne, a brilliant Traveller banjo player, fiddler and seanchaí, a traditional Gaelic storyteller. I sang *Bold Robert Emmet* and was thrilled to bits when one of my heroes, Liam Clancy, came over and complimented me, saying he liked the way I did it. My mate Billy heard all these rebel songs being sung and thought he might be in bother if his cover was blown.

'You won't tell anyone I'm a Protestant will you, Vin?' he said.

'It won't make a ha'porth of difference to anyone who you are,' I assured him.

Ireland felt so safe and Billy was enormously impressed by the friendliness and camaraderie we found there. We left all our gear unguarded in the street while we went for a mooch around and came back a couple of hours later and it was all there, just as we'd left it. If only life was like that all the time.

BYE-BYE, ICI

'Money isn't everything'

Vin Garbutt

Not long after I finished my apprenticeship and became a time-served turner, I entered the annual competition in ICI's works newspaper, *The Wilton News*. The prize was an extra two weeks' holiday and £100, which was a lot of money in those days. You simply had to tell them how you would spend the time off and the best idea won.

I had become pally with Biörn Landahl, the son of the pastor at the Sjömanskyrka, the Swedish Seamen's Mission church on Linthorpe Road in Middlesbrough. I met Biörn purely by chance. He saw me trying out guitars I couldn't afford in Hamilton's Music Shop and asked if there was any folk music on locally. We struck up a conversation and quickly became firm friends.

This is how Biörn recalls that first meeting...

> I well remember when I met Vin the first time, in Hamilton's in Middlesbrough. The year before, I had missed the Dubliners playing in Middlesbrough by a few days, so this year I was concerned not to miss any folk music. The best place to find out was a music store, thought I. The shop assistant didn't know of any folk places. On the second floor was a folky-looking fella trying different guitars. Did he know, I asked, me being a stranger and foreigner?
>
> 'There are loads!' was the reply, and he told me of places every day of the week!
>
> He invited me for a cup of coffee in a nearby cafe and told me he would be in Guisborough that Friday. Not a word of him being a folk singer. Of course, I went. And who was the star of the night? Vin Garbutt! He sang songs including *Red Haired Mary* and *Bold Robert Emmet* in a way that reminded me of my hero, Luke Kelly, and Vin had a new friend for life. As I had my father's car I offered him a lift home to Eston after the gig. We stopped at a ceilidh in Redcar, where he gave an *a cappella* rendition of *The Rocky Road to Dublin*. Two fellas played concertinas for the dancing. At home in Eston his mother was waiting for him with sandwiches. Since then I've seen, met and heard Vin for nearly fifty years.
>
> **Biörn Landahl**

We began going to the folk clubs together and I discovered that Sweden had a rich folk tradition. This gave me and my mate Kevin McLean the idea of entering the competition by saying we'd like to travel around Sweden collecting traditional folk songs. When we won first prize we honestly did fully intend to go there. But our plans were in ruins before we even left the UK. We enquired about ferry tickets at Dover and the lorry drivers warned us we were making a big mistake.

'You don't want to go there,' one said. 'The tickets cost a fortune and you'll starve when you get there because everything's so expensive.'

I've always been quite careful with my money anyway and that was more than enough to put me off. In the light of this new information, we decided to go to Spain instead.

So me and Kevin took the ferry to Calais and made our way to Paris, staying in a little B&B on the left bank of the Seine, not far from Notre Dame – and finding ourselves bang in the middle of the student protests that were raging at the time. We were innocently enjoying a beer outside a café when we saw a wave of students charging towards us. They warned us to scarper because the *gendarmes* were on their way. There were thousands of students fleeing down the street and we ran with them.

The next day we hitched down to the border and across into northern Spain, pitching our little two-man ridge tent in San Sebastian on the Bay of Biscay. It was a stunning city with a beautiful beach, La Concha, and we were just about the only tourists there. We then travelled down to Pamplona, where we took part in the running of the bulls at the San Fermin fiesta, made famous in Ernest Hemingway's *The Sun Also Rises*. I didn't run in front of the bulls with all the local lads, mind – I ran behind them at a safe distance and let the experts lead the way.

Following the main roads, we hitch-hiked deeper into Spain, going wherever our lifts took us. We ate great handfuls of the grapes we found growing by the roadside and drank wine costing one peseta a go in cowboy-style bars where they filled up our glasses and slid them back along the counter to us.

After a few days we took a late train to Barcelona, where we slept on the railway station platform. Rising early the next morning we came across some workers standing around a burning brazier. They gave us a warm welcome, even though we couldn't speak Spanish and they couldn't speak English. In our slowest, clearest English we asked if they were fascists, and they understood that word if nothing else.

'No,' they said, shaking their heads in disgust. 'Comunistas!'

Franco's military government was in power at the time and those words could have got them thrown into jail.

It was a fantastic trip. I fell in love with the Spanish lifestyle and wanted to experience more of it. When I returned to the day-to-day drudgery of working at ICI, my mind constantly strayed to the sunshine and the carefree existence I'd tasted. The following year, as soon as I turned twenty-one, I decided I'd had enough. I handed in my notice and me and five mates planned the adventure of a lifetime.

SIX GO TO SPAIN

'Oh, how we could sing, what fun those nights would bring,
Singing for hours on end…'

Pete Betts, *They Don't Write 'Em Like That Any More*

The plan was to take our guitars and sing and play our way across Spain. There was Pete Betts, Alan Brewer, Joe Jones, John 'Speedy' Bryden and Kevin McLean, my drinking pals from the Oak Leaf in South Bank, the Ship in Eston and the Poverina in Normanby. We all packed in our jobs and bought a cream and green 1959 VW Caravette, which for some reason we christened Sybil Klondyke after the actress Dame Sybil Thorndike.

The six of us were poles apart in all kinds of ways but we made a fine team. A couple of the lads were volatile characters. Pete was a bit of a scrapper in his day and Alan had a terrible temper. He was a fitter and later became an excellent artist – the Cleveland pub in Normanby has a Brewer's Corner adorned with his sketches and paintings. Joe was the grandad of the gang at about twenty-six. He and Pete were both electricians but Joe was a much gentler character. Speedy was mild-mannered like me and nothing seemed to bother him. The gang was completed by my ICI mate Kevin.

> Vin came home from work having recently completed his apprenticeship as a turner. He declared tentatively that he was going to resign from ICI and tour Spain in a VW campervan with his friends. I remember the tension in our living room as Dad said, 'You are going to do what?' – then Mam interjecting in full support of Vin to follow his heart. That didn't go down too well either as Dad continued with his mutterings of 'bloody hippy' and how he should be sticking with a 'proper job'. Our Mam was always a great believer in Vin following his passion, and I'm sure it was her intervention that day that set Vin on his professional career pathway. **Ellen Forrest, Vin's sister**

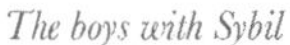
The boys with Sybil

Refreshments available inside Sybil included a tin of Nescafé and a jar of Marvel

After saying tearful farewells to our families and friends we headed off down south and caught the ferry to France. But disaster struck just an hour's drive from Calais – the engine blew up! That was as far as we made it for quite a while and paying for the repairs cost us every penny we had between us. Once Sybil was patched up we set off again from Bethune, feeling a little deflated at the loss of our pocket money.

We'd only made it to Arras, another half-hour down the road, when we heard a worrying 'pop!' sound from under the bonnet. We pulled over and Alan opened the front compartment, which was the boot as the engine was in the back. Inside was a Camping Gaz cylinder that should have been round at the top and concave at the bottom, but instead it was round at both ends. The noise we heard was pressure blowing the cylinder out of shape. Fearing it was about to explode, the rest of us jumped out of the van and took cover at the side of the road, while somebody brave – I can't remember who, but it certainly wasn't me – threw the Camping Gaz container high up into the air. Before it came down again it exploded with a huge bang. Nobody was hurt, thank goodness, but it was a close thing.

Life in Sybil had its challenges, with six of us sleeping head-to-toe and generating an extremely pungent smell in the sweltering summer sun. By the time we reached Paris the heat was stifling, with no air conditioning to provide us with any much-needed relief. It didn't help that traffic in the city was gridlocked. Cooped up together and with very little to occupy us, tempers began to fray until they finally boiled over and a huge row erupted. What began as a silly dispute escalated alarmingly and was quickly on the brink of all-out fisticuffs. Pete and Alan, the two most tempestuous members of the group, were just about to kill each other when I shocked everyone by losing my rag.

'You daft bastaaaards!' I screamed at the top of my voice.

Everybody stopped still in their tracks and complete silence descended. The two combatants were dumbstruck and peace broke out. I'm not usually a swearer, but I learned that day that it's extremely useful to have a truly shocking one in your locker to use when you need it. I was about ten the first time I ever swore. In those days the tin bath came out once a week and the whole family took turns to wash in the same water. Mam told me it was my turn to get in one night.

'Ah f*** off, Mam,' I said.

Well, there was absolute hell on. I was as shocked as everyone else when I saw Mam's horrified reaction to my outburst.

'What?' I said. 'I heard Ralphie Newman say it!'

Anyway, harmony restored within the gang, we continued through the rest of France and over the border into Spain, before enjoying a few blissful days back in San Sebastian, the city I'd fallen in love with the previous year. Cyril Sharman, the landlord of the Ship in Eston, had kindly given us a one hundred peseta note to take with us. There were no *cambios* open when we crossed the border and that money was all we had to spend in Spain. Fortunately, it was more than enough to keep us nicely oiled. We could drink an awful lot of wine at Spanish prices! One afternoon when we were half cut, a man claiming to be a film producer approached us offering the chance to star in his latest production. Full of one-peseta-a-pop vino we were well up for a shot at fame and fortune. But a sensible local came over and quietly warned us that the would-be producer was a dodgy character. He advised us not to go with him and so, somewhat reluctantly, we turned him down. Who knows? We could have all become Hollywood superstars.

After San Sebastian, we spent a night in the tiny village of Berdún, which is perched on the brow of an extremely steep hill. We enjoyed a few drinks in a smashing little bar and then made our way back merrily to sleep in Sybil. The next day we headed off in the direction of Barcelona. Just before we reached the city we parked in the suburb of Badalona and went for something to eat. We returned an hour later and discovered that Sybil had been ransacked and nearly all our valuables had disappeared. I suppose we should have known that nothing good would ever come of Badalona! We didn't have anything of much value, but our most treasured possessions, the guitars, including my prized Harmony Sovereign, were gone. They left just one, Speedy's, which was the cheapest of all. We were devastated that ours had gone and Speedy was grossly offended that his was left untouched.

'What's wrong with my guitar?' he said.

As one man, we all told him.

Deflated but undeterred, we travelled further down the Catalan coast to Sitges, where we settled at a campsite. Sitges is a major tourist town now but was fairly quiet at that time. The Spanish costas were just starting to become popular with the British, although I didn't know many people from Middlesbrough who'd ever been on a foreign holiday.

I'd already found my voice in the folk clubs of Teesside, but Spain was where I found my feet as a performer. From this point onwards we sang in the bars everywhere we went, giving people whatever they wanted to hear, from pop standards to folk, sharing Speedy's cheap guitar between us. By now I had a sizeable repertoire of Irish rebel

Pete and Vin singing for their supper

songs under my belt. It was before the Troubles started and a time when nobody considered them contentious. They just seemed like almost comical relics of times gone by. Pete also sang and Speedy had a lovely voice. He was a handsome lad and he broke a few hearts as all these beautiful Spanish lasses fell in love with him all over the country. The rest of us were dead jealous.

Our first job was in the Tabu bar. We got on like a house on fire with Bob, the affable Liverpudlian landlord. He gave us free drinks and the odd sandwich and we were allowed to pass the hat round after playing a few songs. They weren't what I'd call a listening audience in the Tabu. People came in, had a drink and then moved on to the next bar. It was hard work. We started singing at nine o'clock in the evening and finished at three in the morning. Dawn came early and was always a beautiful sight on the Mediterranean. We were only young, and so once the Tabu closed we packed up and headed off to another bar that had opened for the local workers to visit on their way to start their morning shifts at four o'clock. There we drank a *carajillo*, a small brandy and coffee mixed together in a glass, and after that we staggered off to bed. The campsite was called Los Almendros, The Almonds, because it was also an almond orchard. It had a little bar and I remember The Beatles' latest hit *Get Back* blasting out of the jukebox.

Pete started seeing a Danish girl, one of the biggest women we had ever seen but extremely attractive, and who we referred to as 'The Beautiful Horse'. Pete was delighted because he could go to her hotel for a hot shower, while the rest of us made do with the icy cold campsite washing facilities.

The Tabu gig was brilliant while it lasted and after a few weeks we were able to buy a twelve-string guitar with the money we had collected. Then one day we arrived for our usual session to find the bar locked up. It transpired that Interpol had been to lift Bob – our jovial Scouse pal was apparently number one on their most wanted list. The new manager was from Bolton and spoke excellent Spanish, but in the thickest Lancashire accent I've ever heard. It sounded fantastic and I can still hear him burring, '*Poor favoor, dos cervaysas, senyour, akee!*' Whenever I play in the Glossop area there's a couple in the audience who saw me playing in the Tabu on their honeymoon back in 1969.

Me, Pete and Speedy continued singing for our suppers in Sitges. Kevin stayed with us and passed the hat round, but the two other non-musicians, Alan and Joe, found jobs as deckhands on a wealthy American's boat that was docked in the harbour. Soon they had more money than us and could afford to drink in the upmarket tourist bars. We'd take one look at the price list outside, mutter under our breaths and walk on to find somewhere we could buy a beer and a cheese or squid bocadillo for the same price as a drink in those posh places.

Before long our merry little band of travellers began to break up. Alan returned to England three months into the trip to get back to his family and Pete, Joe and Kevin started making their way up to the Munich Beer Festival. They picked grapes to earn their keep along the way and slept in barns or wherever they could lay their heads down. They were following a well-worn trail used by bar workers migrating north after the summer season.

Not long afterwards Speedy also headed home and I was on my own. I made friends with Paul Leblanc, an American Army deserter I met on the campsite in Sitges. He had been sent to fight in Vietnam twice and decided he never wanted to go back, which was quite understandable after the horrors he'd experienced. When he received his papers for a third tour, he fled to Europe instead. Paul and his Dutch girlfriend lived in an ex-BBC outside broadcast van. It had a hard, rubber platform on the roof that was designed to hold cameras and equipment but was perfect for pitching my little one-man tent on, using weights instead of pegs to hold it down.

Together we drove down to La Linea on the south coast, hoping to cross into Gibraltar from there. But Franco had closed the border so we had to keep driving. Instead, we reached the Rock via a circuitous route that involved crossing the Mediterranean Sea to North Africa first. We caught a ferry across from the port of Algeciras to the Spanish colony of Ceuta, which not everyone knows is one of two Spanish colonies on the African mainland, along with Melilla. The impoverished children of Ceuta left a deep and lasting impression on me. None of them had shoes on their feet but they had the biggest and most beautiful smiles on their faces. I wrote *The One-Legged Beggar* a few years later in 1973 based on my experiences. I finally recorded it in 1978 and it's still one of my favourites.

From Ceuta we crossed the border into Morocco and continued to the historic seaport of Tangier, from where we could catch a ferry to Gibraltar. It took us two ferries

A shot from the 1969 trip to Spain

and a road trip but we finally made it. We parked the van in Catalan Bay and the Rock became our temporary home.

I was skint by now and was almost forced to take a proper job. I saw an advert for a fitter-turner working for the Royal Navy and reluctantly made my way to the naval base to have my first tentative go on a lathe since leaving England. I'd only worked three months as a time-served tradesman after finishing my apprenticeship and had no confidence in my talents as a turner. It would have been a good position to land because I would have been the only turner, but the prospect was a scary one as well. I could just imagine being handed a drawing and told, 'Make one of these…' – and not having a clue where to start. Britain's proud naval tradition certainly wasn't built on craftsmanship such as mine. By not getting the job I did my country a tremendous service.

Instead of taking the Queen's Shilling I started singing in a bar, playing a battered old mandolin that had been overlooked by the thieves who carried out the great Catalan Caravette Caper. The instrument met a messy end when a drunken soldier, who was slouching against a wall listening to me sing, fell over and smashed it into a dozen pieces. He might have been an outspoken music critic giving his verdict on my singing, but I think he was just too sozzled to be aware of what he was doing. Some kind soul realised what had happened and put ten quid in the hat. God bless him or her, whoever it was. Mind you, I'd had so much to drink that night it might have been me!

After three months in Gibraltar I parted company with Paul Leblanc. Paul could be scary at times. He'd seen some horrors in Vietnam and had photographed dead bodies and brought back other thoroughly unpleasant souvenirs of war. People who've seen such violence at close hand are often damaged and hardened. There was a lovely, warm side to Paul and then occasionally glimpses of how his experiences in Vietnam had taken their toll. I wrote *The Ballad of Tim Leblanc* about him, changing his first name, and recorded the song on my first LP, *The Valley of Tees*, which came out in 1972. I never saw or heard from him again after we parted company in Gibraltar. Wherever he is, I'm grateful for his company and hope he recovered from his trauma and has lived a happy life.

Not long after leaving Paul I fell in with a cracking bunch of cockney lads who had found work delivering wine around Gibraltar for a merchant called Saccone & Speed. Together we met a German skipper who was repairing a little fishing trawler and had run out of money. We all chipped in so he could afford to finish the job off and then paid him to take us across the Straits of Gibraltar back to Ceuta in his tiny boat.

I didn't know then that it's an extremely treacherous journey at the best of times, but the conditions the day we set off were horrendous. It was by far the roughest crossing I've ever experienced. As soon as we were out at sea, huge waves began crashing into the boat, drenching the deck and everyone and everything on it. We were all struggling but one of the lads was far worse than the rest of us. He started vomiting and shaking uncontrollably and then just huddled up in a ball, unable to open his eyes and dangerously stricken with seasickness. One enormous wave broke a plank at the top of the cabin and sent it hurtling down into the sea below. Fortunately, the skipper had a Moroccan sidekick who dived in and retrieved the piece of wood as though he was some kind of aquatic creature who belonged down there amid the surf.

It was a truly terrifying experience but we eventually reached Ceuta unscathed and incredibly grateful to put our feet back on dry land. Once we were there some of the London lads went scuba diving wearing gear borrowed from our German skipper, diving off the dockside with oxygen tanks on their backs and no idea what they were doing. You wouldn't have got me down there for love nor money. Looking back it was reckless and dangerous, but when you're young and foolish you sometimes take these risks.

The weather turned even worse and we had to stay an extra night in Ceuta before returning to Gibraltar. You can imagine the blind terror that the very thought of that journey struck into us, especially the poor lad who'd been so desperately seasick.

We went our separate ways soon after returning to Gibraltar, but I kept in touch with one of the boys, Bernie Harrington, who was the son of an Irish fiddler of the same name. A year after returning to England I stayed with his family in London. His dad didn't play any more and the old fiddles were all stacked on top of a wardrobe gathering dust. But when I took my whistle out he reached up for his best fiddle and started playing along. Young Bernie was astonished.

'He hasn't played that for years,' he said.

His dad still had a headful of tunes and I learned most of my early tin whistle repertoire from him. After that night I was delighted to hear that he'd started going to sessions again. Bernie senior was a big pal of the celebrated Irish fiddler Sean McGuire, one of the greatest musicians I ever had the pleasure of playing with. The only complaint anyone had about him was that his fiddling was almost too perfect. Playing in a pub with Sean and Bernie was simply mesmerising. I haven't seen Sean's music in the shops for many years but his fiddling was out of this world, something truly beautiful to behold. Bernie's sister has come to see me a few times and has told me they don't have any recordings of her dad. I might still have some stashed away somewhere in the loft. Two of the other Cockney lads live in Sydney and always bring their families when I play there.

> I and two of my mates, Bernie Harrington and Chris Lewis, left London for our first great adventure to Gibraltar in 1969. I was twenty at the time, the others slightly younger, and we planned to live and work there for six months. We learnt there was a campsite, so on arrival we caught a taxi to our new home. When we were dropped off we thought we were in a car park, as all we could see were trucks and vans parked and not a blade of grass in sight. We were assured it was the campsite and as we investigated we saw some tents erected between the trucks and vans. What caught our eye was that all the guy ropes of the tents were tied to rocks, as you couldn't drive a tent peg into the ground on the Rock of Gibraltar. It wasn't long before we became friends with people from one of the trucks and in particular with this fellow called Vin Garbutt, who was a folk singer. My friends and I all dabbled with the guitar and with this in common we became close friends with Vin. We were also interested to note that this was the start of Vin's professional career as a folk singer.
>
> Our time with Vin was special. We accompanied him to gigs, often taking the hat around for him to top up his earnings, which weren't much. Most of it went on replacing the guitar strings that he purchased locally and were of poor quality. One of his main midweek gigs was at the Lido, just down from the campsite facing the ocean. Here he was guaranteed an audience of at least three people, Gibraltar not exactly being the hub for folk singers. Some gigs were in town, where the place was full of sailors looking for a good time after weeks at sea. They probably wondered what they stumbled into when Vin started singing folk songs, but it didn't take long to win them around with his humour.
>
> Even back in those days we could see Vin was a very special person. His songs told wonderful stories, his guitar playing was superb and his *Ballad of Tonto McGuire* on the penny whistle was amazing. His jigs and reels were excellent too, but it was also his storytelling in between songs that rounded the whole package off. All of these attributes Vin perfected over the years to make him one of the most sought-after folk singers.
>
> **Dennis Grogan**

By the time I parted with the London lads the summer was over and the holidaymakers had all headed back home. With nobody left to entertain, I set off to go grape picking with a lad from Brighton I'd met. We travelled along the Mediterranean coast by a combination of hitch-hiking and the train, crossing the border into France near Beziers. We slept wherever we could. One night we kipped on a fishing boat – whether we were invited or stowed away, I can't quite recall. Another time we slept in a Citroen van after the owner carelessly left its back doors open.

We were hot and sweaty and must have been quite smelly too. We pommies have a terrible name in Australia. They call us soap dodgers because they say we don't wash. In my case, they had a point. I can't remember washing throughout my time in Spain, except when we stayed on proper campsites, and even there the facilities were basic. I'm not sure if the sweaty stench coming from the pair of us was the reason why, but we hardly made any headway after Beziers and nobody would give us a lift. We split up and I ended up hitching on my own, across the border back into Spain and then returning to Sitges. My funds were getting low by the time I arrived and I was running out of ideas as to how I would find my way home again. Just as the situation started to look desperate, I was walking down the street when a familiar-sounding accent called out my name.

'Vinny Garbutt!' the shout came. 'What the hell are you doing here?'

It was someone from home – and for the life of me I can't remember who! I explained what I'd been doing the last few months and that I was now heading for home.

'What a stroke of luck,' he said. 'So are we – hop in!'

So I did – all the way back to Eston!

The young tin whistle pest

VIN GARBUTT

OF TEESSIDE

Songs of Ireland and Britain

GUITAR - WHISTLE
MANDOLIN - LAUDE

QUOTE: "On Saturday, Vin Garbutt proved that he is star material for any club. At Darlington's 'Spinning Wheel' he got through a very entertaining selection of traditional and humorous songs and showed off his instrumental prowess on guitar, mandolin and whistle".

EVENING DESPATCH — NOVEMBER 20th, 1969.

Vin has been singing and playing since 1963, in concerts, clubs and on radio where his wide range of material and sense of humour have made him a firm favourite with folk-club audiences.

Born in South Bank, Teesside, of Anglo-Irish stock, it is not surprising that his material is a fine mixture of songs and tunes from both countries. Perhaps it is this mixture that has given him several grand compositions to his own credit, including JIGS, REELS and HORNPIPES, which although having a definite Irish influence, maintain a noticeable unique difference.

In 1969 Vin spent over six months touring the Continent where he was in great demand by many of the British style singing bars that are dotted along the Mediterranean coast of SPAIN. During the latter weeks of his tour he was resident at the 'Barnacle' Club on GIBRALTAR.

As well as singing and playing, Vin drinks, eats, sleeps, smells and burns, and he doesn't mind people talking about his NOSE and good looks!!!

Available Full Time

32 AMBROSE ROAD - ESTON - TEESSIDE

TELEPHONE: ESTON GRANGE 5 3 4 8

A flyer quoting a review from a 1969 gig in Darlington on Vin's 22nd birthday – Biörn Landahl drove Vin there

An early gig in Redcar

A rare shot of a clean-shaven Vin

THE GIG OF MY LIFE

'The apple groves of Kent, their hops of merriment
Saw me strolling with a lovely Kentish maid.'

Vin Garbutt, *Kilburn Horse*

There really is no place like home, and it was especially good to see Mam and Dad again. I had hardly phoned while I was away because it was too expensive to call and we didn't have a telephone in the house anyway. The only way I'd kept in touch during my six months away was by sending the odd postcard.

Travelling had been a real eye-opener and I particularly loved the Spanish diet. Fresh garlic and onions and tasty tomatoes, oranges and peppers were all cheap and readily available. We ate tons of cheese and onion or cheese and tomato sandwiches in lovely, fresh Spanish bread. I've always been a big fan of rabbit and I had plenty of that too. My palate had been well and truly educated by all these lovely continental tastes and I was soon craving them, so I popped into the greengrocers at Normanby Top on my first morning back.

'I don't suppose you sell aubergines?' I enquired. The lady behind the counter looked back at me sympathetically.

'Ah no, pet, we don't,' she said. 'Have you tried the hardware shop?'

Not only was the food delicious, but the Spanish air seemed to agree with me as well. I enjoyed working at ICI but I had a permanently rattly chest and runny nose. I don't think it was caused by working there, it was more likely the pollution from all the heavy industry in the area while I was growing up. I went to hospital in 1967 to have my sinuses cleaned out so the doctors could try to get to the root of my problems. They stuck lumps of cotton wool steeped in anaesthetic into my nostrils and I sat in the waiting room until my nose went numb and they were able to give it a proper clear-out. But it didn't work and I was soon back to normal, coughing and spluttering. I was due to have surgery when I came home but after living in Spain I was cured, thanks to a combination of sunshine, clean air and a healthy diet. There was no way I was going back to ICI, so the first thing I had to think about now was my new job – as a fledgling folk singer. Dougie Tooth, the landlord of the Dun Cow in Seaton Village, County Durham, gave me my first paid gig in England after

From a publicity shoot in 1970

With The Fettlers at the Transporter Bridge

my return. At the age of twenty-two, I could now call myself a professional musician.

After that the bookings started coming in thick and fast, all by word of mouth, and I had a telephone installed in Mam and Dad's house at 32 Ambrose Road to enable promoters to contact me. The number was Eston Grange 5348. I did everything else by letter, without having the benefit of fax machines and email to help. I somehow managed to keep track of where I was supposed to be and began building up a reputation in the folk world. I started travelling widely, visiting folk festivals all over the country and often singing for nothing. People invited me to stay in their homes after gigs and one booking usually led to another. I wrote down all the addresses and phone numbers and fixed up my own tours.

It was far from being a glamorous existence. I slept on someone else's floor every night, with the occasional settee if my luck was in. My mate Alan Ingledew, who ran Eston Folk Club in the 1960s, was working in Manchester and I stayed with him when I played at the Ring of Bells in Warrington. We took the bus from his house to the venue, planning to catch another bus or hitch back afterwards. But the last bus had long gone by the time the evening ended and no cars were going our way. After walking for a couple of miles, we collapsed in a farmer's field. Tired and tipsy, we each selected our own haystack and climbed in. It was red hot inside and the hay made my skin unbearably itchy. On top of that there was always the worry that a combine harvester with a couple of vicious spikes on it would come and scoop us up at the crack of dawn as we dozed. After settling down we somehow put that thought out of our minds and I managed a half-decent night's sleep anyway.

The gigs continued rolling in and life was brilliant. Everything was new and exciting for me. Then early in 1970 one of The Fettlers emigrated to Canada and I was honoured to be asked to replace him. The Fettlers were stalwarts of the local folk scene and in my formative years I went to Stockton Folk Club every Saturday to hear them singing all these wonderful Graeme Miles and Ron Angel songs. The line-up I played in included Ron, Stewart McFarlane and Frankie Porter, an old mate of mine from Normanby, who joined at about the same time I did. The Fettlers were an excellent band. We all sang, Frankie was a talented guitarist and I played guitar and a bit of mandolin as well.

As well as playing with The Fettlers, I continued doing my solo work – and that's how I came to play the most important gig of my life. It was at the Farningham Folk Club in Kent. The nearest railway station was five miles away and when I arrived I had no idea how to get there, so I found a call box and phoned to tell them I was stuck. The landlord said he would ask if there was anyone around who could help.

A young lass called Pat Austen had turned up early and agreed to come and pick me up. Pat was a regular at the club and had already seen me several times. The Crayfolk were the resident band and Pat's pictured on the front of their LP, *Live at the Coach House*, sitting on the floor in the front row of the audience. I'd been single since returning from Spain. For two years before that I'd gone out with Michelle Warwick, a regular at the folk nights at Anchor House. As teenagers we all went to folk clubs hoping to meet partners. But we had to keep quiet while the singers were on, so it was quite a challenge to get to know each other. They were ideal meeting places for shy people because you

On tour with The Fettlers – Photo courtesy of Biörn Landahl

Playing alongside Stewart McFarlane in The Fettlers

Pat and Vin

didn't have to say much. Michelle later met and married the Middlesbrough footballer Alex Smith.

Pat and I hit it off and met up again when I returned to Farningham a couple of times over the next few months. She was a bonny lass and I was keen to ask her out. But it's a wonder we ever stayed together because two of our first three dates ended in disaster.

I think Pat was born with wheels, unlike me – I've never learned to drive. So when I had a gig at the Peelers Folk Club, which was run by two Irish lads in Bishopsgate, London, she agreed to drive from her home in Orpington and meet me there. Fortunately that first proper date went well and I arranged to see her again.

This time she was picking me up in London and taking me to another gig, in

Aylesbury – but we never made it there. While we were on our way, someone drove into the back of Pat's mini and we shunted into the car in front of us. If that was a bad omen, then the next date was even worse. Pat was taking me to a gig in London but we couldn't find the venue and ended up driving round in circles. Eventually we stopped and went into another pub to ask for directions – and when we came out again the car had been stolen.

Once I'd met Pat, gigs at Farningham always had a special attraction for me. I even managed to persuade them to book The Fettlers while the band were doing a tour down south. When we arrived we were greeted by the sight of a huge poster on the wall publicising the gig. It was a drawing of a coal train (because we were from the North East and, of course, that's what we all do up here). Underneath they'd added a caption saying, 'The Fettlers: Driver – Vin Garbutt.'

Somebody well-meaning had put it up because the audience was familiar with me and had probably never heard of The Fettlers. The others weren't in the least bit bothered but Stew was livid. He was the undisputed frontman of the band. I might chuck in a bit of my daft patter if I was singing a song, but Stew was the main man. He wasn't happy with me doing solo work as well as playing in The Fettlers anyway and he went absolutely crackers about me being given what looked to be top billing. It wasn't as though I'd come up with the poster myself just to get one over on him! After the gig I went to stay with Pat and her mam and brother, and Stew objected to that as well for some reason.

I was only in the band for a couple of years. By then I was becoming too busy as a solo singer and there wasn't much money coming in from The Fettlers after it was split four ways. Singing was just a hobby for the other lads but it was my livelihood. When I inevitably left the band I had the words, 'You'll be back at ICI by the end of next year!' ringing in my ears. That was a side to Stew's personality we were all aware of, although he has many positive qualities as well and we've stayed friendly over the years.

He was wrong about me returning to my job as a turner, though. I continued to make a decent living and at one point I might have even become a pop star. I was introduced to a music publisher through a model called Andrea Hanson, who used to take me to my gigs in the West Yorkshire area. Andrea's mother was from South Bank but the family ran a pub in Wetherby. She was a lovely, outgoing girl and in 1970 she started courting a singer in a rock band from London.

Through him I arranged to meet a music publisher in Wardour Street, in what was at that time a very sleazy Soho. He wasn't interested in my style of music and wanted me to write pop songs for him instead. That was never going to happen but I signed over the publishing rights to some of my earlier songs written before *The Valley of Tees* in the hope that he could do something with them. Sadly for me, that was the last I ever heard of him.

At the Redcar Folk Festival – Photo courtesy of Pete Burham

TAKING OFF

'Now we gaze to the stars knowing they're not so far
As America was to Mr Columbus...'

Vin Garbutt, *When the Tide Turns*

As my reputation grew I spread my wings and started playing further and further afield. My first overseas trip as a pro was to America in 1973, when I stayed with my old pal Kevin McLean and his wife Tina. Kevin, Speedy and another pal, Alan Ingledew, had returned to Spain together in 1970, the year after the six of us had gone out. Kevin never came back. He took a job on a yacht in Tarragona and soon found himself sailing across the Atlantic to glamorous Newport, Rhode Island, where New England's rich and famous hang out, and he settled over there.

While I was in the States we went round the folk festivals together and I played for free and picked up as many bookings as I could. I played gigs from the Eastern Seaboard north of Virginia up through the country to Washington, Philadelphia and New York, then on to Boston and over the border into Canada to Toronto and London, Ontario. I had some fantastic experiences and returned for a month or two for the next few summers.

By this time I was also making regular trips to mainland Europe. Soon after my first US tour I found myself a Belgian agent, Leon Lamal, following a chance meeting in a London underground station. Leon and I were both on our way to Cecil Sharp House, the headquarters of the English Folk and Dance Society. Traditional singers went to raid their archives for unknown folk songs and listen to tapes of old shepherds singing traditional airs. We got off the same Tube train and started chatting as we ambled along the busy footpath and Leon told me he was the landlord of the Mallemolen bar in Hoeilaart. The next thing I knew I had a Belgian tour lined up.

A pal from Eston, Vinny Noteyoung, drove and my long hair and the guitar ensured we got plenty of attention from the customs officials as we left our ferry in Zeebrugge. That was something I became used to over the years, but this time they really went to town. They sent sniffer dogs in searching for drugs and stripped the van, even taking out the cushions, before reluctantly accepting that we were clean and sending us on our way to Leon's house.

The flares date this picture to the mid-to-late 70s

Playing the mandolin in 1972

I love to sample the local food wherever I go and soon realised that Belgian cuisine is fantastic and their chefs are even better than the French. Leon's wife Marijka cooked us a delicious meal called *hutsepot*, a fry-up of potatoes, carrots and onions served with meat. I loved it.

'Oh, Marijka, this is fantastic,' I said.

She smiled and looked towards Vinny.

'Did you enjoy your meal as well, Vinny?'

He looked up, caught off guard by the question, and I'll never forget his reply, delivered in a Teesside accent that's probably even broader than mine.

'Oh, very tasty pet, very tasty!'

Around about the same time I also found a Dutch agent and started going over to Holland. There were a few Brits in the European audiences but they were mostly locals. It was harder work than playing on the established English folk circuit because I was usually just another form of entertainment, rather than someone they had specifically come to see. Us folkies were booked because the bars were usually run by people in their twenties, which never happened at home, where landlords were always much older. They were smoky places but run responsibly and sensibly and they became regular fixtures in my diary. I even learned a bit of Dutch for my stage patter. I only ever use it if I know there's at least one Dutch person in the audience. When I travel abroad people sometimes teach me tongue-twisters to see if I can master the trickier parts of their language. But why would anyone teach a stranger this?

'Ik ben een potloodventer met een puntenslijper op mijn weg naar een Hottentotten tenten tentoonstelling.'

It means, 'I'm a flasher with a pencil sharpener on my way to a Bedouin tent exhibition.' I usually have to say it twice, as even Dutch people struggle to understand it the first time because they're listening in English and not Dutch. Once I give them the translation, I say it again and as the penny drops they laugh their caps off.

Vin, Pat and the children regularly came to stay with us in the late 1980s and through the 1990s. We became friends and I spent time over in Loftus for Redcar Folk Festival and later Saltburn. Now with six grandchildren around us we have less time. But at one point the phone rang in our house. I picked up and heard a voice say, 'Is this the house for lost, bewildered and stray musicians?' It was Vin. He was on the Belgian border with Pat and the four kids. Louis was about one year old. They asked if they could come and stay and we said yes, of course. It took them two hours to reach the house and my daughter Brenda and me had all the beds made, two chickens in the oven and plenty of gravy – Vin loves his gravy. The sun started to shine with the first bite.

It was a wonderful couple of days. When Vin starts to look pensive you know something is up. I was cooking and this voice came from the big table. 'Liesbeth, what is the word for 'flasher' in Dutch?' I told him it was '*potloodventer*' (pencilman). Then a few minutes later he says, 'And what is the Dutch name for a pencil sharpener?' (*puntenslijper*). Somehow he learned about a Hottentotten tent exposition, or in Dutch a '*Hottentotten tenten tentoonstelling*'! So he was sitting there practising saying, '*A potloodventer with a puntenslijper on his way to a Hottentotten tenten tentoonstelling*.' I knew this was going to end up in the gig that night and yes, he was telling a story and threw it in. The audience all turned and looked at me. I looked innocent and they laughed and laughed and still talk about it today.

For some reason people from the North East have a canny ear for Dutch and there are similarities between their dialect and the Dutch language. It probably dates from the fishing days when Dutch boats used to stop off. But when Vin started coming over at the beginning of the eighties and started playing all the folk clubs and theatres he wanted to find out what 'cheers' was. In Vin's dialect 'cheers' sounded like 'chairs', so the guy he asked said *stoelen*, which means chairs. As he went around the country, every time he brought a glass of beer up on stage he would yell, '*Stoelen!*' Eventually one member of the audience asked, 'What are you saying *stoelen* for?' When he said he thought it was the Dutch word for cheers, they all laughed. Vin decided to keep it in, and everybody here in the folk scene still says it when they drink together – it's never the correct word, *proost*, but always *stoelen*. Younger people who have joined will ask for an explanation. We always enjoyed Vin's company and simply love the family as well. They are all lovely people.

Liesbeth Peters and Peter Wesseling

In the mid-1970s a Radio Denmark presenter and producer called Eric Kramsoj saw me at Sidmouth Folk Festival and arranged for his station to fly me over to Denmark.

A familiar onstage pose

He fixed me up with an agent and out of that came a tour with the electric folk band Steeleye Span. I already knew guitarist Bob Johnson and fiddler Peter Knight from their pre-Steeleye days when they led a regular session at Cecil Sharp House. They both secretly played on the Wombles' hits and appeared on Top of the Pops dressed in furry costumes. Peter, who is an excellent fiddler and now has a band called Gigspanner, was Uncle Bulgaria for the show. As well as being pals I also loved their music and thoroughly enjoyed joining up with them. The tour involved making numerous short ferry crossings and we spent most of the time laughing together.

It was around the time that Steeleye had a worldwide chart hit with *Gaudete*, which guaranteed packed out audiences wherever we went. One gig was in a huge theatre in the country's second city, Aarhus. The Danes can be an exuberant bunch and they could give you a hard time if you were the support act and they were waiting for the headliner to come on. I was just launching into my set when somebody up in the balcony shouted what was quite clearly an insult at me in Danish.

'Listen,' I said. 'If you're going to jump, jump!'

The audience loved it and the heckler went quiet after that. The quip was just short enough for them to understand without needing a translation, even though they're all fluent English speakers anyway. Despite my strong Teesside accent I can generally get by in that part of the world. You have a better chance of being understood in Scandinavia if you're from the north of England than if you come from down south. I still speak to Steeleye's lead singer Maddy Prior occasionally and she came to see me last time I played in Carlisle, near her home.

I returned to Denmark in 1977 to sing at what has since grown into one of Europe's biggest music festivals, Roskilde. Even back then it was an enormous outdoor event with 31,000 people attending over three days. I played in between the Ian Gillan Band and the John Miles Band, and Björn from ABBA was in the audience. Dr Feelgood, the Jack Bruce Band and the Chieftains were also in that year's line-up.

Each year I went to the States, Kevin, the former ICI apprentice from Middlesbrough's Berwick Hills council estate, had progressed a little further in his career in the luxury yachting industry. He once smuggled me onto a yacht he and Tina were working on that belonged to a famous author – it was so big that the owner never even found out I was on board. Another time I stayed with them during the America's Cup at Newport, Rhode Island and we formed part of the flotilla of sailing boats that followed the racing ships. I played my tin whistle on the bow of the boat while a TV crew filmed an advert for Salem, the world's first filter-tipped menthol cigarettes. The big sail at the front, the spinnaker, displayed the firm's logo and I stood on the prow in the style of Leonardo DiCaprio in *Titanic*.

I performed in front of 16,000 people on the same bill as Tom Paxton and Kate and Anna McGarrigle at the Philadelphia Folk Festival in August 1975 and thought I'd achieved what British musicians dream of and cracked America.

My 1976 trip was memorable because of the celebrations to mark the Bicentennial of the American Revolution, and the whole country seemed to be bedecked in red, white and blue bunting. The other talking point that summer was the upcoming presidential election when Republican Gerald Ford was being challenged by Democrat Jimmy Carter, a relatively unknown peanut farmer from Georgia. The tour was arranged by my agent at the time, Mick Moloney, and his then wife, Philomena. Mick is a fantastic tenor banjo and mandolin player who found fame in the 1960s with Irish traditional band the Johnstons. He moved to Philadelphia, but had a habit of being on holiday at home in Ireland every time I went over there. It cost a tenner just to pick up the phone to make a long-distance call in those days and I spent most of my spare cash phoning him to find out where I was supposed to be playing next.

Pat and I married in 1977 and for the first time I moved out of Mam and Dad's house. I was thirty-one and it was time to grow up. Pat came out to the States with me for my 1978 US tour, when she was pregnant with our first baby, Emma.

Kevin McLean ended up in bed with us after a gig at the Towne Crier Folk Club in Pawling, upstate New York. We were staying with the club's owner, Phil Ciganer, whose house was full of native African artefacts including shrunken heads and tribal spears and shields. The place gave Kevin the creeps and he burst into our room in the middle of the night.

'I'm not sleeping by myself in here,' he said, and he jumped under our covers!

During the trip we bought an enormous Chevrolet station wagon that just floated along the highway and was long enough for me to stretch out and sleep in the back. It cost us next to nothing and turned out to be much cheaper and more convenient than using public transport to get around. Once the tour finished we planned to store it for the next trip at Kevin's house in Mattapoisett, near Cape Cod, Massachusetts. The final gig of the tour was at New England College in the New Hampshire town of Henniker. They were mad about anything British in that part of the world, so it was a novelty for them to have somebody talking to the students in a regional dialect. They were as interested in my accent as the songs.

Afterwards we filled up the car ahead of the drive back to Kevin's. As we headed along Interstate 95 I was taken aback to hear Chris Rea's *Fool If You Think It's Over* blasting out over the radio waves. Chris was three years younger than me but we sometimes played together at a free session in the basement of the Settlement Centre in Middlesbrough. I'd last seen him on the platform at Darlington station a couple of years earlier. Chris and his girlfriend, Joan, who later became his wife, were on their way to London to sign his first record deal and we were both waiting for the same train. It was good to hear his career was taking off.

We'd only reached Boston, halfway along the two-and-a-half-hour journey, when we hit a serious problem. The Chevy had an external petrol tank and as we motored along it somehow became dislodged and started scraping against the road surface, sending sparks flying in all directions. There was no way we could just stop in the middle of the traffic – but as the sparks turned into flames, feeding off the full fuel tank, the situation became more urgent. Somehow Pat managed to find a place at the side of the road to pull over and we both breathed an enormous sigh of relief. A car swerved in behind us, ignoring the warnings Americans were given to avoid stopping in the area because of the risk of being carjacked. Our Good Samaritans had seen what had happened to us and wanted to help. They found us a local garage, who came out and fixed the damage the same day. The mechanic told us we were lucky the tank was so full because if it had contained more air it could easily have ignited and blown the whole car up. That trip turned out to be my final US tour. Unlike at home, where the folk scene is a network of venues interacting with each other, the places I played over there were all completely autonomous. If you went down well at a festival in England word spread and soon everyone had heard about you. It usually led to another bigger festival and people would come along to see you from other folk clubs and book you for gigs throughout the year. But everything was different in the States. It seemed that nobody talked to each other. Six years after I started going over there I was still doing the same small clubs. I could no longer afford to go just for the craic, struggling to cover my costs. And by then I'd found a much more welcoming market for my music.

BLAZING THE TRAIL

'What's the use of wings if you can't fly?'

Brian Bedford, *Wings*

In 1977 I became the first British folk singer to be taken out to play in Australia, enabling me to reach a whole new audience on the other side of the world. It all started when I received a phone call from Ray Downes, who used to run a folk club in Egremont, Cumbria, asking how much I'd charge to play in Perth. I was mad keen on the idea from the start.

'A shilling and expenses,' I said.

It was just as well I was eager because, as it turned out, I only just broke even. I'd play just about anywhere without any payment back then. As long as they looked after me when I arrived, I'd pack my bags and off I would go. Even now if there's somewhere I haven't played I'd probably still do it for nothing, at least the first time. The idea is that hopefully they'll enjoy the show and pay when they book me to come back.

The big breakthrough came when several Aussie folk clubs banded together and started an English-style folk touring circuit. I had always paid my own way to the States and tried to recoup the outlay when I was there, but this was different. They paid the fare, partly thanks to a folkie called Adrian Eastwell, who worked for an airline and was able to arrange cheap tickets.

This new Aussie folk circuit was brilliant for me. I travelled all over the country, to every major city and town and deep into the outback, with each club paying a standard fee into the kitty. I played in some fantastic places, including the mining communities of Mount Isa and Newman out in the middle of nowhere and right up to Darwin in the Northern Territories and Port Hedland on the west coast.

I met Ewan MacColl and his wife Peggy Seeger for the first time when we all played at a festival in Tasmania and I still have a soft spot for the island. Ewan is a hero of mine and his songs *The First Time Ever I Saw Your Face* and *Dirty Old Town* are two timeless folk classics. He wrote the former for Peggy. She's over eighty now and she emailed me when she was writing her memoirs. She was trying to recall incidents that have stayed with her and asked me what year we met in Tasmania. She recalled me and an Irishman going hell for leather trying to outdo each other with daft patter. She said I

Vin playing the whistle on the yacht Land's End *during a trip to the States in 1974*

won by insulting his mother! I can't imagine doing that – it must have been something comical that he didn't mind. I can't remember the incident but for some reason it's stuck with her nearly forty years later. I told Peggy to write what she wanted about me, as long as I didn't come out as a nasty piece of work because of whatever I said about this poor fella's mam! Peggy invited me to stay at her home near Oxford if I'm ever playing in the area. It was kind of her to do that. I suppose there's a dwindling number of us oldies left, so we can't afford to be choosy!

> Ewan and I were attending the Longford Festival in Tasmania in 1979. I remember a hilarious onstage *flyting* – a traditional versified competition in which each contestant insults the other till one of them gives up. In this corner was Vin Garbutt and in that corner Liam Weldon. They came out slugging in a simple song form and, both being very creative, they dragged it out for fifteen or twenty minutes. Vin won, rendering Liam speechless with anger, unable to continue. I don't remember the actual winning verse, but traditionally the worst insult you can inflict is against your opponent's mother. I once saw a *flyting* in which an outraged Uruguayan broke his guitar over a Paraguayan's head after an insult involving his mother.
> **Peggy Seeger**

In 1986 I spread my wings even further and added a first trip to New Zealand to my itinerary. It turned out to be an eventful one. A folk club in Adelaide had been closing down and had a pot of money left over, so they invited me to go to Australia and do a one-off gig for my airfare and expenses. I jumped at the chance. Once I was booked up I realised it would cost next to nothing to go on from there to New Zealand so I fixed up my own tour, arranging gigs all over both main islands. There was hardly any money in it for me, but it was a chance to show my wares somewhere I'd never been and play to a brand new audience.

I was picked up at Christchurch Airport on Good Friday by a Catholic priest called Father John Faisandier. He was also a folkie and played the guitar and sang. Once we'd made our introductions we set off for the Canterbury Folk Festival. But we never arrived. A few miles into our journey, there was an almighty bang and I was aware of being flung around the inside of the car. Then everything stopped and there was an eerie and complete silence.

My first thought was, 'Am I dead?' I wriggled my toes. They seemed to move and that probably meant I was still alive. My next question was, 'Am I badly hurt?' I was in shock, so there was no real pain at first. I glanced across at John, without turning my head.

'Are you all right?' he said.

'I think so.'

No sooner had we established that we were both alive than the humour kicked in.

'Here I am travelling with a Catholic priest on Good Friday and I could have been killed!' I said.

'That's nothing – at least you'd have a priest to look after you on your deathbed. All I'd have is a folk singer!'

I suppose he had a point. He could have administered the last rites – all I could have done to offer comfort as he breathed his last was sing a song to him.

We were all scrunched up and battered and bruised, but John was incredibly brave and scrambled out of the car and made his way round to help me. We both had broken ribs and my knee was badly cut where it had slammed into the dashboard. It turned out a young couple had driven the other way over some crossroads and smashed head-on into us. Both cars were completely wrecked and pointing in the opposite direction to the one we were supposed to be travelling in.

We were taken to hospital and while we were there a friend of John's came to visit. He was introduced to me as Denis and stayed for an hour or so as we shared a few laughs. After he left I said, 'Who's Denis then?'

'He's the Bishop of Christchurch,' said John.

'Bloomin' heck, John,' I said. 'I'm from the Old World – we're supposed to call a bishop 'Your Grace' and kiss his ring where I come from!'

The tour was cancelled and I stayed with John in his presbytery for a couple of weeks to convalesce. Singing was out of the question and news of the crash and my cancelled gigs was reported in the local papers.

Vin getting to know the actor Geoff Hughes in the New Zealand sunshine – Photo courtesy of John Faisandier

John's recollection of that meeting is slightly different…

> The annual Canterbury Folk Festival was coming up over the Easter long weekend and the organising committee asked if someone could billet visiting performer Vin Garbutt. They said he was a Catholic, which put people off wanting to host him. I was keen.
>
> He arrived on the Wednesday before Easter, having flown directly from the UK. I wanted to make a positive first impression and cook a memorable meal for his first night in New Zealand. This was the beginning of a world tour he was about to make as he zigzagged his way back to England. I thought something distinctly New Zealand would be best and so chose expensive premium lamb chops for us to eat that night. When I told him of the plans for dinner on the way back from the airport he looked at me and said, 'I don't eat red meat during Lent.' Oh dear! What kind of a Catholic did I have here? And me, a Catholic priest, not having any scruples about it. We bought some cheap fish on the way home and Vin showed me a fantastic fish curry recipe which we enjoyed with clear consciences. I've been cooking curries ever since. We immediately struck up a firm friendship. There were serious conversations on all kinds of topics and, above all, playful patter, which generated laughter in huge amounts.
>
> Vin had a couple of days to recover from his jet lag and in that time I heard stories of his travels and his life in Loftus. He wasn't due to perform at the folk festival until late on Friday night, so I looked forward to enjoying his company until then. It was Good Friday and I was due to preach at the local parish for the 3pm service. The theme I chose was how the person of Jesus was rejected by the world because of his ideas and the people he associated with. The parish was rather well-to-do and the people were well dressed, wealthy and generally

didn't associate with folk singers, vagabonds or other people from low-income areas. Vin was there in the middle of them with his shaggy beard and hair. He had told me tales of travelling in England on the train, where he often had a compartment to himself because people would see him sitting there and quickly move on to find a better compartment without somebody like him in it. His presence in the church inspired me about what I wanted to say in my sermon. Few people complimented me afterwards.

When it was time to take Vin to the festival at Amberley, I remember feeling sad that I wouldn't see him again, and so drove slowly to prolong the enjoyment of his company. This turned out to be a blessing. We were travelling along a dark road as the Easter moon had not yet risen and at one bend an oncoming car was out of control and crossed the centreline. There was a moment when our lives turned to slow motion as the two cars smashed into each other, headlight to headlight. We both thought we had died but soon realised that while we couldn't move we were just winded and had very sore ribs from the impact. As we approached the hospital we heard the driver radio through and say, 'We have two minor injuries and will be there in five minutes.' We were both disgusted by his description that we had 'minor injuries'. It certainly didn't feel minor to us in those moments. Fortunately, they were, in fact, minor - cracked ribs and a badly twisted ankle for Vin. We were discharged with instructions to take two Panadol every four hours and Vin was not to travel for two weeks until his ankle was better.

Those two weeks were full of laughter. Once Vin had reconciled himself to cancelling his world tour and informing Pat of the accident and assuring her he was not badly damaged and was in good company, we just had to relax and recuperate. And good company was what we ended up with. Our local newspaper published a story and photo of the accident, which was publicity for the folk festival. The actor Geoff Hughes was in town rehearsing a play that would be touring New Zealand. When he saw the photo he made contact because he loved Vin's music. Within minutes he arrived at our house and over the next two weeks was a frequent visitor with guitar, wine and delicious food to share. Geoff was a larger-than-life character. He took us to a VIP sponsors' tent at the races, we saw his show and most of all we enjoyed having him at our house, where he was relaxed and out of the public limelight.

During these two weeks there was much joking and silly talk but because we both had sore ribs, our laughter had to be channelled elsewhere. We developed the habit of stamping a foot on the floor instead of belly-laughing. That autumn in Christchurch was particularly mild and we spent many days sitting out in the sunshine enjoying one another's company. On a family visit to the UK in 2003 we had the pleasure of staying with Vin and Pat. Geoff Hughes was filming a few miles away and came over for a singalong at the local pub. Those happy times still fill us with warm memories.

John Faisandier

Vin in Tasmania

While I was recovering at John's presbytery I received a phone call from Geoffrey Hughes, who was over in New Zealand appearing in a play. Geoff was a fantastic character actor who was familiar to TV audiences in the UK having been in Coronation Street among many other roles. In later decades he also appeared in shows such as The Royle Family and Heartbeat. We'd met before because he played the bodhrán and often turned up at music sessions in pubs near his home, but meeting him in New Zealand was the start of a wonderful friendship. Renault had loaned him a free car for the duration of his play and he arranged to pick me and John up and ferry us all over the place.

Pat and I became close to both Geoff and his wife Susan from then on and he stayed with us when he was filming Heartbeat at Goathland, not far from us. He wasn't keen on hotels and to be honest I don't think he was that fond of the acting set either. The first time they stayed, our house was still in the semi-derelict state we'd bought it in and all we could offer them was a mattress in front of a warm Aga. He asked me if he was allowed to climb its north face, but I told him it wouldn't have been safe. I reckon Geoff only ever played versions of himself in all his television roles and he would sit around the house in his string vest, just like his *Keeping Up Appearances* character Onslow. He had a couple of nights off during one visit and I wondered if he fancied going out for a pint. He didn't need asking twice and Pat dropped us off at Timms Coffee House in Skinningrove. Everybody knew Geoff's face from at least one of his TV roles and as we walked in I asked how we could expect people to react when they saw him.

'They generally want to be Eddie Yeats' best mate or the bloke who filled him in,' he said in that broad scouse accent. 'If someone comes over and puts his hand around my shoulder, I know I'm all right.'

As it turned out, there were only three other people in the bar and nobody seemed to notice us coming in. Timms dates back to 1704 and looked as though it hadn't been renovated since. We sat and enjoyed a game of dominoes and a lovely pint. After a while one of the regulars sauntered over and stood behind Geoff as if he'd known him all his life, eyeing his hand of dominoes approvingly. Before long he had his hand on his shoulder and was congratulating him on every tile he laid.

'Good move,' he said, nodding his appreciation.

The landlord became curious and I noticed him gawping over with a look of recognition on his face. Seeing that I'd clocked him, he turned his back to me and then glanced in the mirror behind the bar for a double-take.

'Geoff,' I said out of the corner of my mouth. 'I think you've been spotted.'

It was the days before mobiles but the landlord picked up the landline behind the bar and dialled everyone he knew. Within minutes the pub began filling up and the landlord was bringing out big trays of corned beef sandwiches and sausages on sticks. Soon the place was heaving with locals coming in to see Eddie Yeats, and the queue for autographs snaked round the pub.

'Sorry about this Geoff,' I said.

But he wasn't in the least bit bothered. He just pulled some photos from his pocket and patiently signed them for everyone. While Geoff was keeping his public happy, a bloke sidled up to me.

'Can I have your autograph as well?' he said.

'Me? You don't know who I am, do you?'

'Of course I do,' he said. 'You're Eddie Yeats' mate!'

When Geoff was chosen to appear on *This Is Your Life* with Eamonn Andrews the producers asked me to come on the show and talk about my friend. Unfortunately I had a gig I couldn't cancel and I had to say no. It could have been my doorway to stardom! Geoff and Susan had a smallholding in Northamptonshire when we first became friends and later moved to the Isle of Wight. One year our Tim went to the Isle of Wight Festival and Geoff and Susan invited him to stay with them – in a luxury filming trailer in their garden! Geoff was a lovely bloke and we were devastated when he passed away in July 2012 after a long battle with prostate cancer.

On one of my trips to Australia I met up with Eugene McElvaney, who I served my time with. Eugene went to St Peter's School with me and although I can't remember it, he recalls us handing our cards in together and leaving ICI on the same day. I was well known because I kept a guitar in my locker at the Central Workshops on the huge Wilton site and took it out and practised every lunchtime. Everyone knew me as the long-haired bloke who made such a racket in the changing rooms. While I became a full-time folk singer, Eugene emigrated to Australia and did well for himself, starting a successful paint business. He was able to take early retirement and one day in 1994 he was in Port Fairy, Victoria, planning a sailing trip. While he was there he saw a poster for Port Fairy Folk Festival, and on it was my name.

'That can't be the Vinny Garbutt I left ICI with,' he thought.

He bought a couple of tickets on the off-chance and went to his first-ever folk gig. I met him afterwards and I was delighted to see him again. I took him backstage and introduced him to Eric Bogle and Martin Carthy and various other folk luminaries. Eugene loved what he heard and bought everybody's CDs. About a year later I received a phone call. Eugene's family were back in England and he wanted to come to see us. But there was something else he needed to tell me. Eric Bogle's brilliant song *The Green Fields of France* had affected Eugene keenly. The lyrics are incredibly powerful and moving...

Oh how do you do, Private Willie McBride
Do you mind if I sit here down by your graveside?
And rest for a while in the warm summer sun
I've been walking all day, and I'm nearly done
And I see by your gravestone you were only nineteen
When you joined the great fallen in 1916
Well, I hope you died quick, and I hope you died clean
Or young Willie McBride, was is it slow and obscene?

Eugene's grandad was killed in Flanders during the First World War. On their way back home from Australia he took his kids to visit the battlefield and they managed to trace his grandad's grave and recorded a video of the children paying their respects to him. When they played the film to their extended family back home in Grangetown, they noticed something they hadn't seen at the time. The name above Eugene's grandad's in the list of the fallen was a Private William McBride. A chill ran down my spine when he told me. Eric Bogle and I have been friends since the 1970s and I told him the whole story as soon as I could. But Eric had researched the name and discovered that no less than six William McBrides died in France and Belgium during the First World War. It was a sobering lesson that brought home the scale of the slaughter that was inflicted on a whole generation of the world's youth.

I don't know when I first met Vin. It seems as if he's always been a big part of life in South Bank and Grangetown. Vin's mother, Tessie Kelly, was in the same class as my mam, Emily McCabe, and I believe my aunt, Ellen McElvaney, was Tessie's bridesmaid. At St Peter's Junior School, a skinny, curly-headed Vin fitted in and was well-liked by all. In the senior school Vin had plenty of mates but was rarely seen without his best friend and fellow musician, Pete Betts. They used to say that to survive in St Peter's you had to be able to fight, run, entertain or tell jokes. Vin and Pete managed to thrive with their mixture of essential survival talents. Both were school prefects. The somewhat unruly St Peter's students (me included) were easily controlled by the fearsome Pete Betts, but Vin managed to get students' cooperation and commitment by being the most revered of the prefects.

At this stage of Vin's school life, when Beatlemania was at a high, Vin, Pete and a couple of mates developed their ambition to become singers and musicians. However, a trade had to come first and, like many, Vin found himself becoming an apprentice turner at ICI Wilton. Our paths crossed again in March 1969 when we sat together waiting for our final payout and cards in the employment office at ICI. The wages clerk had been called away, so we had about an hour to wait and had a good old chat about our school days and future plans. Vin was going to fulfil his dream of becoming a professional musician in Spain and I was emigrating to Melbourne, Australia, to seek my fortune.

It took Vin only a few years to become an overnight success and in the early 1970s he was touring Australia and the world. Our paths didn't cross again until March 1994, exactly twenty-five years after we left ICI. I was fishing for white pointer sharks out of a small town called Port Fairy on the south coast of Victoria. My hobby was to catch, photograph and release big game fish. These waters produced some of the biggest white pointer sharks in the world and catching them from our small seventeen-foot open boat was the pinnacle for us. Port Fairy was hosting its annual folk music festival and a poster in the main general store proclaimed that one of the festival's main attractions was international sensation Vin Garbutt. My son Craig and his friend Simon didn't quite believe that Vin was an old schoolmate of mine.

Tickets were like hens' teeth but I managed to buy one from a woman whose husband had died that day and so wouldn't be accompanying her to the concert. I met Vin after his performance and he invited me to the festival's green room to have a drink with some of the artists. I had a conversation with Irish singer Mary Black and also chatted with the singer Enda Kenny and Vin's close mate Eric Bogle, the Scottish-Australian who wrote *The Green Fields of France*, the ballad made famous by the Fureys in the late 1980s. I watched every performance of Vin's that weekend and even helped him sell his cassettes. We also had endless drinks while discussing our schooldays and the people of South Bank and Grangetown. With no emails or Facebook then, people lost track of each other and expats like me were starved of news from home.

Over the years, Vin and his lovely wife Pat have visited us in Melbourne and we reciprocate when we visit the UK. Vin has countless friends in Australia. One of the best things about folk festivals for performers like Vin is the extra time over the three-to-four days to bond with the audience. Vin appeals to a range of age groups, but it's the ones between fifty and seventy who respond to his wit the best. At the Port Fairy Folk Festival, after starting a story about his recent heart problems, he told the audience to make sure they turned up the next day to find out whether he died or survived the operations! The venue was packed the next day with a very hopeful audience.

For North East expats, Vin Garbutt is our link with our old homeland. He sings and jokes about the trials and tribulations of the places where we spent our childhood – which helps explain why he performs to packed houses overseas. His songs about the coal and potash miners resonate with Australians who also mine for a living. *The Land of Three Rivers* is not just a song about the geography of the North East, it's about the hardship and mateship that is the life of the Australian worker too. So it's not too surprising that my son James, who works in the gold mining town of Kalgoorlie in the Western Australian desert, came across an outback petrol station owner singing *Silver and Gold* from Vin's album *Persona ... Grata*. The entrepreneurial guy even sold James one of Vin's latest CDs. Vin's songs also highlight the ever-present injustices in the world. Not many people in the UK probably know that *Darwin to Dili* was a rallying song for the resistance to Indonesia's annexation of East Timor. That resistance movement eventually succeeded when a UN vote gave the East Timorese a chance to be a democratic republic. It was an honour to be part of the fight to free East Timor with people like Vin.

Rather than take the huge amount of luggage needed for world tours of up to two months in all sorts of climates, Vin will buy extra clothes to suit the local climate from charity shops. His view is that he is putting money into local charities and when he leaves, he donates the clothes back. Unfortunately, he sometimes not only looks like a 1960s hippy, he often dresses in their original clothes! He's the singing historian. The songs he writes and sings are a living history of the North East and the hotspots of the world. However, his banter is up-to-the-minute stuff that a diverse audience can readily relate to. He has the knack of playing to thousands while making everyone feel he is playing especially for them.

Eugene McElvaney

My audiences in places such as Perth, Melbourne and Adelaide just grow and grow every time I go out. I earn a decent fee and play to up to three hundred people at each gig. There are still parts of Australia that don't know anything about me because they'll never read about me in the papers or even hear of me on the radio. Without that kind of publicity, it's only through word of mouth that I manage to fill the venues I play. I have to hope the audiences enjoy what they hear and buy my CDs.

Ray Downes, the man who took me to Australia the first time back in 1977, returned to his native Cumbria a few years ago. He was dying of cancer and asked me to play at his 73rd birthday party, which he knew would probably be his last. I was delighted to go along and sing a few songs for him. I was greatly saddened when I heard the news that he'd passed away in 2016. Ray was a wonderful man with a big voice and a huge heart. I'll always be thankful to him for that phone call that was to make me the first English folkie to blaze the trail down under.

AROUND THE WORLD IN 23 DAYS

'So he buckled right in with the trace of a grin
On his face. If he worried he hid it.
He started to sing as he tackled the thing
That couldn't be done, and he did it!'

Edgar Guest, *It Couldn't Be Done*

Airfares were plummeting by the early 1990s and I came up with an idea that I thought might allow me to continue singing my songs to the widest possible audience. I reckoned I could save a fortune by buying a round-the-world ticket, enabling me to stop and play at various places along the route to my final destination and a couple more on the way back. I looked at the figures and worked out that sixteen bookings would take me all the way to Australia and back again. I wrote to each club and spelt out the situation as plainly as I could. I quoted them a viable fee and explained that was how much I needed to make it work, stressing there would be no hard feelings if they couldn't afford it. If enough of them took up the offer I could buy a round-the-world ticket and wouldn't need the expense of shelling out for smaller tours to different countries – I could do them all together on the same trip.

The first tour was in 1991 and took me around the world in twenty-three days. I started with four gigs in Canada before heading off for one show in New Zealand and eight spread all over Australia. After that I flew to Brunei, Hong Kong and Singapore before returning to England. I posted LPs out to each venue in advance and managed to sell hundreds of them. The whole scheme was a huge success. Instead of just scraping by, it turned into a lucrative trip and became a fixture in my calendar every couple of years or so.

I threw in the occasional special gig for expats in places such as Bangkok or Malaysia. Expats are usually a wonderful audience. They discover folk music in foreign climes and develop an interest in part of their own culture that they didn't know anything about when they lived back in England. As much as half of a 300-strong audience

The many faces of Vin. At the 2007 Burke and Wills Festival – photos courtesy of Marina Hurley

when I play in Australia might be from the north of England. Many people come to my gigs back in Britain after seeing me abroad. Few of them have heard a lot of folk music until they go out there, but they come along to see a singer from home.

When Pat and I moved to Loftus in 1981 I was struck by the number of houses for sale in the area. It was mainly because thousands of jobs were being lost in the steel industry at that time due to the recession. For some reason, droves of people from our region end up emigrating to Perth in particular in search of a better life. It's nothing new – people have been leaving this area for centuries and there are place names with Teesside links all over Australia, all part of Captain Cook's legacy. Sydney has its very own Linthorpe Street and during my last trip I stayed in a suburb of the city called Loftus. I was inspired to write *The Loftus Emigrant* about a butcher I met during one visit to Australia. Whenever I sing it in a pub session in Loftus people can't believe they're hearing about their hometown. My East Cleveland village is what most people might regard as a backwater and they're thrilled to bits to hear it being sung about. That's the beauty of folk music. It's all about roots and all these songs are roots songs.

> Vin Garbutt is revered among Australian folk music fans, going back to the days when most folk singers here wanted to sound just like him. Nowadays we look to our own land and heritage for inspiration, but in the duffle coat and coffee bar folk days, England was surely the only place worth singing about and every Australian singer sounded as though they originated from Thomas Hardy country. Even though most Aussies now do their own thing, the popularity of the top UK and Irish singers has not diminished, mainly because their greats are such consummate performers.
>
> Vin ranks with the best. He is appreciated in turn for his incisive wit, his meaningful guitar accompaniment – where he never lets the instrument take over from the voice – his superb skill on the penny whistle and, most of all, the quality of his voice and his songs. To me, as a singer Vin is something like Patsy

Cline. Everybody wants to copy his style but nobody ever gets there. I was just the other day listening to Vin's version of Eric Bogle's *Green Fields of France* and nobody could ever squeeze out emotive notes as he can. 'Flu-eu-eu-eurs of the Fo-o-o-oo-re-e-e-esss-tttt,' Vin sang – and I burst into tears. It's like the Welsh choirs as they do the eighth 'Amen'. Nerys and I have had the pleasure of being beautifully hosted by Vin and Pat in Yorkshire and then having the honour of Vin staying with us at Alice Springs, where we organised a delightful house concert. He was such fun and a laugh a minute. Vin ranks with the best in the world.
The Honourable Dr Ted Egan, folk singer and former Administrator of the Northern Territory, Australia

Sometimes expat gigs can bring unique challenges. I once arrived at a venue in the Far East and saw a poster advertising a Christmas dinner and disco – and to my horror, I realised I was the disco! But there can be pleasant surprises as well. I turned up for a gig at the Sports Club of Indonesia in Jakarta and was amazed to find a wonderful pagoda-style building with huge pillars, set in front of a beautiful, shimmering lake. The person who booked me knew his regular audience would be swelled because an English performer was coming over. There were about 250 people there and it was a fantastic night. As so often is the case, most of the audience had never listened to folk music and had certainly never heard of me. They bought their tickets because so few musical Brits pass through Jakarta, apart from a few ABBA clones. They had an enjoyable night and I sold out of CDs.

I love discovering new cultures and playing in places I would never have the chance to visit if it wasn't for my profession. When I went to Singapore I decided to go for a walk to see the sights, before a sign in my hotel room made me think again about venturing out. It read: 'Westerners with long hair may be stopped in the street to have it cut.' I later found out that Led Zeppelin, the Bee Gees and even Cliff Richard were forced to cancel planned concerts in the city-state because of the ban. It was brought in by Singapore's first Prime Minister, Lee Kuan Yew, who wanted to prevent the city's youth from being corrupted by western hippie culture. To this day chewing gum is outlawed in Singapore and you can't take durian fruit on the subway. Durian is an orangutan's favourite food and even though it stinks to high heaven, for some reason Singaporeans can't eat enough of it. It's a little bigger than a pineapple, with a spiky husk that you cut into. I love to eat whatever the locals eat wherever I go, but durian is the one food that's defeated me. I tried to ignore the smell but I almost gagged when I took a bite. It tasted vaguely chocolatey, with undertones of turpentine and notes of raw sewage. I decided to persevere, thinking maybe only the first taste is horrible – instead it became even worse the more I ate. Westerners are unanimously disgusted by durian. Fortunately you can always give it away because everyone else seems to love it.

The worldwide tours took an enormous amount of organising and it was hard work in the months before setting off. I became familiar with the lie of the land in each country and learned about the monsoon seasons in various parts of the globe, and when you

A folk-loving camel on an Australian tour

A publicity shot for the By-Pass Syndrome in the Australian bush

Entertaining schoolchildren in Kuala Lumpur

do and don't want to be in certain places. Agents don't tend to have a grasp of these details, so I made a point of finding out for myself. The problem with the model was that it only took a single cancellation for the whole tour to go to pot. Even with a higher than normal fee to cover my additional expenses, losing just one gig meant a sixteenth of my income disappeared, even though I still had the same overheads to pay out. That happened a couple of times and was incredibly frustrating. One time I'd arranged to fly from Bangkok to Sri Lanka, back to Singapore and then on to Australia but then Sri Lanka cancelled at the last minute.

'Could you come the week after instead?' the organiser asked.

Of course, it's not as simple as it may sound to just change my airline ticket and nip down to Sri Lanka. Most of my employers are hobbyists and they don't always understand that I rely on having a finely-tuned plan, arranged down to the tiniest detail. It was a setback, but I just had to take it in my stride.

On my 1994 world tour I was bumped by Bob Dylan. I had been booked to play for Hong Kong Folk Society, but just before I left I received a phone call from the organiser.

'Listen, Vin,' he said. 'Dylan's just announced an extra date on his Never Ending Tour. He's coming to Hong Kong the night you're supposed to be playing for us and all the folkies want to go. Is there any chance you could hang about for a few days?'

They offered to look after me and throw in a ticket for the Dylan concert. That sounded like a perfect plan to me, and the way the dates fell didn't interfere with any other gigs. Dylan's name might not have meant much to some of the local Chinese population and the audience were mainly westerners. I thoroughly enjoyed Bob's show, although I was slightly disappointed he didn't bother coming to mine. A review of my gig in the *South China Evening Post* a few days later was headlined, 'Move over Bob, Vin's in town.' Unlike Bob, they said, I'd played to a capacity crowd. They didn't mention that my capacity was only a hundred people – about 12,000 seats fewer than Dylan would have needed to fill the Hong Kong Coliseum!

Taken by Graham Whitley at Hartlepool Folk Song Club

At the Transporter Bridge with his trusty 'workhorse' in June 2010. The guitar was specially made for Vin by master luthier Roger Bucknall and is the only Fylde Falstaff with a cutaway

STRIKING A CHORD

'I work hard, I play hard, as hard as I toil'

Vin Garbutt, *The Land of Three Rivers*

My guitar playing style is probably unique. When I first learned I just strummed and then in the early 1960s I developed my own fingerpicking technique. My inspiration came from hearing Devon singer-songwriter Dave Wood playing the American folk classic *Freight Train.* I played the song myself using a plectrum but when Dave performed it fingerstyle it sounded fantastic and he suggested I give it a try. I'd never done any fingerstyle playing up to then.

People like Martin Carthy and Nic Jones were experimenting with open guitar tunings and although I never came round to using them myself, I liked the 'slappy' effect it gave and I tried to reproduce the same sound using standard tuning. Eventually I began using what's called 'drop D' tuning, with the bass E-string lowered to D and the rest in standard tuning. That can give the guitar a fuller tone, but the chord shapes remain almost the same. I don't know anybody who plays open-tuning style on a standard tuned guitar the way I do. I also try to play parts of the melody while I'm slapping away, so I'll sing some of the individual notes at the same time as I'm playing them.

In the early days folk clubs never had PA systems, so you had to hammer the guitar to achieve the extra volume you needed or you couldn't be heard. When I first went full-time I made a mess of my nylon strings trying to project that volume to the back of the audience. Playing a guitar with steel strings solved that problem.

Since early in my career I've played beautiful instruments handmade for me by Roger Bucknall, who runs Fylde Guitars in Cumbria. Many famous musicians play his instruments now, but I owned one of the first guitars Roger ever made, possibly the third or fourth to come out of his workshop. We met when I played at a folk club in Hampshire in the early 1970s. Roger told me he made guitars in his spare time and offered to let me try one.

As soon as I started playing I was blown away – not only did the guitar look stunning, it produced a bright, loud sound that was perfect for my style of playing. I asked how much he would charge to make me one and he very kindly did it for just the price of the

Changing a string

wood. It was love at first sight. Unfortunately, my cherished guitar was badly damaged by hapless baggage handlers at Alice Springs Airport deep in the Australian outback in 1978. Even though it was in a hard flight case, they still somehow managed to snap the head completely off the neck. Ansett Airlines weren't in the slightest bit interested in my predicament. To make matters worse the instrument wasn't insured because the premiums cost a fortune. As soon as I returned home I sheepishly gave the battered guitar back to Roger and after carrying out the necessary repairs he kept it. The string makers Rotosound had commissioned him to make a guitar for them, but when it was finished they realised it would be far too expensive to mass-produce. So Roger offered me the prototype, once again for mates' rates. It's a workhorse, a real guitarist's guitar, exceptionally light and extremely loud. It's been a reliable servant to me and is still my main stage guitar, although it's had more lives than a cat and is covered in dings, dents and scars. Every time I think it's ready for the last rites it's patched up again and just keeps on going. The war wounds only add character.

The first of two major catastrophes this guitar has suffered came at Heathrow Airport after a British Midland flight from Teesside. I checked in and then handed it over to the outsized baggage desk as usual. That should have meant it didn't go on the conveyor with all the other bags and cases when the plane landed. But the handlers carelessly slung it onto the belt anyway and the thin end of the case was dragged into the mechanism. The guitar emerged onto the carousel at the other end resembling a battered coffin. The flight case was in splinters and bits of wood were sticking out all over the place like broken limbs. My good mate Hugh Crabtree, the frontman of the band Feast of Fiddles, had come to the airport to meet me and I could only just hold back the tears.

'Hugh, man…' I said.

Hugh could see how upset I was.

'Leave it with me,' he said.

We walked up to the British Midland desk, with Hugh leading the way.

'I don't suppose you put it in like that?' said the smart young man behind the counter.

'He certainly did not,' said Hugh.

The man started writing something down and Hugh peered over the counter to inspect his work.

'He won't be able to replace it for less than £1,300,' he said, and the man added that to his notes. 'And he has a gig tonight,' he added. 'We're going to have to hire a guitar.'

I was supposed to be playing a private house concert for Robbie McIntosh, who was in Paul McCartney's band at the time. Robbie's an outstanding session guitarist who became a fan of mine after coming to one of my gigs and he later played on a couple of my albums. Before he joined McCartney's band he was in the Pretenders and he lent me a guitar Chrissie Hynde had given him to play that night. Meanwhile, Hugh contacted Roger, who had moved from the south coast to Kirkham, near Blackpool, by this time.

'Just send me all the bits and leave the rest to me,' Roger instructed.

The poor guitar was smashed to smithereens, but Roger somehow managed to perform a miracle once again and put it all back together.

> Vin was on tour and I was picking him up from Heathrow. I managed to persuade my business partner to lend Vin his Guild guitar for the tour while I got on to British Midland and after protracted correspondence persuaded them to pay for the repair, which Fylde undertook. Vin was duly impressed as he told me he'd never have hung on in with such persistence himself, being a mild-mannered folkie and all.
>
> Vin is a performer, songwriter and comic of consummate skill. This is because behind it all he is a profoundly thoughtful human being. A pleasure and an honour to know and now a lifelong friend and influence on my life. I love him to bits.
>
> **Hugh Crabtree, Feast of Fiddles**

The second accident happened when I flew back from Kuala Lumpur to Manchester after a world tour. The clues to the guitar's fate were all there when I stood alongside my fellow passengers to collect our luggage and picked the battered case off the conveyor belt. I nervously unhooked the buckles and was horrified to discover a huge crack running along the entire length of the guitar. As usual, it had been recklessly thrown around with all the other baggage. This time I managed to wangle a new guitar out of the airline. I wasn't insured but they put an article in their magazine about how their generosity had made me a very satisfied customer. Once again, Roger was able to work his magic on the damaged guitar.

Vin was one of my very first customers, even before I formed Fylde Guitars. I met him at the Cutty Wren Folk Club in Hythe, Hampshire, in about 1971 and we made friends instantly – everybody loves Vin. I think he was playing a Yamaha at the time, as were a lot of the younger professionals, and he found that the guitars I was making suited him very well. Some years later Vin bought another guitar from me and left his original with me to update. I wouldn't let him have it back – in fact I still have it! At an even later date, Vin fell for a guitar I had at home and took that away with him, so overall he's had three, but his main guitar has been with him for about forty years. It's been back to me a few times for maintenance and I had to seriously rebuild it after an airline flight. It had become entangled in the luggage carousel at baggage reclaim and came out in several, smaller, pieces. On another occasion his guitar was stolen. After making it known around certain areas, he received a phone call inviting him to collect the guitar from a scary pub where he sang a song as a thank you, possibly to the actual thief!

Whenever I could, I went to see him play locally, and I noticed that the same lovely girl turned up at all those gigs. It didn't matter how far she had to travel, she would be there. Later on, when I moved 'up country,' I still noticed her at just about all of Vin's gigs. That girl, of course, was Pat, now Mrs Garbutt. I'm sure she thinks it was worth it, they have lovely kids and grandkids now.

After one of his gigs in Portsmouth, Vin introduced me to curry. It's all his fault and he's gone on to cook curry at our house and to raid our garden for various strange herbs – I think he's a bit of a white witch. If he feels ill, he makes a potion out of lovage and sorrel and stuff. He sits in our lounge and reels off the names of all the birds and wanders round the garden, writing songs. He was due to play at one of my birthday parties but only checked his diary after he and Pat had set off in the car. Wrong day!

I have travelled far to see Vin play, but the furthest was an accident. I was in New York and saw his name in a paper. I sat in the front row at the Eagle Tavern and when he came on stage I said, just loud enough, 'Hello, Vin.' He looked down and said 'Hello Rog' and carried on – and then did the proverbial double-take. I don't think we found a curry shop that night. Vin's career has been based upon strong songs, off-the-wall humour and amazing whistle playing. At one time he would play solo guitar tunes, which to me were astonishing, like nothing anybody else played.

Roger Bucknall MBE

Roger is a genius but he's suffered for his art. He went through a difficult time after developing a severe allergy to tropical woods. He had to stop making guitars and used his brilliant engineering brain to produce snooker cues for the sport's top stars instead, using aluminium, plastics and brass. He was eventually able to start making guitars again and I was delighted to join other artists at a surprise party in Cumbria in 2016 to celebrate him being awarded the MBE for services to guitar making, music and heritage crafts. It was a fantastic evening with some stunning performances that got the most out of those beautiful instruments. Gordon Giltrap and Eric Bibb were there and a screen displayed video messages from those who couldn't attend, including Martin Carthy.

My Geordie friends Bob Fox and Stu Luckley also reunited to play a couple of songs. Bob played keyboards on my album *Bandalised* and in recent years has been Songman in the West End production of *Warhorse*. I used to tell audiences that to persuade Bob and Stu to join my band I asked them if they fancied coming on tour to Abu Dhabi in the Middle East. Once they were safely signed up I revealed that I'd deceived them ever so slightly. We were actually playing at Derby Abbey in the East Midlands!

> I was working as head of music at a comprehensive school in Rowlands Gill and Vin convinced me that I should really be back on the folk scene as an artist. He suggested that I drive him around on his tours and do a promotional 'floor spot' to secure a solo booking for myself at the clubs and venues he was playing at. I took him up on the offer and in no time I was indeed back performing with a full diary and eventually added a further twenty-odd years to my career, all thanks to Vin.
>
> During the time I was driving him around we had huge laughs. He was constantly working on funny lines based on the things we saw and often these lines would be included in his patter the same night. A road sign provided one of the best. 'Me and Bob were driving here tonight and there was a sign that said 'Hidden dip' – and just round the corner we drove into a big tub of hummus!'
>
> **Bob Fox**

The Vin Garbutt Band put together for 1994's Bandalised album – Paul Archer, Andy McLaughlin, Vin, Bob Fox and Norman Holmes

OCCUPATIONAL HAZARDS

'You can never have enough torches, penknives, glasses or daft caps.'

Vin Garbutt

Being a travelling troubadour comes with unavoidable occupational hazards. I never learned to drive, so I've always depended on the kindness of friends and complete strangers to take me where I need to be. That's how I met Pat, when she came to pick me up for that gig in Kent, if you remember. I usually arrive where I need to be in the end, although there've been a few close scrapes. Probably the closest of all was when I nearly missed the birth of our second baby, Tim.

It was July 1980 and I played a rare gig in Ireland, at the Irish Woodstock, the legendary Lisdoonvarna Festival, as celebrated in the Christy Moore song. The festival took place in a small town in County Clare every summer for six years, until some Hells Angels caused a near-riot and the local council decided they'd had enough and banned it. People camped everywhere and the pubs were full of music and craic. The Chieftains, Clannad, Paul Brady, Richard and Linda Thompson, John Martyn and the famous piper and storyteller Seamus Hennessy were all on the bill the year I was there, as well as Bob Fox and Stu Luckley. My performance went well. People were taken by surprise when I sang my song *Little Innocents*, but it received a positive reaction. Few in the audience had ever heard of me, so they had no idea what to expect, and the words seemed to make them stop and listen. When I phoned home on Monday morning to ask Pat how she was before I set off home, I was surprised to hear her mother answer the phone instead.

'You need to come home as soon as you can,' she said. 'Pat's gone into labour early and she's in Middlesbrough General now.'

I had a return ticket with British Airways to Newcastle, while Bob and Stu were flying with Aer Lingus to Leeds-Bradford. If I flew to Newcastle I had no way of making my way from there to Middlesbrough. But Bob and Stu had a van waiting at Leeds-Bradford Airport and said they'd take me straight to the hospital if I could change my ticket and go with them. Time was rapidly running out and I knew I needed to turn on the charm, so I walked up to the ticket desk and smiled a hopeful smile.

'This is my situation,' I said. 'My wife's giving birth in Teesside as we speak. I have a

British Airways ticket to Newcastle. My friends here are flying to Leeds-Bradford and they'll give me a lift to the hospital straight away if I go with them. Is there any way I can change the ticket?'

The Aer Lingus lady looked me up and down, with a stern expression on her face.

'Give me that,' she said, and she examined the ticket. 'No, we're not supposed to change this. But... you just wait there.'

She disappeared into the bowels of Dublin Airport and I was left sweating on her answer. Five minutes later she emerged clutching an Aer Lingus ticket to Leeds-Bradford.

'Get back home to your wife,' she instructed me.

You wouldn't get that with Ryanair! So I flew to Leeds-Bradford with Bob and Stu, threw the guitars and bags into their van and they whisked me off to Middlesbrough, breaking the speed limit all the way. I hurriedly said my goodbyes and thank yous in the car park at Middlesbrough General and then ran up to the maternity ward, still carrying all my gear. I arrived panting and out of breath and the nurse took one look at me and my guitar.

'You must be Mr Garbutt,' she said. 'You're just in time.'

I had arrived five minutes before Tim was born. It was absolutely brilliant.

> I remember him running into the delivery room and me screaming, 'Hold my leg, hold my leg!' No recognition or relief. I was seconds away.
> **Pat**

Bob Fox also has a clear memory of events...

> I first saw Vin perform as the guest at my local folk club in the Dun Cow, Seaton Village, County Durham, in the very early 1970s. I was still at school and just discovering folk music, loving the stories the songs told, whether they were hundreds of years old or recently written, and here was a larger-than-life character delivering a combination of both with hilarious, zany introductions, superb musicianship, a unique singing style and passion in spades.
>
> Vin was beginning his long road to becoming one of the nation's most treasured and best-loved folk singers, a true troubadour, revered and respected by fellow musicians and audiences alike.
>
> A few years later I also embarked on a career as a folk singer, using him as a model, and during the time I spent in a duo with Stu Luckley we met Vin many times as performers at festivals and other events, forging a strong friendship which lasted for over forty years.
>
> One such meeting took place in 1980 at the Lisdoonvarna Festival in County Clare. It was a great weekend of music and craic, but on the Monday we were due to fly home Vin found out that Pat had gone into labour. We offered to drive him from the airport to the hospital, but Vin was flying back to Newcastle and we were flying back to Leeds/Bradford, so with a bit of typical Garbutt

charm, he managed to change his flight. However, we were travelling in a VW Beetle and the only way we could get him into the car was under all of the bags and guitar cases in the back seat. So for an hour and a half he sat completely obscured under four guitar cases, wise-cracking non-stop, while we made a mad dash for the hospital in Middlesbrough and got him there just in time to be present at the birth of the lovely Tim.

Over the following decade Vin became firmly established at the top of the folk tree. After I stopped touring on a full-time basis we lost touch for a few years, until he invited me to do some backing vocals on his *Bandalised* album. Vin loved the band sound and wanted to do some live gigs with it, so I joined Vin, Andy McLaughlin, Paul Archer and Norman Holmes and we enjoyed many gigs as the Vin Garbutt Band.

Bob Fox

I've heard from countless musicians who've watched in horror as their precious guitars have been flung off planes towards a baggage cart below, only to crash onto the tarmac instead. Baggage handlers just don't seem to care and treat priceless instruments as though they are sacks of coal. As I've already mentioned, I've had my guitars smashed up three times in three different airports.

Damage to my precious guitars is heartbreaking enough, but I feared an even more serious disaster when my plane burst into flames and was forced to perform an emergency landing as I headed home from Australia one time. We'd earlier stopped off to refuel at Singapore, before taking off again and carrying on our journey. Relaxed after a successful tour and looking forward to coming home, I nodded off in my seat. I awoke to hear the pilot addressing the passengers over the PA system.

'Ladies and gentlemen, please return to your seats and fasten your seatbelts,' he said. 'We're about to land in Kuala Lumpur!'

I turned to the young lass sitting beside me.

'What's all that about? I thought we flew over Malaysia hours ago.'

She smiled at me calmly.

'We did, and now we're going back,' she said. 'The wing's on fire!'

I looked out of the window and huge flames were leaping out of the engine compartment and the wing was well alight. As we came in to land I could see the emergency services racing down the runway to meet us. Nobody panicked or screamed, but it was a terrifying experience. Thank God we all arrived safely and I've never been so happy to put my feet back on solid ground.

Then there was the time me and Pat almost ended up being left to rot in a Jersey jail. We'd taken the kids to a festival in about 1985 along with our babysitter, Rachel, who looked after the kids while we went to the gigs. On the way back from my first show we got lost on one of the island's narrow back lanes. We decided to turn back and Pat reversed the hire car through the gateway of a field. As she did so she brushed against the wall and a small piece of plastic snapped off the red reversing light. When we got back to St Helier we were stopped by a pompous police sergeant with an RAF-

Vin with his friend Eddie McNulty

type moustache who asked us if we'd reported the accident, presumably because he'd noticed the damaged light. It had hardly registered with us and we asked him what accident he was talking about, thinking he must have been referring to some bigger incident elsewhere that we were unaware of. The sergeant clearly didn't like the look of me and to our horror he took us to the police station. Rachel and the kids had no idea what was going on and Pat was angry and upset. I tried to reassure her.

'There's probably something going on and they just want to make sure we're not involved,' I said.

But at that point we were separated, questioned and threatened with all sorts. We spent most of the night in custody. Eventually, they told us we were being taken back to the 'scene of the crime'. We couldn't believe what we were hearing. Scene of the crime? You mean the farm gateway we brushed against? It was hardly a case for Bergerac! They phoned the local *centenier*, a kind of magistrate, and we had to lead him to this little track, where the incriminating evidence was lying on the grass – a tiny fragment of orange plastic. They warned us we might have to face the might of Jersey's judicial system in the future and even asked how much money we had on us. Eventually we were released without paying anything and a pleasant young policeman took us back to our accommodation. A few days later we handed the car back to the hire company and told them we'd hit a gate. They weren't bothered at all.

When we arrived home I told the local paper what had happened and the island's director of tourism called me and apologised profusely for the overly officious way we were treated. It was nice to hear, but we'd been shaken up by the experience and I made sure he knew how strongly I felt. I told him I might have expected that kind of treatment in the Soviet Bloc, but not in the British Channel Islands!

Folkies are generally lovely people but they can sometimes be a volatile bunch as well and I've had to talk my way out of more than one scrape over the years. Early in my professional career I was invited to a stoppy-back after a gig at the Old Dyers Arms pub in the Spon End area of Coventry. Finbar, Eddie and George, the legendary Furey brothers, were also there, along with the band's frontman, Davey Arthur. The pub was locked up and we were all enjoying a good drink and a singaround in the back room. I was asked to sing and the room fell silent as I began a traditional ballad, *The Green Mossy Banks of the Lea*. But one poor boozer clearly wasn't aware of the etiquette of these events and continued laughing and chatting away noisily at the bar. My friend Eddie McNulty could be a sensitive soul and always had a tear in his eye as he sang a sad song, but he was also a big, hard man and he flew into a mad rage. He shot across the room and it didn't take a formal invitation for the Fureys to join in as a full-scale brawl erupted. Before long everybody's fists were flying. All except mine, of course. I quietly packed my guitar back in its case and sneaked out of a side door.

> Vin and I have been mates since the early seventies. I first met him at Bromyard Festival. I was along with a mad crowd from the Old Dyers Arms in Coventry and an equally mad crowd from Leamington. On the campsite someone suggested a mass piggyback fight. I looked round for a suitable steed and selected Vin. I didn't know who he was. I just jumped on his back and shouted, 'Giddy-up!' We didn't win but what a hoot it was. I had no memory of this, it was Vin who told me years later.
>
> I went to see him one night in Coventry at the Burnt Post Folk Club. It was held in an upstairs room on a very muggy night. I was standing in the open doorway of the fire escape and he was telling some outrageous yarn when someone in the audience scoffed. Vin paused and said, 'It's the truth I tell ya, may God strike me dead if I'm telling a lie,' whereupon a huge clap of thunder shook the room, followed by a massive flash of lightning! Vin paused, looked up and said, 'Why, I was only joking!' He brought the house down as usual. Vin could have told you a few yarns about our friendship over many years. For me, one of the nicest, most talented people I've ever met – a gem.
>
> **Eddie McNulty**

A different memory of the same incident…

> I've seen Vin many times since the early 1970s. I remember a gig in the

Burnt Post Folk Club in Coventry in the 1980s. Halfway through the gig a thunderstorm developed. Vin was playing a tin whistle solo and just as he was about to blow the final big note this huge clap of thunder deafened us all. Vin had this amazed look on his face as he looked at his tin whistle as if he'd just blown a clap of thunder. Timed it perfectly.
Patrick Tiernan

I played Trowbridge Folk Festival the same year as Bob Geldof, who was with a folky-type band he'd put together at the time. We didn't meet but when I came on stage in front of an audience of about 12,000, I made a gentle joke at his expense.

'Something's just happened to me for the first time in my life,' I said. 'I was standing next to Bob Geldof backstage and somebody said, 'By, isn't Vin Garbutt looking smart tonight!"

That went down well and then I started playing. But a few minutes into my set there was an almighty *boom-boom-splash!* All the lights went off and the sound stopped as well. After a couple of minutes they fixed the PA system but the lights stayed off for the rest of the gig. It turned out a member of the audience had sneaked out to have a wee on a riverbank, but in the darkness he didn't realise he was urinating on an electrical transformer – right in the middle of my set. The transformer exploded, we lost our power and he was blown into the river. When they finally got the lights back the poor man could be seen being carried through the crowd, held high up on a stretcher while everyone cheered. Fortunately, he was all right and was waving to the audience by this time. I wouldn't have liked to have seen his private parts that night though.

I ran into trouble before I'd even left Loftus ahead of my 1996 world tour. Pat was driving me to Teesside Airport on a cold winter's morning. Just as we reached the marketplace on the High Street we skidded on a patch of black ice and skated into the centre of the crossroads, watching in helpless horror as three other cars simultaneously waltzed gently towards us before we all collided in the middle. Nobody was hurt but it was immediately clear that we were all going to be stuck there for some time. I decided to grab my guitar and bags, gave Pat a quick goodbye peck and ran to the nearest bus stop. There were regular services to Middlesbrough and Saltburn and I knew I could take a train to Teesside Airport from either of those. I'd only been there for about five minutes, scrutinising the timetables and trying to work out whether I'd make it, when a stranger stopped his car to go into the chemist and recognised me.

'Hey Vin!' he said. 'Where are you off to?'

When I told him I needed to be at the airport to catch a flight, he generously offered to help.

'I'm heading to Darlington after this – do you want a lift?'

Once he'd collected his prescription, I gratefully bundled my luggage into the back of his car.

'I just have to pop into Saltburn first,' he said as we pulled away. 'And then Grangetown.'

I was slightly concerned by these words but it was too late to do anything about it. In any case, I didn't have any alternative. The icy roads didn't help our progress through East Cleveland and then my Good Samaritan continued to make his way unhurriedly along The Broadway in Grangetown. By the time he eventually dropped me off at the airport it was eleven o'clock – an hour after my flight to London. I thanked him through gritted teeth, wondering what on earth I was going to do. I felt sick. Months of planning and preparation was in danger of going up the spout.

But just as I walked in through the sliding doors I heard an announcement being made over the Tannoy. The flight had been delayed and the passengers were only just being called through to board. Brilliant! There was no queue at the check-in desk and I was soon on my way through security and onto the plane with minutes to spare. I breathed an enormous sigh of relief as we took off and the patchwork of fields around Teesside disappeared below us. Once we reached Heathrow I had four hours before my flight to Toronto. I collected my bags from the carousel and waited for my guitar at the outsized baggage collection area. And I waited. And waited. But it never came out. After twenty minutes everyone else had picked up their luggage and gone, and that sickening feeling returned to the pit of my stomach once again. I collared a passing member of the ground staff.

'I've just arrived on the Teesside flight and my guitar hasn't come out,' I said.

He took my boarding card and punched the details into his computer.

'I'm sorry Mr Garbutt, it would appear that it's still at Teesside Airport,' he said. 'It never made it onto the plane.'

'But I need it – I'm flying to Toronto in an hour!'

He asked to see my ticket and I handed it over.

'You should be all right, Mr Garbutt,' he said. Smiling, he handed it back to me.

'This ticket's for tomorrow's flight,' he said.

After all that worry and hassle, I'd set off from home a day early!

Setting out his stall at a gig in at Lymm – photo courtesy of Colin Mitchell

MUSICAL BEDS

'It's so many years in truth,
That I travelled that great distance…
When I first made your acquaintance,
And your welcome was so warm.'

Vin Garbutt, *Your Welcome Was So Warm*

Somebody should write a book about all the weird and wonderful accommodation folkies stay in. I've slept in thousands of places over the years. I only had a basic formal education but they say travel broadens the mind and I believe that's true. People have opened up their hearts to me and I've heard some extremely poignant and intensely personal stories. I've had the wonderful privilege of staying in the homes of all kinds of diverse, lovely, brilliant people with some amazing experiences to talk about. When I visited London in the early seventies I often stayed with a librarian called June, who had gone to Oxford and captained the St Hugh's College team on *University Challenge*. I met her in the folk clubs and had no idea she could sing. The next thing I knew she was recording albums and I couldn't believe the striking quality of her voice. She's gone on to do quite well for herself and you might have even heard of her. Her second name is Tabor...

I toured Belgium every year from 1974 to 1984 and sometimes went back to play at a summer festival as well. It was a wonderful place to go, but with one major drawback – the accommodation was often terrible. After one of my first gigs over there I kipped on the freezing cold stone floor of the bar I'd been singing in, with only a flimsy sheet to keep me warm. I hardly slept a wink and felt especially badly done by.

It turned out to be the best night's sleep I had on the whole tour. The worst came after a student gig in Namur, home of the Walloon parliament. The students were welcoming and enthusiastic, but my digs were in a condemned building and reaching my bedroom required overcoming an obstacle course. When we arrived I was told to squeeze through some rusty iron gates into an old courtyard. My host then pointed up to a half-collapsed balcony that encircled the first floor above me. We had to climb the spindles that hung down precariously from above, getting a foothold wherever we could. Once we'd hoisted ourselves up, we negotiated the splintered floorboards and tottered towards my room. It had no doors and there was a large fire in the middle, fuelled by wood cannibalised from the rest of the building. The place had all the hallmarks of a squat, with the belongings of the students who lived there littered all over the floor. My only luxuries were a thin, grubby mattress and a well-used sleeping bag. At the end of a long night playing I was so tired that I managed to climb up to the balcony and crawl into the sleeping bag, cursing my luck under my breath before I eventually drifted off. Just as I did so, an enormous black rat scampered over my feet. So this is the glamorous life on the road, I thought.

My accommodation after another Belgian gig made my sleeping quarters that night look like the presidential suite at the Ritz. The ground floor of the building had been abandoned and nobody lived on the first floor either. I was sleeping in a flat on the third floor. The whole place stank to high heaven and I was sleeping on the mankiest, most diseased-looking mattress I've ever seen. There was a cracked sewer down below that I had to use as a toilet during the night. I kid you not, the stench was so bad that I was physically sick. Not surprisingly I took ill while I was there and the lad who arranged the booking managed to find me a decent bed for a couple of nights, which was a tremendous relief.

Over the years I've built up wonderful friendships with the people who book me and those who regularly come to watch. A couple of years ago I was playing in Brussels and enjoyed a happy reunion with some lovely old friends, Dr Franz and Anne Fermont. I'll never forget how they rescued me one night when I was out of luck. They came to see me play and asked me where I was staying that night.

'I think I'm sleeping here on the floor,' I said.

They took me back to their beautiful home in Aalst and after that I stayed with them whenever I went back to Belgium. Their kids were similar ages to ours so we had a lot in common and Pat and the family have been over. During one visit we all awoke in the middle of the night with the house shaking violently. We had no idea what was going on until the next morning, when we heard there had been an earthquake with its epicentre in the Dutch city of Venlo, which was only two hours' drive away.

While Belgium is the undisputed European Capital of Bad Accommodation, it isn't the only place I've found myself wishing I'd booked into the local Travelodge instead of taking the bed that came with the booking. Back in the early 1970s Pat and I stayed at a place in the Catskill Mountains in upstate New York. Our hosts were lovely people and the beds were comfy enough, but every time they gave us something to eat the food was full of cat hairs. I didn't find this too appetising myself, but poor Pat just couldn't bear it and kept scraping her food onto my plate while nobody was looking.

The same thing happened again in England a few years back. At the start of the night the organisers introduced us to a lady and her two daughters who we would be staying with. They were a lovely family and it was a cracking gig, which this lady enjoyed more than most, becoming more and more tiddly as the evening progressed. By the time we left she was very well oiled indeed. We went back to the house and the girls kindly made us some ham sandwiches. Pat picked one up and quickly put it back down on the plate again.

'Aren't you hungry, Pat?' the mother asked.

'No thanks,' said Pat.

The truth is she was starving – she just didn't fancy the cat hair relish that came with the butties! Her stomach was still rumbling as we traipsed off to bed in the hope that a proper night's rest would take our minds off our empty bellies. But when we pulled the blankets back there was a big ginger moggie asleep in the bed. Pat wasn't happy at all. She was a reluctant roadie in the first place and this was the last straw. The next morning we woke up and discovered the mother had gone out to have her hair done. Pat seized the opportunity.

'Let's try to leave without having breakfast,' she said.

We told the daughters we had to be on the road and asked them to thank their mam for us. Then we headed for the nearest cafe and got stuck into a lovely big fried breakfast. On the way home we decided to visit my agent Jim McPhee and his wife Gill, not far away in Kings Heath, Birmingham. Jim had looked after my bookings for twenty years and we were old friends. We knocked at the door and as soon as Gill opened it, Pat broke down in tears. She'd had enough. But Gill has the best shoulder in the world for crying on and after an hour with the McPhees all was well again.

It's not much fun being my roadie either. I was sharing a bed with my mate Speedy in somebody's house after a gig in Rotherham when all hell let loose at three o'clock in the morning. We were woken by the sound of a window smashing and then a wardrobe being hurled down the stairs. It must have resembled a scene from an old Laurel and Hardy film as me and Speedy looked at each other, pulled the covers up to our chins and listened nervously for the next development. We didn't have to wait long. Within seconds our bedroom door burst open and a huge angry bloke stormed in, effing and blinding and ordering us out of the house. We quickly gathered up our belongings and scrambled down the stairs and out of the front door. I never found out what had happened. As we wandered the empty streets of South Yorkshire in the early hours I remembered that John Leonard, who produced the folk programme on Radio 2, lived in nearby Mexborough. I called him and told him about our predicament and he tutted.

'Come on then,' he said. 'I'll make up the bed in the spare room.'

Being on the road for much of your life becomes harder as you grow older. Years ago, when I was a young lad making my name on the scene, I was happy to stay up until one or two in the morning, singing songs and having a few extra drinks with my hosts. As I've grown older I've learned to pace myself. There comes a point when I just want to lay my head down after travelling all day and singing all night. I'm far more confident and relaxed about it now. These days I have no qualms about saying, 'Do you mind if I go to bed?' And because my audience have aged with me, they usually don't.

Making his point – photo courtesy of Graham Whitmore

THE SECRET CONCERT SYNDROME

'I've been to some far away places
With nothing to show for it all.'

Kieran Halpin, *Nothing to Show For It All*

Being employed by folkies can be both a blessing and a curse. Almost without exception, they're wonderful people. While most are also switched on and know what they're doing, a few others have endless admirable qualities but are occasionally a little amateurish when it comes to the art of promoting. Back in the 1980s I played at a club in the Manchester area run by a lovely couple. I arrived early and the phone was constantly ringing as I was setting up.

'It's going to be stowed out tonight, Vin,' the lady said. 'The calls haven't stopped all week.'

Then I heard her answer one of them.

'Sorry, love, we don't sell tickets,' she said. 'It's first come, first served.'

As she replaced the receiver I realised it wasn't going to be packed at all. I wouldn't come if I rang up and she told me I might be turned away when I arrived. Experience has taught me that people will only travel about five miles from home if they can't be sure whether there will be a ticket for them when they arrive at the venue. They certainly won't do a twenty-mile round trip. I was right. The place was half empty.

That was one of my first experiences of what I called the secret concert syndrome. The Lymm Folk Club in Cheshire was another example. I would play to a full house one year and then go back the next time to find hardly anybody there. I never knew why, but something wasn't quite right. Stewart Lever started running the club in about 2002. His family had the Lever Family Folk Club in Warrington in the early 1970s and I knew them all well. The first time I played at Lymm after Stewart took over there was a particularly poor turnout. I was staying with him and decided to try to find out what was going wrong. Now some people are open to a word of advice, while others think you're teaching granny to suck eggs and won't listen, and I wouldn't try to push it. But

Stewart was as disappointed as I was with what had happened and wanted to make sure everything was done right the next time. We discussed it over a late-night beer or two and I asked if he sold tickets in advance.

'No, people just turn up on the door,' he said.

So I told him the conclusion I'd come to over the years. Once you have a ticket you're committed to coming, you're not likely to change your mind. I suggested that even if they didn't sell tickets, if someone phoned up he should take their name and promise they'd get in if they turned up by eight o'clock. That's the nearest you can have to commitment if you don't sell tickets. After that the club was sold out every time I played and Stewart thanked me for the suggestion. He now handles the whole process by computer and sends out an email confirmation that acts as a ticket. I wish everyone was as open to advice as he was.

One of the most spectacular secret concerts I ever played was at a beautiful Victorian hotel in Dunkeld, near Blairgowrie, in 2004. I've always loved playing in Scotland and usually arrange a low basic fee with a share of the takings to top it up. On a good night when a big crowd turns up that can sometimes triple my earnings. Of course, it depends on the gig being promoted properly. My suspicions that the Dunkeld date wasn't being advertised as well as it should have been were alerted weeks earlier. I started receiving emails from six fans in Nottinghamshire who saw the gig listed on my website and wanted to come to see me while they were on holiday in Scotland. They contacted the hotel but the receptionist knew nothing about it. Then they tried the local tourist information centre, whose phone number had been given out as the place to buy tickets – and they were equally in the dark. As soon as I found out what was going on I called my agent, who contacted the man who booked me.

'Don't worry about it,' he said. 'There are two weeks to go yet!'

We had to tell him we knew of at least six people who wouldn't be coming, having done their best to find some information and eventually given up on the idea. In fact, we told him, we didn't know one person who was going. But he was relaxed and confident and insisted that everything was under control.

I arrived early on the night of the gig and walked into a stunning baronial hall, complete with oak and mahogany panelling and a huge open fire blasting out heat. It was undoubtedly one of the most spectacular settings I'd ever been asked to play in. Unfortunately, they'd forgotten to tell anyone about it.

'How many tickets have you sold?' I asked.

The organiser looked sheepish.

'Thirteen,' he said.

I asked if I could remove half of the sixty seats in the room. If only a dozen people turn up they don't look so bad in thirty seats as you stand looking out from the stage, but they look terrible dotted about in sixty. He didn't understand why it made any difference, but I eventually persuaded him to help me do it. In the end we just about filled the thirty seats. Those who turned up all deserved a medal.

'What a hell of a job we've had finding you!' one said. 'We had to come on spec and hope for the best because nobody could sell us tickets or even knew anything about it.'

The hotel staff were friendly and helpful. They couldn't understand why nobody knew the gig was on – or why nobody had told them either! But there was a consolation at the end of it all. I spent that night tucked up in a four-poster bed in a room fit for a lord!

Even though I love Ireland and have visited often, nobody has any idea who I am south of the border. There was one ill-fated trip in 1998 that I'll never forget. Talk about secret concerts, this was a completely secret tour! A gentleman called Gabriel Simpson from Dublin contacted my agent Jim McPhee, wanting to book me for a tour. My conversation with Jim went something like this.

'Is he a promoter?'

'I don't think so.'

'Does he run a folk club?'

'No, I don't think so. He just seems to be a fan who wants to put on a tour.'

'Has he done it before?'

'Er…no, I don't think so.'

I didn't need much of an invitation to go to Ireland, however, and I was up for taking a risk. I'm always keen to play somewhere new and the chance to make a name for myself in Ireland was one I didn't want to pass up.

'Give him three gigs,' I said.

I knew I could handle three failures. Any more than that and I might be upset. Gabriel was a lovely man who had flown over to England a couple of times to see me play in the Midlands. I gave him my stipulations – every gig had to have a decent PA system and a minimum door charge and there would be absolutely no freebies. I knew before I went that nobody knew me, so Gabriel would have his work cut out to pack a reasonable crowd in. There are no folk clubs over there in the way we know them. Ireland doesn't import folk music – they export masses of it instead. The average folk club organiser in England could give you a list of Irish performers, but you wouldn't find anybody in Ireland who could reel off any English singers. They will be familiar with the 'London connection' people and those who made their names in the 1960s' revival – people such as Ralph McTell, Fairport and Steeleye Span – but very few others. I sent Gabriel fifty CDs to give out to radio stations, which was a fair financial outlay for me before I even kicked off. I'd never sent that many in advance of any tour before, but I was keen to make this one a success.

Only thirty-five people turned up for my first booking, at the Purty Kitchen in Dun Laoghaire. Most of those had travelled in from nearby Dublin. But it wasn't such a bad start. 'I've a feeling everything's going to get better from now on,' I told myself.

My second gig was in the town of Ring, County Waterford, in one of the Gaeltacht areas where the Irish language is widely spoken. When I arrived I was surprised to find myself in a teenagers' pub that was heaving to the gunnels. Everyone was speaking Gaelic and, of course, there was no entry charge, despite my instructions specifically banning freebies. The landlord and landlady used to see me singing in London in the early-1970s. When they heard I was in Ireland they booked me for their own enjoyment and took the night off. They sat behind the bar on a couple of stools and listened intently. But they were the only ones in the whole pub taking a blind bit of notice. My usual patter was a complete waste of time, so I just asked them what songs they wanted me to play and if I knew it, I sang it. I was a folk jukebox. I told them to put a CD on when I was finishing my last song, knowing nobody would even notice I'd stopped. The pandemonium carried on and I unplugged my guitar and sloped unnoticed off the stage. But fair play to the hosts, they paid my fee and we enjoyed the rest of the evening together.

The next day I awoke to some atrocious Irish weather. I was travelling everywhere by public transport and took a bus to the Kilmurry Lodge Hotel in Limerick, watching through the window as the rain lashed down on the lush green fields around me. My first impressions of the venue were promising. The building was modern but fairly grand and much more like the kind of place I'd hoped to be playing. When I walked inside, however, my posters were piled up on the reception desk. That was always a bad sign. They should have been up on walls weeks ahead of my arrival, yet here they were on the day of the gig, left where nobody could see them. The room itself had by far the most professional set-up of the tour. There were about a hundred seats set out and a good quality PA system. After dumping my bags, I headed outside for a wander and to take in the beautiful surroundings. But when I returned there was still nobody there. At half-past seven the door creaked open and a young lad of about sixteen walked in. He introduced himself as Declan and explained that his Uncle Gabe had asked him to take the money on the door.

'That's smashing, Declan,' I said. 'I'll just pop upstairs to my room and I'll be back down soon.'

It was March 29th 1998 and my team, Middlesbrough, had played in the Coca-Cola Cup final against Chelsea at Wembley Stadium that day and I was avoiding hearing the result. I flicked through to find the channel that would have the highlights and then returned to the concert room. By eight o'clock there was still only Declan and me there. Half-past eight arrived and it remained all quiet. Still Declan wasn't worried.

'It's early yet,' he said.

Nine o'clock came. Then half-past nine.

'I think you can go now, can't you, Declan?' I said.

'Aye, I think so.'

He picked up his coat, cheerfully said his goodbyes and skipped off home. It's the only gig in my fifty-year career that nobody came to. Not a solitary soul. Just to cap off a perfect evening, I returned to my room in time to watch the highlights as Boro lost to Chelsea – and it wasn't for the first time. Football's just not fair, with all the cups down there! So my Irish tour was a financial disaster, but it was worth giving it a go. It's always a joy to visit the land whose treasury of songs helped me fall in love with folk.

Those nights when we passed the hat round the Tabu bar in Sitges back in 1969 taught me another important lesson, although it took me twenty years to put it into practice. It was my first experience of a phenomenon that I honed into a professional observation over the years – a performer tends to be given the respect the audience has paid for, and not necessarily the respect he deserves. If you give people free entry you can guarantee they'll make a hell of a racket and take hardly any notice of the poor bloke up on the stage. But if they've paid a tenner you can hear a pin drop. They've invested and they want their money's worth. It's not always the case, because some free folk clubs manage to keep good order, but as a general rule it's true.

It wasn't until 1991 that I did something about it. I was playing in a club called the Mill on the Exe, in Devon, which I'd visited at least once a year since the start of my professional career. On this particular night only eighteen people turned up. It was a major disappointment, especially after travelling the length of the country, and it was difficult to lift my spirits and give a decent performance for those who had come.

Afterwards I called my agent, Jim, and told him I'd finally come to a decision. The evidence was there in front of my eyes, week in and week out – the clubs charging more for tickets were considerably fuller than the others. The ones charging three quid (a reasonable amount in 1991 money) were packed out, while the ones charging a pound were empty. I told him I didn't want to play in empty clubs any more. We agreed to set a minimum door charge of three pounds.

> I think Vin was one of the first to use the 'percentage of door against a minimum' fee structure, which caused a fuss at the time but has been widely adopted since.
> **Roger Bucknall MBE**

Not everyone took the news well. A few organisers rang up and said, 'Hey Vinnie, that's not the way we do things here…' But I told them I wasn't asking them to pay me any more – my fee stayed the same. I just wanted them to ask their audience if they thought I was worth three quid. A handful of clubs stopped booking me out of principle and I understand their perspective, but their low rate wasn't good for me or them. Those clubs that did raise the admission price immediately felt the benefit and sold more tickets. It turned out to be the best move of my career.

Vin playing alongside his great friend, Paddy McAvoy, at a pub session

Vin the multi-instrumentalist

WHISTLES AND FLUTES

'Good friends who could see no divide.'

Vin Garbutt, *The Troubles of Erin*

Ireland proved a tough nut for me to crack, probably because the country is steeped in its own musical tradition and sadly has no need to import mine. But I've played in the north of the country many times over the years. There was a different kind of circuit available on that side of the border and I always thoroughly enjoyed going over. In the late 1970s and early-80s I regularly played at free-to-enter ballad sessions that would pay me a fee. The Irish show bands also played them, singing traditional songs in waltz time.

Some of my best experiences were in the Republican heartlands during the Troubles. One memorable tour in about 1979 was arranged by the late Geoff Harden, a journalist and BBC radio presenter from Kent who settled in Belfast in the mid-sixties and wrote a folk column for the *Belfast News Letter*. Geoff always knew where the best sessions were happening on my nights off. Late one evening he stopped the car in what looked to be the back of beyond, beside a few derelict buildings and an area of scrubland. Smack in the middle of all this bleakness was a school.

'What's going on here, Geoff?' I said.

'Cathal McConnell's playing in a session.'

I knew Cathal from his band, the Boys of the Lough. He is an All-Ireland flute and whistle champion who played in the traditional style of his native County Fermanagh. From the outside, the building was in darkness, like the wartime blackout. The only lights were beaming down from a British Army helicopter circling in the sky above us. But when we opened the door we were hit by a wall of sound. The quality of the music was simply breathtaking. People were up dancing and there was no aggro of any kind. It was an unforgettable evening.

Another night I played in a session in one of the little Nationalist enclaves off Belfast's Falls Road, where the end house of a terrace had been turned into a pub. You had to walk through a turnstile to enter but other than that it was just an ordinary house, apart from the security men on the doors and the barbed wire trailing up to the roof. Once again, as soon as we opened the door we were hit by a wave of fiddles and flutes playing all this wonderful ah-diddly-owdle-doo music. I sat beside a lad playing the whistle and pulled mine out and joined in. Between tunes we naturally started chatting.

'Where are you from?' he said.

'South Bank,' I said. I'm not sure whether he knew exactly where that was, but he recognised my English accent all right.

'You do know this is a Provo pub don't you?' he said.

'Well, I didn't,' I said. 'But I do now.'

It turned out he was even more out of place than I was.

'I'm from the Shankill Road,' he said. 'I have to sneak out to come here, but I just love it. They all know I'm a Protestant and there's no problem – we're all just here for the music. It's when I go home that I have to be careful to make sure nobody finds out where I've been.'

I was amazed that someone would risk his life and cross the so-called peace line that divides the city just for the chance to play the music he loved.

I was at the bottom of some stairs at another gig in Downpatrick when a security man shouted up at me from the top.

'Are you a terrorist?'

'No.'

'Why not?'

A few years later I took the whole family to stay with my friend and mentor Paddy McEvoy in Belfast. We were walking around exploring when our Tim said he wanted a wee. He was only about twelve, so I told him to nip down a slope behind some garages. At that moment a squad of British soldiers came round the corner, armed to the teeth and pointing their guns menacingly.

'Tim, quick!' I whispered. 'Zip your trousers up and come back here!'

I suppose we must have looked suspicious, but they let us go on our way.

Another brush with the army came when our car was pulled over at a checkpoint as we crossed from Derry into County Donegal in the Irish Republic. Although the squaddies were supposed to have their rifles at the ready, they relaxed a little when they heard our northern English accents. But all of these experiences gave us a small insight into the way people were trying to live an ordinary life with soldiers on their streets. Not long ago someone asked me to play in Jerusalem, but Pat wasn't at all keen on the idea.

'It's far too dangerous,' she said.

'Pat,' I said. 'We took the kids to the middle of Belfast at the height of the Troubles – we were still more likely to be run over than blown up!'

As well as the thousands who died during those three decades of conflict in the north, countless people had their lives ruined. There were victims on all sides, including the innocent men and women who spent years behind bars after being wrongly convicted of being involved in atrocities. I met one of them, Paul Hill, on a flight home from Australia.

I've always had a knack of being able to recognise people. I've spotted Dave Clark from the Dave Clark Five on a London street, Boyzone at Heathrow, Julian Clary heading for the executive lounge at Melbourne Airport and I once bumped into Bob Geldof in the street in Hong Kong. Bob stood out a mile because he and I were taller than everyone else. I gave him a little nod and he winked back. When I told the people I was staying with, they all said, 'It can't have been him, we'd have heard about it if he was in Hong Kong…' Then the news comes on and there's a story about a surprise visitor to the colony – Sir Bob.

Anyway, I was standing having a drink at the bar on the plane when I noticed Paul Hill. As soon as I saw him I was sure who he was, having read so much about his case. He was one of the Guildford Four, who were accused of killing four soldiers and a civilian in a horrific pub bombing in 1974. He served fifteen years behind bars, including five in solitary confinement, before eventually being cleared of all wrongdoing. Even though another IRA active service unit nicknamed the Balcombe Street Gang owned up to the bombings during a court appearance in January 1977, the Establishment stubbornly refused to admit their mistakes until years later.

'I don't want to pester you, but you wouldn't be Paul Hill would you?' I asked.

We started chatting and it emerged that we both knew Christy Moore, which led us into a conversation about music. We were still talking as we walked down the steps of the plane together towards customs at Heathrow.

'I suppose you attract plenty of attention when you pass through here?' I said.

'No,' he said. 'They haven't been too bad since I was released.'

When we reached the desk they completely ignored Paul and I was pulled to one side and given a thorough body search instead. That was quite a common occurrence for me – I can't think why! It was at its worst during the Troubles, when I think they were looking for guns rather than drugs.

I sometimes wonder if we've learned anything from miscarriages of justice such as those inflicted on the Guildford Four and the Birmingham Six, who were also entirely innocent Irishmen. I saw pictures in a newspaper not long ago of two or three Muslim men with what was supposedly bomb-making equipment in the kitchen of their flat. I looked at it and realised it could have been our kitchen in Hummersea.

'There's a bag of chapati flour and a couple of demijohns bubbling away in the corner,' I thought.

They were placed under house arrest but the jury thought the case should be thrown out and there was a campaign to have the men released.

I can't imagine how it must feel to be on the wrong end of such an injustice. I met a lass from Eston on the quayside at Newport, Rhode Island, in the 1970s. I knew her from Eston Folk Club and we had one of those daft, 'Eeee, what are you doing here?' exchanges. Shortly after that I was back on Teesside and read in the *Gazette* that she'd been chatted up by a bloke who persuaded her to take his bag home. It was back in the days when we weren't aware of the risks involved – and the bag turned out to have an explosive device inside.

I've known Christy Moore since long before he achieved his current status as a folk music superstar. Christy was a bank clerk in Ireland who first came to England during a long bank strike in 1966 and ended up settling in the Halifax area. Back then he was a jovial Irishman singing songs like *Paddy McGinty's Goat* and *The Rocky Road to Dublin* and he even recorded an album called *Paddy on the Road.* He regularly played at Eston and Redcar folk clubs and Anchor House on Grange Road, Middlesbrough, which later became the John Paul Centre and was run by the Catholic Church. Christy was never a big Catholic and if a priest walked in, which was fairly normal at Anchor House, he could be a bit naughty with them. I remember him saying, 'Look out, here's another Pill-pusher coming through the door!'

Our paths often crossed on the road and he could be witty and good company. Like me, Christy was on Bill Leader's Trailer record label and he became a familiar face on the folk circuit. In 1971 he recorded his second solo album, *Prosperous*, featuring the musicians who went on to form Planxty with him. A *planxty* was a tune written by the old pipers and minstrels and dedicated to the Lord of the Manor. There are dozens of them, like *Planxty Irwin* and *Planxty George Brabazon*. The musicians in the new band included Christy's old school friend Dónal Lunny and two more exceptionally gifted musicians in Liam O'Flynn and Andy Irvine.

When the band started up Christy packed in touring the English folk circuit and returned to Ireland. At that time Irish bands always had brilliant musicians and the music was first-rate. But nobody had developed much in the way of stage presence. I like to think Christy learned the secrets of showmanship while he was treading the boards of the English folk club scene. Back home in Ireland he was one of a small number of performers who had recognised the importance of stagecraft. Combined with the excellent musicianship of the other members of his band, it made for a truly magical blend and Christy was a major element of what made them special. They became hugely successful internationally, helped by the inter-Celtic connections that stretch across the world to America, Australia and everywhere else. Sadly, the English don't have an equivalent musical network.

> When I played the Eston Folk Club in 1967/8, I met Vin for the first time. I reckon he was about 18 or 19. He came up and played the whistle and he was simply brilliant. There was a great vibe and the audience clearly loved him. It was great to watch his career develop as he went on to become one of the authentic voices of the English folk revival. He always proudly represented his North-East, Teesside roots. We played together at the Redcar Folk Festival in the 1970s. It was always good to meet Vin.
> **Christy Moore**

I've ended up in hot water over the years because of my songs about Ireland. When I wrote *Mr Gunman*, which was on my first LP, *Valley of Tees*, somebody came over and told me I was out of order singing an anti-British, pro-Irish song. The same night somebody else congratulated me on getting the balance right. The second Troubles' song I wrote was *Welcome Home Howard Green*, about the Green Howards infantry regiment that was made up predominantly of young lads from the Teesside area. The song is more about humanity than politics. Again, I tried to achieve a balance, but not everyone agreed that I'd managed it.

In 1998 I was invited to sing at half-time during a game against Liverpool at Middlesbrough Football Club's Riverside Stadium. They were putting on entertainment every week at the time – the week before me it was an opera singer. Boro had only been promoted to the Premier League the previous season but were sixth in the table and on a long unbeaten run. It was Boxing Day and even though it was chilly and a winter storm had played havoc with the country's electricity supply in the run-up to Christmas, there were still 34,626 fans crammed into the stadium, by some distance the biggest audience I've ever faced.

'Hope you're going to give them something cheerful and upbeat,' Boro's media man Dave Allan said as he led me down the tunnel and onto the pitch. I think I might have disappointed him. Middlesbrough and Liverpool share a strong Irish history. It was the year of the Good Friday Agreement and hopes were high that the near thirty-year conflict in the north was over at last. So I decided to sing *The Troubles of Erin...*

Oh, remember the civil rights marchers
Who were battered with clubs to the ground,
And the very last squaddie to lay down his body
And part with his soul for the crown.

Chorus
May the troubles of Erin be over,
May the bubble of peace be preserved,
May the white dove inspire the children of Ireland,
Peace is the least they deserve.

And remember that cold Bloody Sunday,
When the troops opened fire on the crowd,
And the people of Derry again had to bury
Their loved ones, and pay for the shroud.

And the tragedy of Enniskillen,
When a bomb broke the heart of the town,
And that elderly man, who held out his hand
To the killer who cut his girl down.

And the boys in the bar room at Poyntzpass,
Good friends who could see no divide,
A cold heinous crime cut them down in their prime,
Their blood was as one where they died.

Oh, the prisons are filled with their number,
The angry, the anguished, the shamed,

But the wire must come down in each county and town
For the ghosts of the past to be laid.

So let's pray for the day of forgiveness,
When the weeping and wailing will cease,
And may love reconcile all of Erin's green isle,
May the living and dead rest in peace.

I think it's one of the three best songs I've written, which is why I was disappointed when I sang it in Holland one night and an Irish woman picked out one line that she disapproved of...

That elderly man, who held out his hand to the killer who cut his girl down.

I can't understand why anyone would have a problem with that. To me, Gordon Wilson is a hero of the Troubles. He inspired me with his complete forgiveness after the IRA killed his daughter and eleven others in the Remembrance Day bombing in Enniskillen in 1987.

I knew singing *The Troubles of Erin* to thousands of football fans was risky, but I'm glad I chose it. I had confidence in the song because it was about hands reaching out in peace, as opposed to fists being held up in violence. The song went down well as they were eating their pies and drinking their Bovril and I thoroughly enjoyed singing it. As I sang I was counting the crowd in front of me and thinking even if only half of them bought a CD, I'd still be able to retire! The only black mark on the whole day was Boro's 3-1 defeat, the first time they'd lost at home in over a year. I hoped nobody would blame me for bringing bad luck but a few days later I was in the Station pub in Loftus and a big fella in a leather jacket sidled up menacingly at the bar.

'All right,' he said.

'All right.'

'I saw you at the Riverside on Saturday.'

'Did you?' I said. 'What did you think?'

He took a long swig from his pint before he answered.

'You were the only professional on the pitch all day!'

THE TALE OF THE TAPES

'If you can... watch the things you gave your life to broken,
And stoop to build 'em up with worn-out tools.'

Rudyard Kipling, *If*

For a long time I looked after bookings myself. When you start in the folk business you want an agent but can't get one because agents need to make money and don't want the thankless task of trying to flog bookings for a singer nobody's heard of. Then when you have enough work anyway, after treading the boards and generating the demand for your services, every agent in the country suddenly wants you. You've become a saleable asset. But by that point you don't need an agent because you're busy enough and you don't want to give away a cut of your takings in commission. It's a Catch 22 situation.

I battled away for a while until I had more bookings than I could handle on my own – I was on the road too much of the time to take care of all the arrangements. It was so easy to find an agent by this stage that I had two, Jean Oglesby, who died a few years ago, God bless her, and Jane Winder. Jean lived in Islington but was originally from Hartlepool, where she helped run the Nursery Inn Folk Club. She married Bob Davenport, a stalwart of the Tyneside folk scene during the fifties and sixties, and last time I heard he was still going strong, singing around London in his mid-eighties.

It was Jean who introduced me to the record producer Bill Leader at Loughborough Folk Festival in 1971. Born in New Jersey, Bill was a prolific collector of music and amassed a huge archive, including recordings of elderly shepherds singing centuries-old pastoral songs. He learned his trade as a recordist for Topic Records, the left-leaning label that's still going strong today. It began as a sideline of the Workers' Music Association in 1939 and is said to be the world's oldest independent record company. The great Ewan MacColl, the brilliant guitarist Martin Carthy and family group the Watersons were all involved with Topic and it played a major role in what was called the British folk revival. Once he'd mastered his craft Bill left Topic and set up his own label, Trailer. He then recorded dozens of folkies, including Christy Moore, Bert Jansch, Davey Graham and John Renbourn, and I was thrilled to bits when he asked me to join the list.

The image used on the cover of 1991's The By-Pass Syndrome

My first album, *Valley of Tees*, came out on the Trailer label in 1972. I recorded most of it at Cecil Sharp House, the headquarters of the English Folk Dance and Song Society in Camden Town, near Bill's home. As with a great number of his recordings, *Valley of Tees* was what you might call low-tech, just the guitar and me and a little bit of double-tracking. Someone else played tin whistle and I added a second whistle over it. The title track was an early environmental song – as one magazine later put it, I was green long before the Greens were green! It was a big success and I released another two albums with Trailer, the live LP *The Young Tin Whistle Pest* in 1975 and the cheekily-titled *King Gooden* in 1976.

Everything was going swimmingly and I would have probably stayed with Trailer for the rest of my career if nothing had changed. And then in 1977, without a word of warning, poor old Bill went bust. I was in America when I heard the news. I spent at least a month there every year between 1973 and 1979 and I was just about to play a gig in Boston, Massachusetts.

Transatlantic Records, who distributed for Trailer, were supposed to send a batch of LPs over for me to sell at my gigs but for some reason they shipped them to Toronto instead and I've no idea what became of them. The irony of Transatlantic failing to transport my LPs from here to America was not lost on me. It was as though they were thinking along English lines, that you could drive from London to Birmingham and pick them up – but it was a couple of days' drive from Boston to Toronto. Maybe Bill couldn't afford the extra money needed to send them directly to where I was. There could be a couple of hundred Vin Garbutt LPs still gathering dust in a warehouse somewhere deep in Toronto Airport for all I know. I wouldn't mind buying them back and I keep checking eBay just in case they turn up.

After Trailer folded I signed up with Topic Records themselves and recorded *Eston California*, which was released in 1977. The name came from the old mining hamlet in Eston called California, just up the road from Normanby, where I moved with my family when I was a kid. It was in the Eston Hills that 'rusty gold', also known as ironstone, was discovered by Bolckow and Vaughan in 1850, which brought about the birth of Teesside as we know it. The recording was all done on reel-to-reel tape equipment and the process was still basic. But I didn't need anything more to put my songs across.

> Our gang of ten- and eleven-year-olds had been up Eston Hills, the playground of our youth. On our way down we passed through Eston Square. Outside the Eston & California Social Club, a bloke stopped us and asked if we wanted our picture taken. Without hesitation, we all agreed. Penny whistles were quickly passed around and we were told to sit on the kerb next to each other and make out we were playing them. The image was taken and soon afterwards the movement of band equipment from the club to the car park began.
>
> Not knowing who these rock stars were, I followed the main man down the sloped access of what was Walter Willson's, asking him for his autograph. He stopped, picked up a matchbox, tore it open to expose the inner and rolled his thumb over the cardboard to make a print. Then he handed me the box and said, 'Take this to South Bank Police Station, they'll tell you who I am!' It was a joke that at the time I didn't understand but stuck with me until this day. We were instructed to look out in the *Gazette* for the picture.
>
> Some months later my sister brought home a copy of the finished product, the famous *Eston California* album. It was that day I was introduced to his name – Vin Garbutt. The album was stocked and sold at Peter's Records in Eston and we purchased a few. I followed Vin from a distance and almost forty years later I was in the North Stand watching the Boro when I saw him climbing the stands to his seat. After a brief reintroduction it was agreed that a re-enactment of that photo would be attempted. After a couple of years, most, but not all, had been tracked down and were up for a get-together. I'm the young lad on the far right with the purple jumper.
>
> **Paddy Walsh**

The following year, 1978, Topic released *Tossin' a Wobbler* and in 1980 I recorded a live album while I was on tour in Australia. It came about through good fortune more than anything. Someone turned up at my gig in the small Queensland mining town of Mount Isa with all the best gear money could buy and asked if they could record me.

'No problem,' I said. 'As long as I can have a copy of the tapes!'

Shy Tot Pommy was a full-length LP, although there were only six tracks. LPs were a maximum of twenty minutes each side and with all my daft patter during a live performance, that's all there was room for. But they included *El Salvador*, which I think is one of the best songs I've ever written. *Shy Tot Pommy* still hadn't come out by the time Topic released my next studio album, *Little Innocents*, in 1983. My relationship with Topic started to go a little bit awry after that. They didn't seem to want to use *Shy Tot Pommy* at all – for a long time I kept asking when they were going to release it. I couldn't work out why they were dragging their feet. I don't think it was just a coincidence that my last album for Topic was *Little Innocents*. Perhaps it was the reaction in the months that followed that changed their attitude so dramatically. But more about that later.

With Topic suddenly losing all interest in me, I was left in limbo. However, the future started to look a little bit brighter when I was approached by my old friend Dave Bulmer, who ran his own record label, Celtic Music. Dave was an excellent accordion player. I first met him when he booked me for gigs at Leeds University during his student days and we always got on well. He remembered me telling him I'd recorded *Shy Tot Pommy* and asked what had happened to it. When I told him it was on Topic's shelves in London, he offered to release it on Celtic instead. I had come to the conclusion that Topic had clearly gone off me and so I handed the master tapes over to Dave. He tidied the recordings up and it was released in 1985. (To this day, most people don't understand the pun in the title of the album. The picture on the front shows me changing my guitar strings while sitting on a bench beneath a palm tree. A little girl on the other end of the bench is looking at me coyly. She was the shy tot and I was the pommie. I'm going to leave you to work it out for yourself. I specialise in jokes that don't offend anybody – even if it's sometimes because nobody else understands them!)

After that Dave suggested getting my Trailer tapes back. I agreed to let him try, as long as it was all civilised and he didn't take poor old Bill to court or anything like that. I was happy for Dave to find out where the masters were and see if they could be retrieved. Well, he got them back all right – but I never saw them, sadly. Instead, they ended up at Dave's home near Harrogate, along with master tapes belonging to several other folkies.

It won't come as a surprise to anyone who knows me that I was never that savvy about the business side of music. I had a diary full of bookings and was so preoccupied with the real world that I didn't want to deal with all this wrangling and falling out with record companies. After what had happened with Trailer, Topic and now Celtic, I was sick and tired of the whole record business. I didn't make a record for another four years. I just continued doing what I loved, playing live to audiences all over the world.

Then, to my surprise, Dave contacted us again in 1989. It sounds crazy looking back on it, but not long afterwards I released another LP on Celtic, *When the Tide Turns*. I paid for the recording myself and no paperwork ever changed hands between us. It was produced by Alan Whetton, who played saxophone for Dexy's Midnight Runners and became a fan after being given a tape of my music by Trevor Burton, the guitarist with the Move.

The whole arrangement with Dave was by way of a gentlemen's agreement. As it turned out I never actually received any cash off him at all. Instead I bought the LPs and CDs off Dave and sold them at my gigs. But not long after the record came out, the taxman started asking difficult questions about my dealings with Celtic. The time had come for us to make our relationship official. Pat and I did everything we possibly could to persuade Dave to settle the books with us. Our accountant was tearing his hair out. He told us we just couldn't continue like that and he needed to know how much we owed Celtic Music and how much they owed us. Dave never gave any straight answers, but I'm sure he owed us a lot of money. He simply wouldn't comply with our requests and our relationship became extremely awkward.

Somehow we muddled through without falling out completely and we agreed he would release my next album, *The By-Pass Syndrome*. Once again I paid for the recording myself. But soon the disagreements over money started again. The situation just wasn't right and one day I decided I'd had enough. I didn't want the hassle any more and I walked away from Celtic. Eventually, me and Pat decided to ask him for all my tapes back. But we were in for a shock.

'You can't have them,' Dave told us. 'They're all part of my portfolio now.'

We didn't put up much of a fight. Up until then I was one of the last people still defending Dave because we'd always been friends. I'd heard grumbles from other performers who perhaps weren't as well established as I was and who were scraping a living.

Things could easily have been worse, though. At one stage I had a ticket for a train to Harrogate in my hand and was on my way to sign a contract with Celtic Music. Something nagging away in the back of my mind didn't feel right, but I decided I was going to do it anyway. If I'd reached Harrogate I would have signed away the rights to *When the Tide Turns* and everything else Dave had the master tapes for, which was just about my entire back catalogue. But just before I set off I received a phone call from Chris and Geoff Key, who came to see me whenever I played in the Derby area. Their seventeen-year-old son Haydn was dying from a muscle-wasting illness. They said Haydn loved my songs and asked me to sing to him during his final days. I felt drawn to go because I knew Haydn liked my serious stuff. He didn't want me to go and cheer him up, he wanted to hear about these important issues one last time. I was deeply moved that a young person leaving this world would still want to be thinking this way and I couldn't refuse such a request. So instead of signing my life away to Dave Bulmer, I went to Derby and sang to Haydn in his last hours. It was a very special honour and I also have Haydn to thank for that near miss.

> We first saw Vin on May 19th 1990 at the Feast of Folk, Derby Assembly Rooms. Our son, Haydn, thought he was brilliant. Haydn was physically disabled (something similar to MS) at fourteen years old. When Vin came to Burton-on-Trent Folk Club, Haydn wanted to see him again, so we took him, carrying him and his wheelchair up the stairs – probably against all fire safety regulations! We went a few times and each time we bought a tape, until he had quite a collection. In 1993, Haydn's heart began to fail and he was very ill and we asked if Vin would come and sing to Haydn at our house. Vin, being the most caring chap he is, said yes. It was an amazing few hours: he sang songs,

with Haydn joining in, played tunes on his whistle and made a seventeen-year-old lad very happy. Four days later, Haydn passed away. Since then we've become firm friends. We've put Vin and Pat up at our house on odd occasions and been up to stay with them when we went to Saltburn Folk Festival in 2009. If he's in our area, we always try to go along. It's now twenty-four years since Vin came and sang to Haydn – where does time go? We love him and Pat. Vin has a heart of gold, which is felt in many of his songs. Haydn's favourite was *Carol Ann Kelly* and we played *The South Wind* at his funeral.
Chris and Geoff Key, Hatton, Derbyshire

I don't quite understand what Dave Bulmer was thinking of. I have no idea what he planned to do with the tapes. Just having them in his attic didn't make him any money. Pat has a theory that he hoped to sell the whole catalogue one day. She gets angry about what Dave did to us, although I don't. It seems to me that Dave loved having friends, but he loved having money even more, and that's sad. In the end he lost almost all of his friends. How can it ever be worth putting money before friendship?

Fed up with the whole business, Pat and I decided to launch our own record company, Home Roots Music. We never actually wanted to run our own business – I was too busy performing and writing to look after all that side of my career as well. But I had become so uncomfortable dealing with the music industry that we felt we had no choice.

Home Roots released its first record, *The By-Pass Syndrome*, in 1991, followed by *Bandalised* in 1994, the live album *Plugged* in 1995 and *When the Tide Turns Again* in 1998. The latter was *When the Tide Turns*, which had been released on Dave Bulmer's Celtic label in 1989, with one additional track added, *The Court of Cahirass*. By now the technology existed to produce a high-quality reproduction of the original recording without having access to the masters. My agent took the photograph on the front, which shows a rusty barrel washed up on a beach, so we owned the copyright for that. We redesigned the back cover and then waited to find out if Dave would pursue us through the courts. He didn't, of course. I'd like to think we can do the same as we did with *When The Tide Turns Again* with all the other recordings.

I never saw Dave Bulmer again and he passed away in the summer of 2013. I still haven't recovered those invaluable master tapes, the missing milestones of my early career. I didn't want to pester his widow and kids after he died. But I'd love to contact them and ask, diplomatically, whether we can settle our differences. Maybe one day we'll have those precious tapes back.

DAFT PATTER, SERIOUS SONGS

'Comedy and tragedy live side by side.'

Vin Garbutt

Making people laugh is a wonderful feeling. But songwriting is a serious business for me. I'm not keen on singing humorous songs and only have two in my repertoire, *They Don't Write 'em Like That Any More* and *Fell Off the Back of a Boat.* I worked out early in my career, though, that if you just hammer away at an audience's sensibilities with constant social comment it can become more like a sermon or a lecture than a concert. I could understand people who weren't used to it saying, 'That's not for me.' Instead I developed a technique that enabled me to get away with singing the serious songs that are key to my performance – by filling the spaces between them with patter.

I've always been a humorous person. My dad was a patter merchant and I followed in his footsteps. What I can't stand, though, is the humour being promoted ahead of the music. I shudder when a poster reads, 'Vin Garbutt, comedian and singer.' It's an insult to what I do and to the songs because they're about important issues and they need to be heard. As soon as I see those posters my heart sinks. The humour then becomes the lowest common denominator. I've learned that if people turn up expecting a comedian they sometimes can't handle the issues in the songs and go away disappointed. But if they come for the songs or for the whole package, the humour's a bonus. The people who come back to see me over and over again are the ones who understand what I'm singing about.

Some people have described my stories as surreal. Others have said they're just daft. By wearing those two masks of comedy and drama, I'm able to entertain an audience who aren't all hardened folkies with songs about places and people they might never have heard of. After softening them up with patter, they're ready for the serious content. I might randomly tell them that William the Conqueror has a lot to answer for because he's the man who brought Norman wisdom to Britain. Then, as people are gradually

A serious studio portrait

A more familiar pose

working it out and a titter starts working its way around the room, I launch into my next song, which could be about genocide in East Timor, child prostitution in Bangkok or a story from much closer to home.

Sometimes I'm inspired by what I see around me or events I experience on my travels around the world, and I've also written about places I've never been. I learn about them by absorbing as much high-quality news as I can, with as much variety as possible. I don't read much fiction but I'm an avid news reader. When I'm travelling I often have two or three newspapers with me. I was once on a train from London with a group of journalists behind me on their way back from a conference. They were looking around the carriage and analysing what people were reading and why. I had the *Independent*, the *Socialist Worker* and the Catholic paper the *Universe* laid out on the table. When they came to me they just shook their heads and gave up! I used to read the *Guardian* but I switched to the *Indy* until it closed its printed edition. I liked it because it was left-wing, but not in the manner of those left-wingers who say, 'We're all the goodies and they're all baddies.' I'm just searching for the truth and you can only do that if you hear different slants on what's going on.

I watch CNN to find out what the Americans are hearing and I also like tuning in to Al Jazeera for a different perspective altogether, especially after an incident such as the attempted coup in m. Al Jazeera is based in Qatar and is generally pro-Western but also pro-Muslim, so you become aware of an angle you won't hear elsewhere about what's happening. Russia Today also offers a fascinating alternative viewpoint. I view the Russian-speaking Ukrainians as the victims in the fighting going on there, with one of the biggest ever mobilisations of NATO troops taking place all along the border area. When I visit the States there's a lot missing from the news they're fed. They also hear some news we don't, but there's so much they just ignore. During the 1980s you never heard a word about the terrible miscarriages of justice going on in Nicaragua and El Salvador. At that time the Reagan government was going to extreme lengths to keep out what it perceived as the creeping threat of communism in its own backyard. In Nicaragua they armed the Contras who, by all accounts and according to all the research I did, were terrorists. The CIA also trained and financed the death squads of the military junta that were responsible for countless murders during El Salvador's long, bloody civil war. Both ended up as the subjects of my songs. But similar atrocities happened in countless other places. I'd love to write a song about Diego Garcia, a British territory in the Indian Ocean whose inhabitants were all shipped off to Mauritius or other islands to make way for a US military base in 1971.

There are also injustices going on that we're not told about by the BBC. I've learned about some of them in completely random circumstances. A friend who used to live in Loftus celebrated her wedding in the stables at Chatsworth House and I sat next to the bridegroom's sister, who was in her late fifties. She told me she was married to a Muslim from Western Sahara. It's close to the Canary Islands and was fashionable with French and Spanish tourists and at one time with the English. United Nations troops are stationed there and it isn't recognised as a country in its own right. This poor woman had to be smuggled in, covered up in traditional clothes and pretending to be asleep in the car. She needed to avoid being questioned because the Moroccan government, which controls much of the territory, didn't want any foreigners there. Her husband's family are forced to live in Algeria because it's too dangerous for them to go back until their homeland is liberated. I just went to a wedding and ended up learning about events we never hear about on the news.

Hearing songs with messages behind them, stories of hardship, injustice and workers being oppressed, was life-changing for me. There's a song by the folk singer Dick Gaughan called *A Different Kind of Love Song*. It describes the way folk songs are about love for other people. It's not a sexual love, it's a brotherly and sisterly love for the dispossessed and the poorer members of society - not just your own people, but caring about what's happening to those living in other parts of the world as well. It's easier for Celts to listen to songs with messages behind them than it is for the English. English people can enjoy the sensory side of music and tap their feet along with it, but the tradition of listening to what I would call a heavy song has been lost. The Irish and the Scots hear the words. When you start singing a serious song in an Irish or Scottish pub, the place falls silent. Here in England you can see people shuffling awkwardly and whispering, 'What's he on about?

Most songwriters look inwards and talk about their own experiences, usually in the form of love songs. But in my songs I write about my observations of other people, rather than about myself. I don't open up my soul and tell the world about my personal heartbreaks and I don't tend to be self-reflective in what I have to say. Pop songs are usually sensory and you have to be able to tap your feet to them. You don't necessarily have to listen to the lyrics, you just need to feel good about the sound you're hearing. I'm not knocking pop and rock songs at all. I enjoy them enormously – and, of course, you can make vast amounts of money if you have a talent for writing them. I listen to Chicago sing, 'If you leave me now, you'll take away the biggest part of me,' and wonder how anybody can write such words. It's a beautiful sentiment and makes me want to cry. Nothing of that nature ever flows from my pen though. The nearest I've ever come to writing that kind of song is when I pinched Bach's melody to write *The November Wedding*, which I recorded on *The By-Pass Syndrome*. I haven't told anybody before, but it's about my wedding to Pat. I've tried my own melody to go with it, but so far I'm struggling to beat Johann's.

My lyrics can evolve over the years. I've recorded songs and later realised something isn't right, so I've altered the words when I sing them live. But sometimes there's nothing you can do to fix them. There's a line in *The City of Angels*, which I recorded on *Word of Mouth* in 1999, that says, 'They pay off the debtors.' A teacher friend kindly pointed out to me that you don't pay off debtors, you pay off creditors. A debtor owes money. That was an 'Aargh!' moment for me. I've hardly sung it since then, even though most people wouldn't notice. I would have to change it to 'They pay all the debts off' and it doesn't quite fit.

Perhaps the most satisfying compliment I ever received for any of my songs came from the American folk superstar, Tom Paxton, who has always managed to combine humorous songs with songs about injustice throughout the world. I'd met him a couple of times, including playing on the same bill in Philadelphia back in the 1970s, but I didn't think he would have heard of me. Then during the *Bandalised* era in the mid-1990s we both did a 'secret' festival at Coombe Abbey in Warwickshire. There was a fantastic line-up but no publicity and consequently hardly anyone turned up. Tom recognised me backstage and I was stunned when I saw him heading over to chat. A few years later Pat was in an internet cafe in Malaysia when she realised we'd received an email from him about my song *When Oppressed Becomes Oppressor*. It's about the way history is littered with people who suffer terrible injustices but who themselves then go on to commit crimes against others. The exchange between Tom and Pat is priceless…

Vin,
I heard your piece re: Oppressor on the Huntingdon Folk compilation (what a great venue, no?) and must say, steady on, my son! You're making the rest of us look bad. What a great piece of work that is. Well done!
Tom Paxton

Dear Tom,
Just a brief message to say thanks for the vote of confidence. This is Vin's wife, Pat. We are in Kuala Lumpur on the way to Australia. It's a bit hit and miss getting our email but I just have to ask is this THE Tom Paxton that I'm talking to? I am answering the mail as Vin is in his usual place – asleep in bed!
Pat G

Hi Pat,
If there is a THE Tom Paxton, I guess I'm the guilty one. Don't wake him up. Let the darlin' sleep! Have a good one in Oz and tell them love from me.
Tom

When Oppressed Becomes Oppressor

When oppressed becomes oppressor and the best becomes the worst,
When the meek become the mighty and the blessed become the cursed,
When the flame of faith is failing and the light of love has died,
When the fruit of truth decays upon the tree of human pride.

'Send me your huddled masses,' cried America the free,
Then from Saigon to San Salvador
The streets were filled with refugees.

The Jew who braved the ghetto wearing David's sacred sign,
In the promised land with stick in hand,
He beats the child of Palestine.

The Chinese peasant army faced the capitalist gun,
Then their long march to freedom ended
In the Square of Tiananmen.

The world expelled the man Saddam
From a defenceless Kuwait,
Then the torturers of Al Sabah sent hundreds to an unknown fate.

The Chetnik fought so bravely to fend off the fascist horde,
Then his sons went raping Muslim girls
On orders from a Serb warlord.

Will we ever learn from history?
The memory fades so fast,
But we're destined to repeat the sins
If we forget the past.

When oppressed becomes oppressor and the best becomes the worst,
When the meek become the mighty and the blessed become the cursed,
When the flame of faith is failing and the light of love has died,
When the fruit of truth decays upon the tree of human pride.

Deep in the moment

I've relearnt some of my old songs that weren't particularly popular when I first sang them and they go down much better years later. I've been singing *Nawa's Song* about Saddam Hussein gassing the Kurds in Halabja. I wrote it in the late 1980s, before the Gulf Wars and when Britain was still supporting Saddam. Sadly, history is repeating itself in Syria, where exactly the same thing is happening. *Nawa's Song* didn't receive many comments the first time around, but when I sing it now it brings a very positive response.

Danny Danielle has also experienced a resurgence more than forty years after I recorded it on *Valley of Tees*. It was my attempt to write in a traditional style and if I'm honest the style of the melody was heavily influenced by Martin Carthy's *Sovay*. It has that slightly Eastern European sound. I was trying to write in the traditional style, as a new songwriter just experimenting.

I recently relearnt *The Royal Blackbird* from *Little Innocents* and although I don't sing *The By-Pass Syndrome* much these days, my friend Paul Tilley has inspired me to relearn that too. He sent me a video of him singing it to his kids and I thought, 'That's not bad!' He kept chucking in compliments in between lines as he sang – 'Brilliant, Vin, brilliant!' If I was feeling down on myself and fishing for compliments, Paul's the man I'd call. He's a Grangetown lad who now lives in Scarborough. He's a top-class musician and has been a professional singer-songwriter for donkeys' years, though he's more of a rocker than a folkie. He plays keyboards and guitar and has earned his living in the way the folkies do, by building up a following. Paul discovered my music when he was a kid and we became friends. He played the drums for me on *Bandalised*.

I've never recorded any of Paul's songs but there's one called *Better Days Ahead* that I mean to learn one day.

Occasionally, I've had to give up and put a song I've written away and leave it alone for years because I find it too hard to play. For a long time I just couldn't learn the guitar part for *Waits and Weeps*, which Bob Fox does brilliantly. Some songs on my more recent albums might have been written twenty years or more before I come round to recording them. But folk songs don't go out of date. They're about real events that still go on all the time - ordinary people's experiences that are happening all around us now, if only we open our eyes and look for them.

> I was the youngest of seven and my oldest brother Dave was a massive Vin fan, so I knew all the songs on those early classic albums at a very young age. I learned to play piano and guitar and by thirteen I was singing the Vin classics. He was like Paul McCartney to me. I went to see Vin live when I was fifteen and I was mesmerised by his all-round performance and down-to-earth approach. I was amazed that someone from the same area as me was performing in our accent and singing songs about our part of the world. It made me proud to come from Teesside.
>
> His politics were a big influence on me and although I didn't agree with everything, I admired him greatly. I went to see Vin whenever I could and I found his patter would often creep into my everyday speech.
>
> Pat saw me playing at Redcar Folk Festival when I was about eighteen and told Vin about me and we struck up a friendship. I went off to London to do a music degree and he would often stay at my house there. As part of my degree I did a tribute to Vin and played songs such as *Not for the First Time* and *When the Tide Turns*.
>
> Vin asked me to play on his album *Bandalised* and then I recorded some of the tracks and played on the *Word of Mouth* album. He also asked me to transcribe the music for his *Songbook*. Vin and his family were often at my regular monthly gig at the Station Hotel in Loftus and Vin would get up and sing with me. I played there every month and became close to all the family, often popping round for tea beforehand.
>
> **Paul Tilley**

I'm not sure which is the best song I've written, but I'm especially fond of *When the Tide Turns* because it reflects my life's philosophy. It's an ecological song. I can't remember when I started writing it, although I can picture myself cogitating on a double-decker bus from Coventry to Warwick University as I tried to finish it off. I still have the little notebooks I used to carry to write down song ideas when they came to me. Now I don't travel by public transport any more, those notebooks are hardly touched. I don't seem able to write without complete solitude.

When the Tide Turns

When Columbus set sail, sophisticated men wailed,
Calling him a fool, saying: 'You'll topple over.'
The top brains of his day said: 'That can't be the way,
You know the world is flat – think on that, foolish rover.'
Now we gaze to the stars knowing they're not so far
As America was to Mr Columbus,
But the brains of today tell us that's not the way,
They say to concentrate on reducing our numbers.

Chorus:
When the tide turns, a black priest will come,
When the tide turns, to England, my home.
When the tide turns, a new rising sun
Like a bright flame will burn, when the tide turns.

Sophistication can't kill nations quite as much as starvation;
See it in the eyes, hear the cries of the West's depressed.
For the weak we've no room, now the womb is a tomb;
Tomorrow's world must die if the mighty say it's for best.
Oh, there once was a time - Oh, there once was a time
When these people of mine coexisted, one with the fauna and fields.
Where Mother Nature gives breath to the soil with each death
Her simple symbiosis produces her yield.
Human life, like the grass, in one season does pass;
Fall and feed the soil, as our seeds feed tomorrow.

Every man, every beast, host and share the same feast,
Giving back the earth quite as much as we borrow.
But as man's chart unfurled, his materialist world
Has turned away from Nature's advice and God's wonder,
And with our hands in Earth's till, starving millions we kill,
Naively denying our part in the plunder.
But the brains of today, they shall not have their way;
Tomorrow's world belongs to the weak and the needing,
For the meek still give birth and inherit this earth
While we, now used to greed, overfeed and cease breeding.

I've often wondered if Archbishop John Sentamu would appreciate the first line of *When the Tide Turns*. It's about the West exporting Christianity and then years later having problems recruiting clergy of their own, and the former colonies sending missionaries back the other way to these islands of ours.

When my lifelong friend Pete Betts was dying in hospital his wife, Faith, who's not a Catholic, asked if we should call a priest.

'Pete's always been a closet Catholic,' I said. 'I think he'd like that, yes.'

The priest who came was a black African.

When the Tide Turns was heavily influenced by two issues that were dominating my life at the time I wrote it. I was a new parent and a passionate organic gardener. The words try to show how you can end up believing something just because everybody else does. Thinking there was only so much food to go around, the people of the fifteenth century expected to keep fighting each other for the land that seemed to be available. And then Christopher Columbus decided to go off and find out if he could discover some more, defying the logic of the wise men of his day.

Today, the rich, materialist nations of the earth are worried about overpopulation and claim it's out of concern for the wellbeing of everyone. But it's not altruistic at all, it's because they're frightened that if the poor keep breeding there will be less food and fewer natural resources for them to exploit. That leaves me feeling acutely uncomfortable. I'm not too worried about people outgrowing the world. I've read that more baby boys than girls are born for the next couple of decades after a war. Something ecological happens. To me, it's God's plan – what some call Mother Nature is what I see as the divine.

When I wrote that 'sophistication can kill nations quite as much as starvation' I had to look up the word 'sophistication' to make sure I was using it correctly. I discovered that it derives from the same root as the word 'sophistry'. A sophist is someone who will tell you a lie if it helps them win an argument. You might accept what you're being told and say, 'If you know that and I don't, thank you for giving me the truth.' Then you find out it wasn't the truth at all, they just wanted to win the argument. That's sophistry. I would hate to be accused of that.

I'm a Catholic and happy this way. My religion means a lot to me and I've confirmed my membership of the Church in adulthood. I love the painting *The Light of the World*. Victorian artist William Holman Hunt depicts Christ standing outside a closed door, holding a lantern. To me, the message is that you have to welcome Jesus into your life – he won't force his way in. The more I open that door, the more I find out what it's all about. Pat didn't have that when she was growing up - she was from an Anglican home but not a churchgoing family. She thought I was Irish when she first met me and her mother used to say to her, 'Are you still seeing that Catholic communist?' We eventually became friends, but at first she wasn't too keen on the idea of her daughter being with a left-footer. Pat only has one living relative, her brother Dave, who lives in Loftus, but she loves the Garbutts and embraces the wider Catholic family. She doesn't display much spirituality herself, but if something's lost she'll say to me, 'You'd better get St Anthony on the job, Vin!' It's a sort of faith by proxy.

Thankfully, this Catholic-Protestant problem isn't a big issue in England any more. We have the white-black divide instead, although it's not as wide as you'd think if you just read and heard about it from the media. Britain is a better place for multiculturalism. There's just not enough support for those people who cross the divide. There weren't many Asian people in Eston and Normanby a few years ago and I loved playing in Bradford. It was like going abroad for me. There was a thriving Pakistani community, the food was always delicious and the place was so warm and friendly. I remember reading how the crime rate dropped in Bradford in the mid-1970s because of the influx of Asian people. I thought it was brilliant that the city could absorb the peaceful influence of the incoming Asian community and benefit from it. Sadly, we now live in a more violent culture, and some young Asians have adopted our British ways instead.

Back in the seventies I saw English lads and lasses courting Asian lads and lasses and I thought it was fantastic. There's a song on *Persona… Grata* called *Punjabi Girl*, about a young couple in an all-too-common situation. It's set on Teesside and is fictional but based on the experiences of real people. A white Middlesbrough lad and a young Asian girl whose father came over from India fall in love and both families disapprove of their relationship. The parents just can't bear the thought of their children marrying someone from a different culture and the couple have to fight the system to stay together. It's a battle for them, but they end up marrying and having children. It struck me that not so long ago the Irish-English situation was exactly the same. Back in my mam and dad's day it was incredibly difficult for them to go courting. Dad was a Methodist from Normanby and Mam was an Irish Catholic, born in South Bank. Talk about mixed marriages! At that time there were regular fights between gangs of Catholics and Protestants on the Trunk Road in between South Bank and Normanby.

Children really are the future. We make our mistakes and then our kids are there to grow up and rectify them. Pat can be a pessimist, but she's extremely astute as well. She says kids grow up prepared for life in the society they were born into. They don't reach adulthood and look round in shock at all the horrible happenings around them. They've lived with it as they've grown up and they just get it. She's right. As long as you can give them a firm grounding so they can cope with the experiences life will throw at them, they'll be okay.

It's been thirty-odd years since I wrote *When The Tide Turns* and in that time I haven't changed my mind about any of the lyrics. I'm pleased with the melody but I'm especially proud of the lyrics. They sum up so much of what I believe.

TAKING A STAND

'Think, be philosophical, question yourself.'

Vin Garbutt

I'd left school by the time the 1967 Abortion Act made the termination of certain pregnancies legal in England, Scotland and Wales. I was aware that the Catholic Church said abortion was wrong, but that was as far as my knowledge went. But as the 1970s progressed I became more and more concerned about what was happening in our society. The first time I remember speaking out about the subject was during a United States tour in 1973. I became involved in a conversation at a party about a girl who'd had an abortion.

'She fell pregnant, so she just got rid of it,' someone said.

I was quite shocked by the casualness of the remark.

'That was a bit drastic, wasn't it?' I said.

I wasn't aggressive or angry, I was just adding my honest response. As the discussion went on, two women became upset and started crying. I realised I'd touched some raw nerves and later the hostess came over to me.

'You were a bit over the top with what you said there, Vin,' she said.

I was completely caught off guard by this. I had no idea what I'd done wrong and went outside for a walk to clear my head. At that stage I wasn't a committed pro-lifer by any means. But it was the moment I realised just how important the issue was – and how dangerous even talking about it could be.

As I explored the issue further over the years that followed, it became more and more apparent that my opinions were out of step with many other people's and were going to bring me problems. In one discussion, Ewan MacColl, one of my all-time musical heroes, told the company we were in that they were wasting their time talking to me about it.

'You'll never convince Vin,' he said. 'He's a Catholic, so he won't be able to make up his own mind.'

He was saying that Catholics take their instructions from the Pope in Rome and can't form their own views or think for themselves like everyone else can. My intellect was under attack because of my religion, and that got to me. I decided to go away and question everything I had believed up to that moment in my life. I wanted to examine whether I had been conditioned or brainwashed as Ewan suggested. I wanted to be true to myself as well, though. My Christianity was a gift from my family and school and was passed on to me out of love. There was no hardship in my background, I only experienced love as a child. I wasn't going to let go lightly of the principles my upbringing had taught me. If I genuinely searched for the truth, I knew I might discover that the beliefs I had cherished up to then were false. But something better would have to come along to replace them first. And however hard I looked, that never happened. Instead, the more I studied, the more convinced I became. I immersed myself in the subject, researching as much as I could about it. I was innocent, even naive I suppose, so it all had to be learnt from scratch. On every level, even the merely practical, the Church's teachings made more sense to me than anything I could find anywhere else.

The moment I decided I had to take a public stand came when Pat was expecting our second baby, Tim. We were overjoyed and Pat went for a routine appointment with the doctor.

'Do you want to keep it?' he said.

Pat was shocked by his words. There was nothing to indicate this wasn't a normal, healthy pregnancy.

'What do you mean?' she said. 'This isn't a crisis. I haven't come to you crying and panicking. This is a happy, wonderful moment in our lives.'

We didn't think it was a question a doctor should ask. According to the law, a woman is supposed to be in seriously dire straits before a termination is even a possibility. I realised then that we'd somehow sleepwalked from abortion being legalised as a desperate measure in extreme circumstances, under the strict terms of the 1967 Abortion Act, to it being a casual matter available at the stroke of a doctor's pen. It had become routine.

When Tim was born I tried to put an announcement in the local paper's Births, Deaths and Marriages column. It said, 'On Sunday he was our foetus, on Monday our son did greet us, for the rest of his life may we help him in strife, and please God, the world won't defeat us.'

But the *Evening Gazette* didn't want to publish it. They phoned me up and said they couldn't print it because it made some of the girls in the office feel sick.

'Really?' I said. 'Why's that? We're thrilled to bits and want to share our happy news with the world. Why would the girls feel sick about it? We were all foetuses once.'

I spoke to somebody higher up at the paper and they eventually agreed to publish the announcement. But by now I felt so strongly about the issue that I started writing songs about it. *Little Innocents (A Civil Rights Song)* was the first one. It drew a parallel between the babies destroyed by King Herod as he tried to kill the new baby king in the New Testament and the babies being killed by abortion in our day and age...

An unfamiliar freedom now belongs to common man,
It's hard for us to say, 'No thanks' - we're told, 'You can, you can.'
We've even won the right that evil rich men always had,
It seems true forbidden fruit is priceless even when it's bad.

So let's scrutinise the package deals we're offered,
Like Anti-nuclear, Save the Whale, Abortion on Demand,
We may feel we're so liberal and enlightened,
Like him who to defend his rights did napalm Vietnam.

Chorus
Oh, cruel world, you try to make a beast of honest men,
You hand out rosy spectacles and then
You slaughter little innocents whose own lives can't defend,
If you'd the right to choose, would you do it to Jesus again?

During all this time I continued finding myself in more and more heated debates and sometimes even arguments. If anyone said anything that challenged my own beliefs, I would go away and study their reasoning to find out if they were right. All it did was inspire me to write further verses. I learnt important lessons about intelligence and arrogance, and realised that you can never lose an argument if your objective is to search out the truth. If the other person convinces you, then you've found the truth and so nobody loses – you've both won.

In 1983 I released the *Little Innocents* album. It included several anti-abortion songs as well as the title track. One of them was *Lynda* and I donated all the proceeds from the album to the national anti-abortion charity SPUC, the Society for the Protection of the Unborn Child. The reaction was mixed and I lost some bookings. A few students in the back row at Bradford Folk Club caused a bit of bother because they disapproved of my words. But most of those who objected came up to speak to me afterwards and give me their opinion instead. That's fine. Dialogue is good and a song should open the doors to dialogue. I'm not too keen on people shouting out during my songs, though. I have no problem with anybody talking to me about something they feel strongly about, but you can't discuss the subtleties of an argument with a heckler, because there might be a thousand people in the conversation.

One of the greatest challenges at that time was the way my views brought me into occasionally fierce conflict with some close friends. I spent many sleepless nights worrying about it. One fallout was particularly painful. A friend I sincerely respected told me my views were just my own prejudices, my own little 'package deal'. That was a backhanded reference to one of the lines in *Little Innocents* – 'Let's scrutinise these package deals we're offered...' Once again, my Catholic faith was being brought into the debate. The song was my way of questioning the way people of a left-wing political persuasion lumped a pro-abortion stance in with their other views, perhaps without ever thinking about why. But this friend turned it back on me, saying my religion was also a package deal, a Catholic job lot. The argument caused a deep rift between us and for years we weren't on speaking terms. Thankfully, that's never happened with anyone else before or since. The reason I was so hurt was because of this man's immense integrity. I held him in the highest esteem in every way.

Then one day the telephone rang.

'You're right,' said the voice on the other end of the phone.

'Who's that?'

The voice simply repeated, 'You're right.'

And then I realised who it was, and said his name. He told me that years earlier his wife had undergone an abortion. As soon as I put the receiver down at the end of the call I broke down and wept. I thought back to the time when I was writing *Little Innocents* and had asked her, 'Does this line sound okay?' I was blissfully unaware of the emotional hurt and anguish it must have caused her.

After that, the couple both became pro-life activists. They even took a girl into their home after she fell pregnant and her lover told her she had to decide between him and the baby. We're the best of friends again now, but it was difficult for a long time. I learnt so much from the integrity of this intelligent man, who made sure there was no corner of my brain unweeded in the search for the truth.

Several times it was said and written in newspaper and magazine articles that I was abusing my position by singing my songs. That's slightly ironic when you think about the longstanding folk tradition of exercising free speech. People such as Woody Guthrie and Bob Dylan sang about the subjects that mattered most to them. The difference is that folk singers generally sing about what are considered to be left-wing issues and somehow being anti-abortion is considered to be right-wing. What's all that about? I don't understand how on earth that's happened, I just can't get my head around it. If being left-wing is about defending the weak and vulnerable, why is it not left-wing to want to defend those who are most vulnerable of all – unborn babies?

So I'll sing working-class songs about the trials and tribulations of miners and steelworkers, and then sing an anti-abortion song. That went completely against the grain, particularly in the media. There were cries of, 'Traitor! What does he think he's doing?' And what was I doing? I was thinking for myself. When it comes to abortion, I've heard no new information to convince me to change my position and I can't understand why there are millions of people on the other side of the fence. I've done plenty of soul-searching, but the people over there don't seem that interested in considering the possibility that they might be wrong as well. It looks to me as though the world is a more convenient place for them to live if they have the ability to stay in control of their lives in that way.

At the same time as I was exploring the theoretical side of the issue, I was also gathering more first-hand feedback about the repercussions of abortion than just about anybody else I knew. I was in a unique position where women who had undergone abortions and heard my songs came to me and gave me more information about what they had been through. While some people were telling me I was out of order, those who knew best – the women who'd had abortions – were saying, 'I know what you're talking about because I've been through it.'

One young woman handed me a handwritten note at the end of a gig in London and the words it contained cut me to the bone.

'We're not all bad people, you know,' she wrote.

I was devastated that she thought I was judging her because she'd had an abortion.

I most certainly wasn't. I thought I'd made it plain that I don't think women who go through abortions are bad people at all, but I obviously hadn't. None of my beliefs come from hate – they come from love. I don't think a woman who has an abortion is evil, but lost. I see two victims in every abortion that takes place. More than that, I think society as a whole is damaged by the act.

Even though it hurt her, this woman came to see me again after the first time she heard me sing *Little Innocents*. She heard it a second time and still she came back. After the third time she was brave enough to hand me that note and I thank her for that, even though I was extremely troubled by what she wrote. My song *The Secret* was a direct response to her.

I'm sorry if I've hurt you, singing my piece,
It's the last thing I'd ever intend.
The truth is impelling, it's painful in telling,
But well, it heals wounds in the end.

I had come to the belief that when a woman is pregnant she's not going to have a baby, she already has one. Even if she has an abortion, she's already a mother and she remains a mother for the rest of her life. She's a mother without a child and her physiology and psychology have to cope with that. Society tries to convince her everything's fine and that she's back in the position she was in before she became pregnant. I wrote *The Secret* about those poor women who are told by the state and even by their friends that their problems have been solved and they can just get on with their lives. They are victims of abortion, every bit as much as their babies are.

Back in the 1970s there was hardly any support available for pregnant women in crisis. I first went to meet volunteers from the pregnancy-support charity Life because I wanted to find out if what a friend told me about them was true.

'They're a nasty bunch,' he said. 'They persuade women not to have abortions and then, when it's too late for them to do anything about it, they just abandon them.'

I found it hard to believe that anyone would do anything so callous and heartless. But it was an intelligent, educated person telling me this, so I gave some credence to his words. I decided to find out for myself and arranged to visit Life's office in Middlesbrough. The first thing I noticed was the thank you letters from women and young girls pinned up on the noticeboard. I stopped to read them and they were heart-wrenching.

'I don't know what I would have done without you getting the flat for me,' one wrote. 'I can't believe I even contemplated having an abortion.'

'Why haven't you sent these letters in to the local papers?' I asked the volunteer who was showing me around. 'I only ever hear negative comments about what you're doing.'

But her only thoughts were for the people they cared for.

'These women are the victims,' she said. 'They've been through enough already.'

They told me all about the flak that came with the territory. Some of that was to come my way in the years that followed, and when it did, I thought about how Life volunteers had to put up with that kind of insult every day. But the heartfelt gratitude expressed in those wonderful letters far outweighed any harsh words they might be subjected to. That visit to Life marked an important milestone in my pro-life journey. I've done an annual fundraising concert for the charity every year since about 1980. I was immensely touched by the papal blessing presented to me in recognition by Father Pat Day at the concert in 2015.

Sadly, my involvement with the pro-life movement at national level wasn't always as positive as my experiences of the amazing work volunteers do locally. SPUC ended up with piles of *Little Innocents* LPs in their London offices because they couldn't get them into the shops and didn't have the marketing nous to sell them themselves. Eventually, I decided to take matters into my own hands. I collected the records from SPUC headquarters and carted them around the country with me to sell around the folk clubs. It was better than seeing them go to waste. One day I'd love to use the internet to enable all of them to be downloaded and shared as widely as possible.

My beliefs continue to be backed up by real women's testimonies. So many women have told me about their experiences of abortion after hearing me sing. They don't come to play hell, but to confide in me. I can't express how much I appreciate those women, nor can I emphasise how much they inspire me. They're my letters on the noticeboard. Each one means far more than a thousand people attacking me for speaking out about what I believe in. I've had emails from women all over the world telling me how my songs helped them. A woman was brought to my gig in Etton, near Beverley, by her father, who told her about my pro-life stance on the way. Her dad didn't know it at the time, but she was pregnant and later gave birth to a child with Down's syndrome. She wrote to tell me my songs helped her decide to keep her baby.

Countless people were in that position and talked to me about it. But I couldn't ask for their support or use them as witnesses in my defence when people were writing to the newspapers complaining about me and my songs. Would I dream of asking them to come on stage with me and explain their experience to my audiences? Would I ask them to write down what they have told me? Would I use their names to defend myself? No, of course not. I know they've already been through enough. Somebody had a go at me about *Little Innocents* after a gig at the Arc in Stockton, telling me I was out of order. He wasn't abusive and made his case in fairly reasonable terms. I started responding to him myself, but then a young woman stepped in and took over. She told the man I was right and he was wrong. She revealed that she had undergone an abortion herself some years ago. It became a double tragedy for her when the baby's father died shortly after she had the operation. She didn't realise the first event was a tragedy until the second one came along and then she was devastated. But that incident was the exception. Most of the time I can't elicit the help of my supporters because they're victims. I know these women, who carry their experiences every day like a cross. *The Secret* is for all of them.

> *Little Innocents* had a big impact on our family. We loved the song *Lynda*. It's so powerful and with Vin's voice it raises the roof. I'm not religious but I

was a midwife and when we were expecting our second child we declined amniocentesis, a blood test that gives a warning of possible spina bifida. Because we loved Vin, *Little Innocents* and *Lynda*, we couldn't risk our baby's life and she was born with spina bifida, which was operated on. Sadly, Jessica had Edward's syndrome and she died at the age of three weeks. We had no regrets and remain grateful for the compassion for the unborn child and disabled people that Vin brought to our consciousness. He has a presence, something very special.
Maureen Taylor

I planned to include *For an Explanation* on the *Word of Mouth* album in 1999. It was about a baby who was due to be aborted but survived the operation and lived. Anthony Hamilton, the consultant gynaecologist, underestimated the age of the foetus, thinking the mother was twenty-three weeks pregnant instead of her actual thirty-three weeks. Mr Hamilton was accused of failing to provide the treatment the baby urgently needed. The baby was eventually taken to a special care unit where nurses called him Timothy John. Against all the odds he survived and was later adopted by another family. A charge of attempted murder against the doctor was dismissed the following year. That child didn't have a voice and I wrote *For An Explanation* to give him one.

Just as my album *Word of Mouth* was being finalised at Norman Holmes' home studio in Sedgefield, I received an email from my agent Jim McPhee.

'Do not put that song on this album,' it said. 'It's taken us fifteen years to persuade the folk media to stop mentioning you and abortion in the same breath and they're just starting to accept you again.'

Pat agreed and other people I trusted urged me not to put it on, saying I would lose my credibility all over again. So I didn't. But six years after *Word of Mouth*, I recorded *For an Explanation* again for *Persona… Grata*, and this time I sang it better than I had the first time around. I'm glad I finally did it because it's so important to me.

Most of my audience these days aren't even aware that there was ever any controversy and I receive a better reception for some of my harder songs than ever before. There are still some negative reactions, but many more positive ones. Audiences seem more able to cope with the subject matter now. It's as though those who just wanted to be entertained in the past now realise there's more to my music. Young people are more open to questioning. The generation who have lived through these changes in attitude – that's my generation – have now matured and some people who were angry at me back in the 1980s have softened their stance. But will our children think we made the right decisions? My song *Be As Children*, on the album *Bandalised*, is directed at people of my age. In it, I'm saying, 'Will we reap what we've sown?'

Something's got to be done immediately
For those little ones lost on the cruel sea
Of selfish waters, fate has caught us,
Drowning our sons and daughters.

But the time it will come when they'll arise,
When we're old and frail they'll gaze into our eyes,
We'll feel their hatred burn or love returned;
The wages we've earned.

Will we be the first generation to be euthanised, since we are the ones who approved of killing at the other end of life, when it's just beginning in the womb? Once we say yes to abortion, we hand society the right to choose who is worthy of living and who isn't. I know the compassionate case for allowing what they call 'dying with dignity' can be compelling. But I've told Pat, even if I end up in a terrible state and I'm screaming to be put out of my misery, please don't because if they are allowed to do it to me, they'll use that power against someone else who doesn't want to go.

I wrote *You Just Can't Fade Away* in 1983 after I read a book called *Return to Auschwitz* by Holocaust survivor Kitty Hart-Moxon. She was only sixteen when the Germans took her and her family away because they were Jewish. One of the most chilling passages was the way neighbours and friends watched people they had lived beside being herded into cattle trucks to be sent to Hitler's death camps. They didn't witness them being killed, and perhaps would never have imagined the horrors that awaited them. Or maybe they didn't want to think any further about what might happen after they saw them fade away into the distance on that train. I love some of the imagery, although the words aren't quite right yet.

Now each human creature is conceived at the start
Of its life; without this feature, from life we can't depart.
If this truth we deny then the truth we call a lie,
For we cannot be conceived and then not die.
'Cos you just can't fade away, you just can't fade away.

I read about a Jewish man trying to flee Germany with his terrified family before the war. His son was crying as they scurried past the soldiers in the street. The father knew they might not escape but he said, 'Son, it will be over one day.' He was telling the boy that whatever happened to them, the evil that was going on around them would eventually be defeated. I genuinely feel that abortion is so wrong that it just cannot win. One day people will look back and hear what happened and say, 'They didn't really do that, did they?' I had friends who used to be very despondent about the future at the height of the Cold War - they thought a nuclear war was inevitable. I never believed that would happen. I feel the same way now. Goodness will win in the end.

The truth is sometimes painful to hear and sometimes it's painful to tell as well. I still worry about the words I sing. I know they have to be just right. I want to sound sympathetic to the situation women are in because I genuinely am. But when people ask me if I wish I'd never released *Little Innocents*, the answer is simple – absolutely not. Without any doubt, it's the most important record I've ever made.

THE MEDIA SHADOW

'Wot, No Vin?'

The 'Bring Back Vin' campaign

Cambridge Folk Festival is one of the most important annual events in the folk world. According to their records, I played there in 1975, 1977, 1980, 1982, 1985 and 1990. The current organiser has a different memory of why I've never been back since, but this is my version of the story. I sang *Little Innocents* there without any problems and the original organiser of the festival, Ken Woollard, continued to book me. I think it was singing *The Secret* that started all the trouble.

There was a smattering of heckling as I introduced the song. At that time I expected that. My policy has always been to avoid being drawn into debates with hecklers – my response is already in the words of my songs. When I finished my set I was told that a woman wanted to talk to me backstage. It could have been anyone and I was a bit apprehensive, but I went over and said hello. She looked straight into my eyes and thanked me. She had kept her own experience of abortion bottled up inside her for years. She told me she'd never heard anybody who understood her story before and I'd just sung it to her. One of the folk magazines printed a review of the concert afterwards and said Vin Garbutt had managed to upset women in the audience, unlike Christy Moore, who put his message across without offending anybody. But the fact is that the only woman who spoke to me had been profoundly moved by the song. As usual, I couldn't call her to my defence.

Sadly, Ken Woollard died in 1993. For a couple of years after that last performance I asked my agent, Jim McPhee, if there was any more interest from Cambridge, but there never was. If you're famous, Cambridge will approach you and ask you to play. If you're not, your agent has to tout you by sending them a promotional pack every year. I suggested that it might be time to give them another try.

'Shall I send them a CD with *The Secret* on it?' I said.

'They won't even open it,' Jim replied.

And that's the way it remained until I won the BBC award in 2001. By then Jim had retired because of heart problems and Chris Jaeger from Worcester was my agent.

Rob Henderson and friends fronting the campaign to bring Vin back to Cambridge Folk Festival

Chris called one day to tell me Eddie Barcan, who was then running Cambridge, had been in touch and wanted to book me for the following summer. The problem was that I already had a booking elsewhere that day. I mulled it over and then decided to honour my prior commitment.

'I don't owe them any favours, Chris,' I said. 'Just tell them I'm already booked.'

If I'm honest, I took some pleasure in that. They've never asked me since then, despite the campaign to bring me back. I saw a photograph of fans at the festival site wearing t-shirts with the slogan 'Wot, no Vin?' I'm even told the singer Eliza Carthy had her picture taken with the protestors. I console myself by saying it's never been one of my favourite festivals. Much of the music tends more towards rock than folk. But the truth is I would love to play there again.

> I saw Vin play and mentioned I was going to the Cambridge Folk Festival.
> 'Oh, I haven't played there for ages,' was his reply.
> So, being very drunk, I thought it would be funny to make a 'Bring Back Vin Garbutt' flag for our camp flagpole.
> The first night's rain brought down the flag! All it was good for now was as a sunscreen, until my mate dared me to get 'WHERE'S VIN?' tattooed on my chest with henna. Drunk as I was, I agreed.
> Getting the tattoo was the start of a snowball effect. The conversation went...
> Me: 'How mush to get WHERSH VIN on me chesht?'
> Vendor: 'About £10 mate.'
> Me: 'Mint.'
> Vendor: 'Why the hell do you want WHERE'S VIN on your chest?'
> Me: *explained what I've just explained to you*

Vendor: 'Excellent! Here's £5 back. Can I sign the flag to start a petition to hand in to the festival organisers?'
Me: 'Wahey! Letsh do it!'
Waking up in the morning, I found myself with Eliza Carthy and the Mayor Of Lewisham's signatures on my flag, along with more of the last night's less-than-sober folk.
Back home and thinking it was all becoming a distant memory – how wrong I was! My father got an email from the Mayor of Lewisham, who had set up a website with me as campaign leader. Not only that, but our local paper had got hold of the story!
Rob Henderson

For a few short years during the 1970s I was part of the worldwide music machine – albeit a tiny cog. Transatlantic Records, who distributed for Trailer, had some clout in the industry and were able to put my LPs on the shelves in Australia, Canada and the United States, as well as in Ireland. But after *Little Innocents*, everything changed. I was on my own. I was still incredibly busy in terms of live work – I've had a full diary since about 1977. My first national agent, Jean Oglesby, looked after some of the biggest names on the folk circuit, brilliant singers such as Richard Thompson, Martin Carthy, Bob Fox and Stu Luckley. Later I moved to Jim and Gill McPhee's Acorn Agency and again they said the phone never stopped ringing for me. My agents didn't need to be proactive. Without being big-headed, I knew I was one of the top draws on the folk scene.

However, as well as no longer having a distribution deal, leaving Topic after *Little Innocents* also meant I lost the London connection. If you ask a non-folkie to name a folk singer they might come up with Richard Thompson, Ralph McTell or Steeleye Span. They're all exceptionally talented, but if they were based up here in the North East of England they might still be doing the local circuit, no matter how good they were. The London connection played a crucial role in their ongoing success. Hundreds of thousands of people all over the world have seen me perform live, and yet most of the influential London media circuit have never heard of me. The few who have, don't read reviews or interviews or hear my music on the radio, they hear from someone who has seen me. It's word of mouth – which is why I made that the title for one of my records.

What was going on didn't start to become clear to me until years after *Little Innocents* and all the furore it caused. The gigs were still pouring in and I was one of the busiest performers in the folk world. But publicity-wise, nobody would touch me any more. My eyes began to be opened in 1994. I'd assembled an excellent band to make the album *Bandalised* and we were invited to play at the Cropredy Convention, Fairport's annual festival in Oxfordshire. Cropredy was always a wonderful experience. It's a chance for Fairport to bring together fringe-folkie rock stars they've met over the years. I first met the band in the late 1970s when I supported them at the Rainbow Theatre rock venue in Finsbury Park, London. I snapped a string during my first song and had to battle my way through the set with only five, but I somehow got away with it.

Katie, Pat, Louis and Tim with Vin after he recieved his honorary degree from Teesside University

Cropredy is the biggest event of its kind and our 1994 spot was directly before Fairport, the headliners on the last night. I knew it was a tremendous opportunity for us. There were close to 20,000 people there and we went down a storm. But having such a low media profile, hardly any publications tend to publish reviews of my albums or shows. The only article that made it into print about that concert was in *RnR* magazine. It was a little footnote saying: 'The Vin Garbutt band had sound troubles…' I don't know where they got that from. I wasn't aware of any problems when I was on stage and the crowd certainly didn't seem to think there was anything wrong either. *RnR* is based in Cumbria and the editor, Sean McGhee, is always very friendly when I meet him. But over the years I've realised he doesn't come to my gigs, and I get the impression from the way he talks about people he's interviewed that I'm not famous enough for him. I checked the coverage of the festival in the other folk magazines and we didn't have any mention at all. It was bitterly disappointing because I needed those quotes to sell the band and make a success of what I was trying to do. But that one line about us having sound troubles is all you'll find in writing about the history of that talented little group.

The Cropredy coverage gave me an insight into what was going on, but the real epiphany moment came two years later, in 1996. I was staying with my friend John Faisandier, the priest who was in the car crash with me in New Zealand. John was putting on my concert in Wellington. By this time he had left the priesthood and was working as a counsellor, using psychodrama to help business executives to de-stress. We were chatting in his house one evening and I opened up to him about how I was feeling. John listened intently to what I had to say and then led me on a journey through the major milestones in my life as a musician. He challenged me to think about the issues that emerged from our conversation. He gathered up armfuls of cushions and started throwing them onto the floor to map out the path of my career. He began when I started out with no worries in the world back in 1969. We continued forward and he questioned me about my feelings at the time of the Trailer break up in 1977. I told him I was still fairly contented – it was a testing time but I could cope with it. Up to now the cushions were all laid out in a straight line. Then we reached the fallout over *Little Innocents* in 1983 and the line suddenly forked. Work-wise everything was still going well and I was chock-a-block with bookings, even at the height of the flak I came under. Throughout the 1980s and the '90s I played to packed audiences in folk clubs all over the world. But John said this fork was something else – it was all about the media. As soon as I heard this I knew he was right. That was the moment the penny dropped that a 'media shadow' had made me invisible. There was an artificial glass ceiling on my career, preventing me from ever reaching the top table of my profession.

John wanted me to focus on the fact that the rest of my life was going well and stop worrying about things I couldn't affect. That was easier said than done. If I'd never become aware of the media shadow I suppose I would have remained blissfully ignorant. However, I became frustrated when I realised I couldn't go any further without having to work so hard that it would compromise me artistically. Shortly afterwards I talked to a music distributor who'd never even heard of me.

There was another problem besides being in the media shadow. About twenty years ago I started thinking about slowing down and edging closer to what should have been retirement. When I looked in shops around the country, though, I realised my music wasn't in them.

My 1998 Irish tour may have been a complete washout, but I did learn one lesson when I visited a major Dublin music shop while I was there. They didn't have a folk music section, of course, because what we call 'folk music' is what the Irish just call 'music'. They stocked a few English folkies, though, and I was envious that even though I'd been professional for all those years I still wasn't capable of getting my CDs into a shop there.

I genuinely haven't a clue how many albums I've sold in my career. Not an inkling. I couldn't even tell you which records have been more successful than others. But I've gone from having my LPs in shops all over the world to the point when you can't even buy one in a record store in my home town. If you go into HMV in Middlesbrough you won't find my music on display. Ask at the desk and the assistant will tap my name into the computer and order a CD for you. They still don't end up in the racks, however – until they're collected they stay under the counter (where they used to keep a certain kind of magazine until a few years ago!). I can confirm this because I tested it out. If a hundred people came in and ordered a Vin Garbutt CD, I asked, would a record be made of all the enquiries? If so, the manager would become aware of the interest and might say, 'Hey, we'd better stock up on Vin's CDs, they're going like hotcakes!' But the answer was no.

Even if we never sell another record in the shops though, we're better off financially as we are, doing everything ourselves. My reason for wanting to be in the shops isn't for the sales. It's the fact that without that presence, I'm the only publicity I have. It's simple – as soon as I stop travelling and playing gigs up and down the country and overseas I will disappear.

Receiving the BBC Folk Award for Best Live Act from Barbara Dickson in 2001

Others live here in the media shadow as well, invisible to the press and radio even though we have full diaries and entertain audiences all over the country. Kieran Halpin, from Dundalk, in Ireland, is a prolific songwriter. He lived in the Scottish Borders before moving to Germany, where most of his work is. He has a big following in some areas and yet the media aren't aware of him at all. He came with me on a tour of six gigs down south to promote himself to a new audience. I arranged in advance to have his name written on the bill as a special guest performer and he picked up at least three return bookings.

We've all done that. It's sometimes the only way to get your name out there. In my view, Jez Lowe, from County Durham, is the best act on the English folk scene. He's a brilliant songwriter and there isn't a folk club in the world where someone isn't singing one of Jez's songs. I can't speak highly enough of him. He writes wonderful songs, both humorous and serious, and he has an excellent stage presence as well. He's also a gentleman. I went to see him at Redcar's Cutty Wren Folk Club not long after I cancelled a tour because of illness.

'Look, Vin,' he said. 'I know you're not selling your new CD because you're not gigging. If you want me to sell them at my gigs, I will.'

People don't usually have enough money to buy two CDs, so Jez knew doing that would dilute his own sales, but he did it anyway and sold dozens for me.

> After emerging from a Vin Garbutt concert many years ago, our voices hoarse from singing along, and our sides aching from laughing so much, we all wondered, as many times before, why the Teesside Troubadour wasn't a megastar, a household name, such was his unique but all-inclusive appeal that came across in each and every performance. Martin Carthy, England's leading folk singer and a cult-figure himself if ever there was one, once offered his opinion on this conundrum: 'Vin flies better under the radar,' he said. I suppose there was much truth in that.
> **Jez Lowe** (reproduced courtesy of the *Northern Echo*)

The subject of the media shadow chewed away at me for a few years afterwards. Then came two twists that turned my fortunes round. Firstly, I decided to spend some money on publicity and advertise myself for the first time. *fRoots* is the main magazine for the UK folk music scene, but I'm just too difficult for them to handle and they tend to ignore me. The only way I could get a mention was by paying for a full-page advert for my upcoming round-the-world tour. It cost me £700, which was a considerable investment, but it turned out to be money well spent. It brought home to some people just how busy I was. Unless you were one of those people who went out and listened to live music you wouldn't have heard of me at all. It reminded people that I was still around and still doing all right.

Soon after the ad went in, things started happening. I was presented with a major national folk award, followed by an honorary degree from Teesside University. The award was Best Live Act at the BBC Folk Awards and I was also nominated for Best Folk Singer. Some people tell me it was a big honour and that I should be proud of it. To me, though, it wasn't an achievement, it was a gift. If the whole nation had been voting, or even if all the folk clubs had been asked their opinion and thought I deserved the award, I'd have been thrilled to bits thinking how these thousands of people thought I was worthy. In my heart of hearts, however, I knew it was just a meaningless token. We were told the names of all the winners in advance and it didn't take me long to notice a link between some of them. Once they'd given out the minor honours, the real meat in the sandwich often seemed to be connected to the big record labels. The whole awards scene is dominated by the music industry. They'll always dole a couple of gongs out to safe bets with no business connections, someone who's not going to upset the applecart and will help legitimise the system, such as me or an obscure young fiddle orchestra from the Shetland Islands. The main course of the night, however, the top honours such as Best Original Song and Best Album, usually go to people who suit the interests of the people who run the awards.

My experience of the folk awards was a real eye-opener but I realised it was going to do me a power of good. I was soon being noticed again. Someone commented shortly afterwards on the BBC website: 'I thought Vin Garbutt had packed in after all that furore over his rabid anti-abortion stance.' That person had never heard of me since 1986 and there I was receiving a folk award in London fifteen years later! Some of the media started to look at me again and I was given a big spread in an Irish music magazine, using an interview I had done four years earlier that wasn't used at that time. So I decided to make the most of it. I felt a twinge of guilt, knowing deep down that the award didn't mean anything. But we put the award on all our publicity and capitalised as much as we possibly could.

Along with the decision to place that ad in *fRoots*, the other breakthrough that revived my career was the arrival of the internet. It was the best thing that could have happened. Pat and I had started our Home Roots label in 1991 as a necessary vehicle to continue bringing out albums. However, the online revolution enabled it to become a fully-fledged cottage industry. It allowed us to bypass the music industry and shift thousands of CDs by ourselves, without relying on the media for help. I read an article in *fRoots* about the average sales for a folk album and realised that even though my records aren't in the shops – which is why we handle sales ourselves, through our webshop, mailing list and at gigs – I'm still selling more CDs than some mainstream artists.

ON SONG

'Words are important, don't waste or fail to use them.'

Vin Garbutt

I sing within the constraints of the sound from the guitar, and my singing style is intertwined with the way I play. I would have been a better singer if I didn't play the guitar. If you take my guitar away from me now, though, I'm uncomfortable singing a song on its own. I enjoy having a go at singing unaccompanied and I'd love to do it more often, but I find the thought of it daunting. The first time I sang with gusto unaccompanied was *The Chemical Worker's Song*, which is fantastic. I've also sung *When Oppressed Becomes Oppressor* and *Waits and Weeps*, which took me years to learn, and I sing the melody I put to Rudyard Kipling's *If*. I love the old traditional Irish ballad singers who sing everything unaccompanied. With no restrictions rhythm-wise, they can slow down and speed up as they want to. Singing unaccompanied gives you the freedom to do that – you can do it with a guitar as well if you're good enough, but I'm not!

There's a traditional Irish song called *John Mitchel* that I sang in the 1960s but it just never sounded right with a guitar. It ruined the flow. I've never had the guts to record it unaccompanied, but to truly put his story across I think that's how it should be sung. One of these days I'll bite the bullet and do it. It's set in 1842, during the potato famine, about a rebel who finds himself being transported to Van Diemen's Land. I visited the Maria Island penal colony in what is now Tasmania a few years ago. The island is uninhabited but has one town, Darlington. There are lists of all the poor souls who were transported there and the huts they lived in have been preserved in the hot, dry climate. I found myself pondering whether it might be the exact place John Mitchel was sent to. Looking at the dates, everything seemed to be about right.

We stayed in a village called Richmond back on the main island of Tasmania. All the dry stone walls round there were built by stone-wallers from Richmond in North Yorkshire. Outside the door of St John's Church in Richmond, the oldest Catholic church in Australia, there was a child's grave. It was the baby of another Irish political prisoner called Thomas Francis Meagher, who escaped the colony and fled to America and ended up becoming a brigadier general in the army and then Governor of Montana. There's a statue of him on horseback in the state capital Helena to this day. While we

Kate Clarke's stunning artwork for Vin's final album, 2014's Synthetic Hues

were in the church I read its history and noticed that when the banns were read before Meagher married, there was an objection from a Mr John Mitchel. Meagher's wife-to-be, Katherine Bennett, was the daughter of a convicted highwayman; maybe that's why Mitchel objected. There might be a thousand John Mitchels, but I couldn't help wondering if he might just be the one I've often sung about.

I've never had to practice much, because I spend so long out on the road singing live and always found rehearsing a chore anyway. But now I've cut down on the number of gigs I play, I try to run through any songs I might be unsure of before setting off. I usually take the guitar out and sing in my living room, ideally when Pat's not in or is busy doing something else. She doesn't appreciate me belting out *The One-Legged Beggar* in the middle of *Coronation Street*. Some songs have been fairly constant in my repertoire over the years, but many of my early ones are almost unknown to my current audiences.

When you're a professional singer you can't just sing what you want to. You don't just turn up at a gig and think, 'I feel like singing this today,' because the folk clubs might be full of people singing that same song. As a pro, you're paid to give your audience songs they haven't heard anywhere else. They want to hear their favourites as well, but I'll soon lose their allegiance if I just keep giving them the same set every time. I have a few of what I call my 'Christmas hits', crowd-pleasers that I'm regularly asked to play live.

Even though a journalist might occasionally write something like, 'If you've heard Vin Garbutt once, you've heard him a thousand times,' I can guarantee that ninety per cent of my audiences won't know the majority of the songs I sing when they see me. There are a few real stalwarts who have heard most of my repertoire, but even they won't know everything. I only usually sing a song for about three years before it's rested and then I forget it for five or even ten years. That way it's fresh when it comes back round again. If I was famous, people would already know them all, but instead they're brand new songs to most of my audience when I bring them out and dust them off.

I soften my strong accent so I can be understood in some places and I think my diction is quite clear when I'm on stage. People might not understand me at first but the words are there to be heard and they tune in once they've seen me a couple of times. I've had a few critical comments about my singing style, although not too many, fortunately. I wouldn't have earned a living singing all over the world for forty years if people didn't like my voice. I suppose it's horses for courses – you're never going to be everyone's cup of tea. A review in the *Guardian* a few years ago said, 'Vin Garbutt is a good musician, but I can't share in the widespread enthusiasm for his singing. He has irritating vocal mannerisms, and a penchant for not over-brilliant contemporary material.'

I kept a more positive review from a fairly unlikely source, the trendy music magazine *Melody Maker*.

'I met a guy recently in Manchester who actively dislikes Vin Garbutt. The discovery came as a shock, for I assumed there wasn't a soul who wasn't captivated by the man and his music.'

Maybe the chap he'd run into in Manchester was the reviewer from the *Guardian*! One of my favourite reviews said I turned the auditorium into my living room. That was pleasing. I feel contented when a night's going well, I can relax and feel at home and the audience does too.

Although it can be disappointing if people don't turn out, the size of the audience I'm performing to doesn't usually bother me. If the crowd know me and my music I can be sure the night will be all right, no matter if there are a dozen of them or twenty thousand. If they don't know me, whether the numbers are big or small, it can be awkward.

I always do my best to give it my all on stage, but sometimes I arrive at a gig exhausted from a long journey and just not looking forward to it. By the end of the first set I might be thinking, 'This isn't going too well here…' Then I receive a tremendous reception from the audience, giving me all the energy I need for the second half. It can be difficult to judge how well a show is going from my vantage point up on the stage. I remember coming off after one gig I thought had been a complete damp squib.

'That was hard work, Pat,' I said.

'You're joking,' she replied. 'Why?'

'I could hardly hear any reaction from the audience at all.'

'You should have heard them at the back,' she said. 'That's one of the best gigs I've ever seen you do!'

Lost in music

Playing live in the 2000s

Other times I'll come off buzzing and Pat brings me crashing back down to earth by saying, 'They were a bit deadpan, weren't they?'

I've seen the British folk circuit change dramatically over the years. In the 1970s there was a thriving student scene and just about every university and college had a folk club. I played at Oxford and Cambridge and all the major London universities. Then, as the last of the old members left, the clubs gradually ran out of enthusiasts to keep them going. The next generation of students hadn't a clue what a folk club was and by the late 1970s they'd all folded. If students heard folk music at all it was because they found it themselves, as it all but disappeared from the mainstream and was no longer played on the TV or radio. Warwick University remained a regular gig before it disappeared into the Oxford Triangle. That's what I call the area between Milton Keynes, Gloucester and Stratford-on-Avon, where for some reason I rarely got bookings.

I've had the privilege of singing my own songs in some of the world's most beautiful churches. In the late-1980s I was staying in Father John Faisandier's presbytery in New Zealand and he asked me to sing *Little Innocents* to his congregation during Sunday Mass at the Cathedral of the Blessed Sacrament in Christchurch. It was a beautiful, renaissance-style building that won George Bernard Shaw's admiration when he visited the city. Singing there was a special moment in my life and I was saddened when the cathedral was badly damaged in the 2010 earthquake. Then in the year 2000 I was invited by a Middlesbrough priest, Father Peter Keeling, to play at York Minster as part of the commemoration of Archbishop Oscar Romero's assassination. I was delighted to be asked, not only because it was such an important cause but also because it's a fantastic church. It was unusual for me to perform in any place of worship, and even more so in an Anglican one. Somehow that made it all the more special. Archbishop

Romero was shot dead while celebrating Mass in San Salvador. His murder came the day after he preached a sermon calling on the army to put their Christian faith first and refuse to carry out orders that oppressed the basic human rights of the Salvadoran people. During the service in the Minster they played a recording of an impassioned speech that Archbishop Romero had made on behalf of the poor. I sang my song *El Salvador*, making the most of the superb acoustics, and I treasure the crucifix made in the country that I was presented with afterwards.

Something happened in 1989 that brought home to me just how fragile and fickle a career in the music business can be. I was preparing for a gig in the village of Nettlebed in Oxfordshire when I lost my voice. I tried to talk but the only thing that came out of my mouth was the sound of silence – and it wasn't as catchy as Paul Simon's version. I was staying with my mate Hugh Crabtree in Reading. As well as being a successful businessman, Hugh is also an excellent melodeon player and the frontman and founder of the band, Feast of Fiddles. He took me to the venue where I was supposed to be playing so I could show them I genuinely couldn't speak and wasn't just making excuses. The MC explained to the audience that I'd lost my voice.

'We did manage to persuade Vin to sing one song,' he said.

Then Hugh crouched down behind the stage and sang the verses of *The Chemical Worker's Song* while I mimed, before the audience joined in with the chorus.

> I recall doing a Vin voiceover at Nettlebed Folk Club when it was still meeting at the Bull in the village. As usual Vin stayed at our house. Unfortunately he lost his voice, so the organiser had to gather up alternative entertainment at the last minute. That involved me and some others from the local scene – notably Simon Mayor and Hilary James. Vin was only able to play his whistle and croak a few words until the start of the second half when he sang *The Chemical Worker's Song*. Or to be more accurate, I sang it *à la* Vin, concealed behind him while he mimed. Needless to say he got the biggest laugh when he included the ventriloquist's trick of drinking while singing! Unsighted, I had no idea what all the noise was about and just carried on with the song, which became even funnier to the audience.
>
> **Hugh Crabtree**

We all had a laugh, but I could tell Hugh was worried about me. Early the next morning he drove me to the Royal Berkshire Hospital in Reading. I was sent to the Ear, Nose and Throat department and before I knew it, a white-coated doctor was peering down at my tonsils. He was amazed by what he saw and shouted over for another consultant to come and have a look.

'Hey, Rupert,' he said. 'I think you'll want to see this…'

Soon, half-a-dozen doctors were gathered round, all staring into my mouth. I don't know whether it was because I was a singer but he said he could look further down my throat than he could with most people. They gave me a laryngoscopy and showed me the video they made of my vocal cords smacking together as I coughed, explaining this was what happened every time I cleared my throat. They instructed me never to clear my throat by coughing, but to gargle or swallow instead. The diagnosis was voice abuse. I didn't yet have any nodes, which are noncancerous growths on the vocal cords that some singers suffer from. But I soon would have if I kept on going the way I was, they warned. That would have just about put me out of business. I was told to take three months off work, and worst of all, I had to stay completely silent for weeks on end.

Not being able to speak was a form of torture for me. Even after I recovered I was ordered not to raise my voice above the level of ambient noise. That presented another challenge because it was too loud in the noisy venues where I earned my living to be heard without shouting. But I took their advice and developed the ability to speak quietly, although it could be frustrating because people sometimes didn't understand that I wasn't just being rude. I was also sent to a speech therapist, who told me I was singing from my throat and needed to learn to project my voice from the diaphragm instead. I ended up singing better than ever before and putting less strain on my vocal cords at the same time.

Recording albums is hard work. I'm usually too tied up in the business of travelling around the globe gigging to find the time, and when I come back from my travels I've heard enough of my own voice and can't listen to myself for a while. I'd like to make an album each year, but because I'm not famous I can't sell enough CDs to make that worthwhile. So it became about every three years, until a long barren period between *Persona... Grata* in 2005 and *Synthetic Hues* in 2014. I have to sell most of the previous CD before I can get cracking on another one.

Once I've recorded an album I find it hard to settle on a title. A few years ago I was struggling as usual and Pat suggested *The Finger-Wagging Bore*. It was a quote from a review by Raymond Greenoaken, editor of the folk music magazine *Stirrings*.

'Vin Garbutt has turned into a humourless, verbose, finger-wagging bore,' he wrote.

I assumed he just didn't appreciate me or my music, but a few years afterwards he came to a gig and was very pleasant and I understand his opinion of me had softened over time. Even though I was amused by the quote, I decided against using it as an album title. When I finally do settle on one I usually know it's just right. *Persona Non Grata* is a phrase we often hear for someone who's not welcome anywhere, so I had this idea of *Persona...Grata*. The title is all about the word that isn't there, that 'non'. Because there are a few people who aren't that keen on me, I thought I'd let them fill in their own 'non' – not that they're likely to buy my CDs in the first place, but the three dots are there for them anyway. A priest friend pointed out that the actual meaning of *Persona Grata* is slightly different from what I had thought – 'a person with grace'. I like that. Grace is a good old fashioned word.

When it came to recording the album, Tony Leonard, who I used to meet and chat with at gigs and who later moved to Loftus, helpfully took me over to Norman Holmes' studio in Sedgefield and gave me feedback on the tapes we made. That took some of the strain off Pat. With me being a non-driver, Pat would have had to give up a day's work to take me over to recording sessions. Norman, who played the flute on *Bandalised*, has a studio in his home and was totally accommodating. Day or night, even if I just wanted to record one song or a single verse, he would do it. He's extremely gifted and is possibly England's best flautist. He took to the computer age with ease and became brilliant at the technical and engineering side of recording. *Persona Grata* was launched with a performance at the Sage in Gateshead in October 2005. It was nearly a decade before I would release another album.

Synthetic Hues came about after I played at the Gala Theatre in Durham to celebrate the golden jubilee of Canon Bob Spence, in 2013. (Canon Bob's a devout Newcastle United fan. The club's manager Ruud Gullit once personally drove him the fourteen miles from his parish in Lanchester, County Durham, so he could sprinkle holy water on the St James' Park pitch to remove a curse. It was just before the 1999 FA Cup final, but the Magpies still lost 2-0 to Manchester United so the poor man's still waiting to see his beloved team lift a trophy!)

Another brilliant flautist called Anthony Robb was in the audience that night and he emailed me the next day to say he'd loved the show. Anthony is heavily involved in the Northumbrian Pipers' Society and knows his music inside out. He'd recently retired and treated himself to some top-quality recording equipment and installed it in his home (which, like Norman's, is also in Sedgefield), and he said I'd be welcome to come and record there. I was in two minds at first because I had no idea whether Anthony knew how to use this equipment, but the offer came at just the right time. And when I went over to meet him I could see that the set-up was fantastic.

I was delighted to have Becky Taylor, who comes from Middlesbrough, playing Irish pipes, Northumbrian pipes, fiddle and whistle on the CD. Dave O'Neill, who used to be in the Eric Bogle Band and ran the National Folk Festival in Canberra, played the mandolin. Dave is so talented that he once joined me on stage without even practising - he was fantastic, and afterwards I asked him if he was planning to visit England soon. By chance he was, so I invited him to come and stay and we went to Sedgefield together to record his parts.

What I loved most about Anthony was his enthusiasm. I'm a live performer. I need an audience, which is another reason I'm not keen on recording. Being in the studio with Anthony felt like having an audience. After I recorded a song he would immediately come bounding through.

'Where did you find that one?' he'd say.

He radiated an infectious exuberance. When I was singing to him I was thinking, 'He'll love this one.' It was just what I needed and the resulting album was the business.

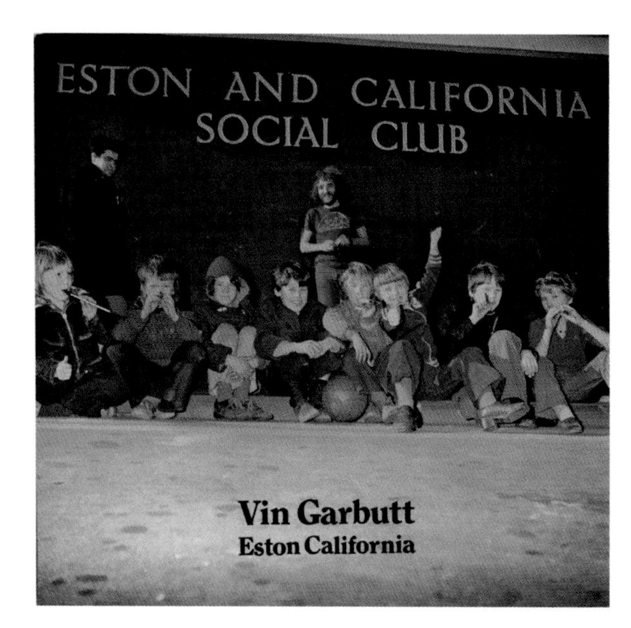

1977's Eston California

2010's Teesside Troubadour

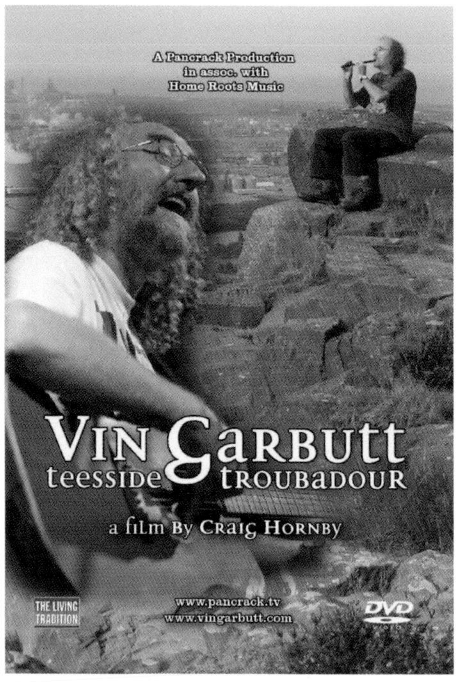

TEESSIDE TROUBADOUR

'Though the world has its wonders and beauteous sights
With my north country none can compare.'

Vin Garbutt, *Valley of Tees*

I've no idea what Craig Hornby expected when he first came to listen to me sing, but it wasn't what he heard. I went to see *A Century in Stone,* the film he made about the birth of Teesside and its industry, *and* over the next couple of years he became a regular at my gigs. Craig didn't look like your average folk fan – standing six-foot-seven-inches tall, he was more into punk rock than my kind of music. But he was bowled over by my songs.

Craig, like me, was a South Banker who went to St Peter's School, albeit twenty years after me. Some of the kids who were lined up outside the Eston and California Social Club on the cover of my 1978 LP *Eston California* were his mates and that photograph was the only thing he knew about me when he was growing up. It was Craig who came up with the idea of making a film about my life. He wanted to emphasise the way I travelled all over the world singing songs about the area and yet Teesside people knew nothing about me. He saw parallels between the protest messages in my songs and the ones he was used to hearing from punk bands.

He came with me to Holland and Belgium, where we looked at war graves together, and then joined me on one of my world tours, to Ireland, Canada, Malaysia and Australia. Most Aussies couldn't tell you where Middlesbrough is, even though two of their nation's biggest icons come from the town. Captain Cook was born here and the Sydney Harbour Bridge in Australia has 'Dorman Long, Middlesbrough, England' stamped on its girders. I always said that if I got a gig at the Sydney Opera House it would make it a Boro hat-trick. And I did, eventually – when Craig filmed me playing the *Wilfy Mannion Jig* on my whistle on the steps outside.

The result of all the travelling and filming was *Teesside Troubadour*. Craig came up with the title.

> I first heard of Vin when I was eleven or twelve in the late 1970s. My mate, Dave 'Jaffa' Jefferson, brought into school an LP that had him and a bunch of other local kids on the front cover. It was *Eston California*. I was fascinated

Craig Hornby and his cousin, Raymond, Christmas 1967

Craig and Vin in Sydney

to discover that a local bloke had made a record and that he was an ex-pupil of our school. It must have sown a seed of interest in local history in me and that came to fruition many years later with my film *A Century in Stone*. Ironically, that told the story of Eston and California, the 'iron rush' that gave rise to industrial Teesside.

The first time I met Vin was in 2004 when a mutual friend, Ian Luck, took me to see him play his local in Loftus and the same week brought Vin to see my film down the road in Lingdale. People had been telling me to go and see him for years but I was no folkie, I was into punk and noisy stuff. But finally there I was utterly blown away and laughing myself silly. He was as daft as a brush and deadly serious. Very local and totally global. Film ideas began racing through my head. This was an international cultural story from Teesside and one that TV would never tell. I thought a film could help expand his audience outside of the folk scene, especially if I could get it on at Cineworld in Middlesbrough as I had with *A Century in Stone*, and also, just maybe, get it on the box. Vin gave me a bunch of CDs and a copy of his *Songbook*, which told the stories behind some of his most famous songs. We got on a storm and religion aside (we were diametric opposites, with me being an atheist) we had much in common. We had a shared love of nature, adventure, history, politics, music and humour.
Craig Hornby

By an amazing coincidence, I had written a song many years earlier about a Middlesbrough woman I had read about in our local paper, the *Evening Gazette*. She had a baby in the 1960s who was born with spina bifida and she was told he wouldn't survive and that operating couldn't save him. She had to fight to make them operate and her baby did survive and lived to be fifteen. What struck me about the article was the way the mother insisted that despite all the difficulties she had experienced, she would go through everything again. It was a deeply moving story and inspired me to write a song, without using the real names of the mother and her son. The first time Craig heard me singing *Lynda*, while we were planning the film, he immediately recognised the people whose story it told. The woman who I called Lynda was in fact Craig's Auntie Joan and the baby I called Kevin was Craig's cousin, Raymond. Craig told his Auntie Joan, who was delighted to think that audiences all over the world had heard about her beloved son.

Lynda

Lynda's doctor told her things were bright right from the start,
A baby due in January to warm her longing heart,
But no sooner had she chose the name
When she heard that her child couldn't ever be the same
As the ones in the street with the nimble feet playing out a 'normal' part.
Her doctor said that later tests had led him to believe
That things were far more serious than first he had perceived,
He said her child could be deaf or blind,
With at least a definite defect of the spine,
And her friend said, 'If the choice were mine, I'd see you were relieved.'

Chorus

Lynda, your kin can't know the torture they put you through,
Or else they'd go head in hands in shame.
Our hearts are true, but in the wrong place,
You know we'd never say to your face
Anything we thought would cause your pain.
Your life is one long giving,
And we've the nerve to say it's not worth living,
And you say you'd go through it all again.

To Lynda in the final days that advice sounded good,
She knew her friend meant well but take a life she never could,
So her boy was born on a winter's morn,
With a hole in his back, an unholy crown of thorns,
Still Lynda smiled on her child newborn, as she had sworn she would.
Her doctor said, 'There is no hope, but I'll do what I can,'
Lynda said, 'As long as I'm not dead, he'll grow to be a man,'
So with optimism and operations, and to Lynda's own great expectations,
Science saved the situation to Mother Nature's plan.

Now Kevin's almost seventeen, his O levels he's passed,
His mother's heart's a storehouse for the pride that she's amassed,
She knew the going would be rough, but because she's made of the stuff that saints are made of,
She says she's been paid back with enough love her life to last.
That life is still a struggle and for all, it's plain to see,
How she ever copes remains a mystery to me.
But I know if we could be born again in a kindlier world of supermen and women,
Then like the person Lynda is, the rest of us could be.
Yes, I know if we could be born again in a kindlier world of super men and women,
Then like the person Lynda is, the rest of us could be.
Still at least young Kevin's grown to be less handicapped than me.

Joan was my dad's sister. My cousin Raymond was about eighteen months older than me and died in 1980. The subsequent *Gazette* article made quite an impact at the time. None of the family, however, had a clue that a song had been written until twenty-four years later. Auntie Joan was in tears when I told her. I planned to film Vin meeting her, but sadly she suddenly died a few months before filming started. Nonetheless, it was personal now and the film had to be made.

I thought Vin was a trad folk singer who mixed in a bit of humour. I had no idea how funny and often surreal he was. It was fascinating filming him telling daft stories to audiences in Belgium or Kuala Lumpur and leaving them in stitches. I certainly had no idea his music had such a political dimension until I went to see him. I loved the way he could be singing about the decline of South Bank one minute and genocide in East Timor the next. Watching him sing *Darwin to Dili* in Australia was especially poignant. Another live powerhouse was *When Oppressed Becomes Oppressor*. No instruments needed. Just the man. Real heart-on-sleeve, belting it out. You can't rattle off those songs. They can only be sung with 100 per cent conviction, and by him. To see that passion night after night around the world was a true measure of his integrity. Touring is exasperating and exhausting and he and Pat were no slouches. So often, times were frantic, getting lost, rushing for buses, trains, planes. Rarely was it not fun.

I filmed Vin's life sporadically, at home and on the road, over four years. I went through every cupboard and every drawer in their house looking for old pictures and negatives, I prised and haggled rare archive film from the BBC and spent most of 2010 in the cutting room where I finished it, to quote Vin, '800 times'.

Vin was the first folkie ever to have their life flash before them on the big screen. And being ever the humble chap, he was slightly ill at ease watching himself. Just over 1,000 people saw the film at Cineworld in November 2010. It went down a storm and packed out shows across Teesside and at Sage Gateshead too. The film received excellent reviews and made the TV news

> but, alas, no TV slot. That didn't surprise me when even regional TV has less regional content than ever. It's still infuriating, though, when you know that a multitude would have become instant converts.
> **Craig Hornby**

The film had a sellout run at Middlesbrough's Cineworld multiplex and if it hadn't been for the new *Shrek 3D* film being released and shown on every screen, we would have had another week! I played a short set after the premiere and then answered questions from the audience. It was a thoroughly enjoyable experience.

Craig and Vin prepare for the premiere of Teesside Troubadour at Cineworld, Middlesbrough

Pete Betts and Vin – Photo courtesy of Jo Betts

FOLK HEROES

'Reuse, recycle.'

Vin Garbutt

I don't know where my songs come from. It's a mystery to me. When I sing them to an audience for the first time and they go down well I think, how did that happen? Songwriting comes from somewhere else and the very best songs emerge out of the cosmos.

Ewan McColl's *The First Time Ever I Saw Your Face* is one of those songs. I heard it in the sixties before it was famous and immediately knew it was a truly exceptional piece of music. It saw Ewan's family set up for life in royalties. It's tricky to play but Ewan was an unaccompanied singer, so he didn't have the restrictions of a guitar holding him back. The chords people play to accompany the melody are quite unusual. I guess he wrote it without an instrument, unless he played the piano. A piano lets you go wherever you want to and if you can play well it must be a considerable help for a songwriter. But while Ewan's song became a worldwide hit and has been recorded by everyone from Roberta Flack to Elvis, other wonderful songs never make it out of the folk clubs. If somebody famous had discovered Brian Bedford's *Wings*, which was on my *Plugged* album, or Keith Hancock's *Absent Friends*, which was on *When the Tide Turns Again*, they could have been huge worldwide hits.

People are writing songs all the time and they might never sing them outside of their local folk clubs. Someone who doesn't understand folk music might think both the singer and the song are rubbish, but a true folkie can appreciate the qualities of a song, even if it's not being sung particularly well. Folkies hear the song underneath the performance. They also appreciate a singer giving it their best. I consider it a privilege to be able to travel around the country and hear someone who might work in an office singing a song he has written about what goes on during his day. I love songs for their own sake and sometimes find myself listening to a floor performer in a folk club and thinking, I need a copy of that.

I always record some songs written by other people on my albums, as well as some of my own compositions. I don't just lift them off other CDs though, I know the writers personally. The songs have often been recorded only by the writers themselves before I

Vin with Frankie Porter, Biörn Landahl and Ron Angel in Sidmouth, 1973

get hold of them. I don't want to sound like I'm blowing my own trumpet, but they're usually thrilled that I'm singing their song. That's what's supposed to happen to a folk song and I'm just carrying on that tradition. I'd like to tell you about some of the special people whose songs I have been privileged to sing…

Pete Betts was born just a week before me and we grew up together. But unlike mine, his wasn't such a happy childhood. He was usually fighting and he got away with it because he was such a big, strong lad. He was a handy friend to have while I was growing up. When we were older we started knocking about together and played alongside each other in The Mystics as teenagers, singing Beatles and Hollies songs. Pete thought he was a good singer and we could harmonise together because we knew each other so well. I don't think we were much cop, although Pete was always brimming with confidence. He was also the first of my mates to have his own transport when he bought himself a van. We were stopped by the police on the way to Scarborough with about ten of us in the back. They asked Pete if he had a C licence, which he needed to prove he was qualified to drive a commercial vehicle and I decided to help him out.

'It's a van, not a boat!' I shouted from the back.

After training as an electrician in the tram sheds at South Bank, Pete drifted into contracting, before we packed in our jobs and went off to sing in Spain for six months.

I loved *They Don't Write 'em Like That Any More* from the first time I heard Pete sing it. The style of the song isn't particularly me, but the experiences it describes certainly are – all those people going back to the house after the club closes for the night and having a good old fashioned sing-song together.

Ee, how we could sing, what fun those nights would bring,
Singing for hours on end.
Once we found the key - Oh! What harmony
Those boozy voices could lend!
'Heart of My Heart', just for a start,
Or 'Walking My Baby Back Home'.
When it comes to an end, it's - 'Let's sing it again!
They don't write 'em like that any more.'

I like to think Pete was pleased when I started singing his song and I recorded it on *Tossin' a Wobbler* in 1978. I sang two or three harmonies on the chorus and I wanted someone to play the piano, but the guys at Topic Records put me off. I still think it would have been good. It's a hard song for me to sing and play at the same time and it doesn't work down south, because the way of life described in the song is a distinctly northern one. The further down the country you travel, the more you can feel the audiences becoming less able to relate to it. But it's a cracking song for northern people and loads of people have sung it.

Pete made a few pennies from me recording it and then a few years later he was watching TV one night when the actor Robson Green introduced what he said was 'a traditional Geordie song'. He then launched into his version of *They Don't Write 'em Like That Any More*! I don't know where he'd heard it but Pete was livid, even though it earned him a decent royalty payout. He contacted Robson Green and told him in no uncertain terms that it wasn't Geordie at all and was very much a Teesside song. Pete wrote other songs as well, including a cracker called *The Critic* that I'll have to learn one day. It's about doing a brilliant gig and then reading a review that says you were rubbish – something that's happened to me once or twice!

He couldn't sing
He couldn't clown
No - his heart it lay in putting people down
He couldn't play
But he could write
And with his pen he broke a heart again tonight

> Vin and my dad were a funny pair together – almost like chalk and cheese, but with such a deep love and bond that ran through the years.
> **Jo Betts**

Pete suffered a stroke in September 2015. Before that he'd been fit and well. His death came as a dreadful shock and hit me hard. I was on the mend from my own health problems before that, but the emotional upset put me right back and I went into acute atrial fibrillation at his funeral. My old ICI mate Kevin McLean phoned up from a yachting trip somewhere in the Mediterranean. The news had hit him like a ton of bricks as well. They never used to be the best of buddies, but that trip to Spain forged a lasting bond between the six of us and Kevin was very emotional on the telephone as we reminisced about Pete. Kevin has homes in Buzzards Bay, Massachusetts, where they filmed Jaws, and in Fort Lauderdale, Florida. The lads who went to Spain in 1969 are legends to Kevin and Tina's sons, Owen and Brendan, and they love to hear us reminisce. They've heard the stories about our trip so many times and make a fuss of us whenever we meet them. Sadly, I was there in 2008 when my sister phoned to say poor Mam had passed away. As usual Kevin, who has remained my lifelong friend and support, moved heaven and earth to help me change my plans and get back home.

Pete treated me as a brother. He was a rock for me and Pat. When he died I was touched to hear what my siblings said about him. They hardly ever saw Pete but there had just never been a time when he wasn't around and they all said they would miss him dearly. And so do I.

Like *They Don't Write 'em Like That Any More*, *The Chemical Worker's Song* was written by another great friend of mine and came to be an important part of my repertoire. The writer, Ron Angel, was in The Fettlers with me and went to teacher training college in Middlesbrough. I once sang for Ron in the college and the principal asked me if I wanted to join the course without having to pass any formal qualifications, just on the strength of what he heard in my songs. He said I'd make an excellent teacher. It was pleasing to hear that compliment, although I never took him up on the offer – I knew that music was my career. *The Chemical Worker's Song* is all about the harsh realities of life working at ICI. I was performing to 16,000 people at the Philadelphia Folk Festival in 1975 when all the lights went off because of an electrical fault. With no amplification, I decided to sing unaccompanied and started blasting out Ron's song. It was an unforgettable experience to hear thousands of Americans joining in with the chorus in the dark, singing about the trials and tribulations of a Teesside process operator.

A process man am I and I'm telling you no lie
I've worked and breathed among the fumes that trail across the sky
There's thunder all around me and poison in the air
There's a lousy smell that smacks of hell and dust all in me hair
And it's go boys go
They'll time your every breath
And every day you're in this place you're two days nearer death
But you go

A few years ago I was watching TV in a hotel room in Montreal when a Canadian band called the Great Big Sea came on and started singing Ron's song. As soon as I arrived home I phoned Ron and asked if he'd ever registered the copyright. He told me he'd never got round to it. I broke the happy news that it was being broadcast all over the TV and radio in Canada, so there were royalties in the kitty for him. Sometime after that the phone rang.

'Thanks for telling me to register my song,' said Ron. 'I've just received a cheque for £300 from the Performing Rights Society!'

Ron died in September 2014 at the age of eighty-three. It makes me sad when I think of all the cracking songs he wrote and collected that may not even be recorded. Martyn Wyndham-Read has recorded dozens of songs by another fantastic Teesside songwriter, Graeme Miles, but Ron had so many as well, both traditional songs he'd collected and his own work.

I've missed out on Ron's songs but I want to have another look at Mick Sheehan's. Mick's family were involved in running a folk club at the Golden Cock in Darlington and he came on my first trip to Ireland in the 1960s. He's an excellent songwriter and published a new CD of his songs a few years ago. He lives in Richmond now and runs Alt-Berg walking boots, which has factories in Richmond and Italy. Mick could easily have done what I did and gone full time. He's in the film *Teesside Troubadour* singing an unaccompanied song with me and Pete Betts in a pub in Staithes.

Sometimes it's obvious straight away that a song is for me, while others take a little longer. My friend Shep Woolley took his guitar out one morning when I was staying with him after a gig on the south coast.

'It might suit you this, Vin,' he said.

I had a train to catch and was distracted and kept looking up at the clock as Shep sang. I was eating an egg sandwich and he had no bread, so it was really just a floppy egg and there was yolk getting all tangled up in my beard. Shep sang his heart out and I honestly wanted to listen to the words, but I was just too anxious, trying to wolf my floppy breakfast down so I could catch the train home from Portsmouth.

It was only months later when I played the tape that Shep had handed over that I realised what a special song *Down By the Dockyard Wall* was, and that it did indeed suit me. Unlike me, Shep is a comedian first and a songwriter second, but he was inspired to write as he watched the Falklands veterans returning to Portsmouth. It's about a woman waiting for her true love to come home. Shep wrote it shortly before the fortieth anniversary of the end of World War II and it struck him that nothing much had changed in all that time. Whether it was written two hundred years ago, in the 1970s or just yesterday, it's a never-ending story, sadly – the words still resonate throughout the ages.

Down by the dockyard wall, I will wait for you
As you come across that walk ashore in your suit of blue
My love for you will never change, my heart is always true
Down by the dockyard wall, I will wait for you

Phil Millichip is one of my favourite songwriters and has many songs I could have learned. The one I did sing was *If I Had a Son*, and it's become one of my 'Christmas hits'. It's a beauty. I met Phil when he did a floor spot in Newport, South Wales, about thirty years ago. I became friendly with him and his brother Bryn that night and have stayed with him several times since. Newport has a transporter bridge and a steel industry, as Teesside has – or used to have, anyway – so there's a big connection between the two areas. As soon as he started singing that song I knew I loved it. It tells the story of a man who gives the best years of his life to working down the pit and the terrible experiences he endures. An elderly man told Phil about his memories and experiences of surviving a pit accident where the coalface collapsed on him and his fellow miners. He said, 'If I ever had a son he'd never go down the mine', inspiring the song.

If I had a son, he would never go down there
To work all his days in a damp, dingy hole
They can close every pit from Bedwas to China
They've broken me, body and soul
In search of the dirty black coal

Silver and Gold is another brilliant mining song that has become a favourite with my audiences. It was written by Bryn Phillips, who lives in the West Midlands. Again, I was playing at a folk club one night and Bryn just stood up and started singing. When he came to the chorus for the second time, the audience sang along with him. That got me interested. It's always an encouraging sign when an audience sings along with a song they've never heard before. It's about a coal miner, John Gates, who became a successful embroidery teacher after being made redundant at the age of fifty. One of his proudest achievements was embroidering a wedding dress for his daughter.

Give me the silver and gold,
Give me the silver and gold,
My hands must be clean as I'm picking the seam,
Not black with the dust of the coal,
Give me the silver and gold.

I love the juxtaposition of the images of a coal seam and the seam of a wedding dress and the fact that this grimy-handed coal miner embroidered a pure white wedding dress for his daughter. When they closed the pit John Gates would have been distraught and worried about what he would do next. To think that a coal miner could make such a dramatic transformation is inspirational. He became an ambassador for lifelong learning and lectured widely on the benefits of learning new skills.

> You can imagine how pleased I was when Vin told me that he liked the song and asked if he could use it. It was several months before I heard back from him and when I did I was delighted he had learnt it and said it was going down well with audiences. Later, when I saw him at my local folk club, The Woodman, in Kingswinford, West Midlands, I felt proud to hear him perform my song and loved his arrangement. He told me he enjoyed playing it at The

Woodman as he knew the audience would know the chorus off by heart and do a great job of it, which of course they did! Since then I have heard him play it both in folk clubs and at festivals. He told me he found it a good song to end his festival spots with, as he gets the whole audience singing along. It was quite a thing for me to hear a large festival audience singing along to the chorus of my song.

As well as hearing him perform it myself I frequently had reports from friends who had heard him play the song in various venues, including one report from Australia. It made me realise he had taken my song and given it wings. If I had been the only one singing it, the song would have stayed in clubs, pubs and festivals around the West Midlands. Vin took it everywhere and I still get enquiries from people who have heard his recording and ask whether I am happy for them to perform it. I am forever grateful to him for giving my song such wide exposure.

One of the best pieces of news was from John Gates himself. One of his friends, who was interested in folk music, knew Vin was performing in the area and took John along to his gig. John introduced himself and, of course, both he and Vin were pleased to meet up. I saw Vin a year or so later and he told me he was thrilled to meet the hero of the song!

Vin always gave me full credit for the song and when people told me they had heard him perform it, they also told me about the introduction which often contained embellishments in typical Vin style. One that has stuck is when he changed my name from Bryn Phillips to Brynph Illips and to this day I occasionally get jokingly referred to as 'Brynph'.

Bryn Phillips

Graeme Miles was the Bard of Teesside. He was a world-class songwriter who never made a penny out of the masterpieces he created. He had a brilliant mind and back in 1952 he embarked on a mission.

'The Geordies have all these wonderful songs and Teesside doesn't have any,' he said. 'So I'm going to write some.'

He gave himself twenty years to complete his task, and I don't think he wrote another song after 1972. Graeme understood how songs can give people a sense of identity. During that golden period he produced songs such as *Ring of Iron*, *Blue Sunset*, *Guisborough Road* and *Where Ravens Feed* – all, quite simply, masterful works of art. There seems to be a growing interest in his legacy these days and he commands huge respect from people who are familiar with his music. As well as being a superb musician, he was also an extremely talented artist.

There was a fantastic event in his honour called *Across the Vale* held in Saltburn in the summer of 2016. It was an eye-opener even for me, with songs I'd never heard before and an exhibition of Graeme's drawings, including some from his National Service days in the 1950s. When he travelled to Brazil with his French wife, Annie, in the 1980s he didn't paint the big Spanish haciendas as other artists might have, he drew life in Rio's famous slums, the *favelas*. It was the same approach he took to his songwriting and art back home in Teesside, telling the stories of ordinary people. The whole night was devoted to Graeme's music. I knew three of his songs well, but I might have been a bit shaky on a fourth. So the man who put on the art exhibition suggested that after singing Graeme's *Ring of Iron*, *My Eldorado* and *Guisborough Road*, I should sing my song, *The Valley of Tees*, to explain how I'd been influenced by Graeme. I thought that was an excellent idea.

Later that year there was a second hugely successful event in Graeme Miles' honour, during Hartlepool Folk Festival. It was called the Ironopolis Project and consisted completely of Graeme's songs and writings, which were brilliantly read by the narrator Kevin Hall, a proper folkie from the old days. I relearned *The Iron Moulder's Wedding* for the occasion. It mentions taking the train to Urlay Nook for a wedding and I sang it years ago with The Fettlers. Hartlepool Town Hall was packed and people travelled from all over to be there. There was a tremendous standing ovation at the end of the concert and the audience didn't want to sit down. People will have returned home to all corners of Britain and abroad with more knowledge about Teesside history than the average local because it's all there in those songs.

I visited Graeme in his Middlesbrough home during the filming of *Teesside Troubadour* and the last time I saw him was about a year before he died. The English Folk Dance and Song Society awarded him their gold badge award in 2012 – coincidentally, my old producer Bill Leader received one the same year. I'm pleased Graeme's genius was recognised alongside previous recipients including Nic Jones, Eliza Carthy, Dave Swarbrick, Ewan MacColl and Peggy Seeger. Annie told me it was Graeme's most treasured possession because it was given to him by his fellow folkies. He had it with him when he died on Good Friday, 2013.

Among the musicians who came and sang at *Across the Vale* was Martyn Wyndham-Read, who is probably Graeme's greatest advocate. He recorded a whole album of his songs in 2001 entitled *Where Ravens Feed*. He interprets Graeme's songs so well. Martyn was a major figure on the folk scene in the 1960s. I first met him at Eston Folk Club, where he played a couple of times a year during the late 1960s. He was travelling widely as a professional at that time and he heard me singing and offered to take me to his gigs so I could try to bring in some work. I was already on the circuit at that time but only playing in the North East. Doing the rounds with Martyn was a big breakthrough for me and introduced me to a whole new audience down south. I picked up numerous bookings on the back of it.

As well as giving me a foot in the door Martyn also drove, and he kindly took me all over with him. One time he had been in Manchester when I was playing in Leeds. There was no M62 then and there were no mobile phones either, but he came over and picked me up at the roadside. We drove down to Newdigate in Surrey, where I stayed with him and his wife, Danni.

Later, Martyn and Danni bought a property in France where they used to hold courses. A few years ago I was doing a summer songwriting seminar there. On the first day I explained to my enthusiastic group of students about the structure of songs and how they're written. To illustrate what I was talking about, I used a beautiful song called *The Flowers and the Guns*. As I started singing, and slightly to my consternation at the time, one of the students got all excited and flipped open a mobile phone.

'Listen to this,' he said. 'Vin Garbutt's singing my song!'

I wish I'd bought a lottery ticket that day because that must have been a chance in a million. There in my group sat George Papavgeris, the writer of the song I'd picked out as my example. I'd never met him before that but had learnt it because somebody else heard him singing it and thought it would be perfect for me.

George is Greek and has lived in the Aylesbury area since 1970. *The Flowers and the Guns* looks back at the experiences of my generation, the people who grew up during the 1960s. It was the days of the hippies and the flower power movement, when an American student famously stuffed carnations down the barrels of the National Guards' rifles as a peace gesture. Hopes were high that we were going to change the world and make it a better place. The song asks whatever happened to those principles and ideals in the decades that followed…

Where are the flowers that we put into the muzzles of the guns?
Dried out and pressed inside a frame, they never get a second glance.
The love that we would banish war with, on bombed-out streets now naked stands,
Where are the flowers that we put into the muzzles of the guns?

There was nothing I could teach George Papavgeris about songwriting.

My wife, Danni, and I had a property in France called La Jeusseliniere, an old farmhouse which needed a fair amount of work. With the help of friends we managed to convert it into a respectable venue for holding week-long folk music courses. It was situated in a very beautiful rural area on the border of Normandy and Brittany. We said we'd used up all our luck and would never win the lottery, as we had the best neighbours you could wish for. Our La Jeusseliniere courses ran from May to September and we had a wonderful range of tutors who came for the week – Dave Fletcher and Bill Whaley, Eric Bogle and John Munro, Joe Broughton and Kevin Dempsey, Stan Graham, Mike Silver, John Dipper, Harvey Andrews, Iris Bishop, Bob Fox and, of course, Vin Garbutt.

One particular year we received a phone call from a longstanding friend of Vin's. He knew him back in Teesside and went off to live in France for years and became fluent in the language. He had seen that Vin would be at La Jeusseliniere and asked if he could come over and meet up with him to catch up. We were delighted and so was Vin, and the date and time were duly arranged. Wednesday was always a half-day when people could go off and enjoy the area and so it was chosen as the day for the visit. There were religious crosses dotted about the roads and we had one at the top of our drive, which was a useful landmark for finding La Jeusseliniere.

After lunch, Vin and his friend decided to walk up to the nearest village, Larchamp, about a mile away. This meant they would pass by our dear neighbour, Mme Claire Caree, a retired French farmer who could not speak one word of English. Her house overlooked the road and she spent time looking out of the window and saw anything that passed by. On this occasion she saw Vin and his friend walking, so as they were strangers she went down to talk to them in her usual friendly manner and they passed the time of day. Later that same day Claire came down to visit us and told us excitedly about a great miracle that had happened earlier that afternoon. Jesus had descended from the cross and was walking towards the village, so Claire had come to speak to him and, lo and behold, he had an interpreter with him.

Martyn Wyndham-Read

When Martyn retired from running the workshops and was renovating his house in France, he found the time to work on a completely different project. His father had been shot down over France during the war and Martyn decided to try to find out more about the circumstances. He managed to track down a woman who remembered seeing the incident and he went to visit the village where the plane had come down. Amazingly, it was just a stone's throw from where Martyn and Danni lived. Something or someone must have been guiding them to *La Jeusseliniere* when they bought that property.

Martyn is shy and not one to blow his own trumpet, but he has had a long successful career and his contribution to folk music is immense. He lived in Australia for seven years from 1960 when he was just eighteen and amassed a wealth of fantastic Australian songs from old farm hands he worked alongside on the sheep-shearing stations. He's a prolific collector of songs and you can tell how much he loves the music he plays. From the 1970s onwards folk audiences began to demand more from their performers and I think it was hard for him to accept that he had to try to be an entertainer – glitz and glamour are just not his style. When he played up here on Teesside, even if he knew that I was away touring, he would turn up at our house with a bunch of flowers for my mam. That's the kind of guy he is - a top bloke, very modest and a true gentleman.

DOCTOR'S ORDERS

'If you can force your heart and nerve and sinew
To serve your turn long after they are gone,
And so hold on when there is nothing in you
Except the Will which says to them: Hold on.'

Rudyard Kipling, *If*

I'd always avoided antibiotics and prescription medicines, preferring my own herbal remedies made from plants I picked in the fields around me. But I arrived home from a world tour in March 2004 with a nasty, hacking cough. I'd played gigs in Canada, New Zealand, Australia and Kuala Lumpur and was worried because it was the time when people in the Far East were coming down with bird flu. All the talk in the papers and on television was the danger of it turning into a pandemic that could wipe out millions.

I saw my GP and he wasn't concerned at first. He told me to just keep taking the herbal remedies as I always did and I'd be fine. But when he placed his stethoscope on my chest, his expression changed.

'What the hell is that racket?' he said.

He thought he could detect a heart murmur. An echo scan at James Cook Hospital in Middlesbrough that June confirmed I had a mitral valve prolapse. They said it might not cause any problems and they'd just keep monitoring me. So I carried on as usual, fulfilling all the gigs in my diary and giving it rock-all on stage as though nothing had happened.

In January 2005 I was enjoying a musical sabbatical on my own near Fuengirola on the Costa del Sol. I love going away with just my guitar and a tape recorder to rehearse, learn new songs and write in solitude. Even if I didn't get any songs out of it – because you can't make them happen – I always came back with at least a new whistle tune. During the last few days I was away I developed a rattle in my chest. It got worse when I lay down and it started keeping me awake at night. I decided to come home early and made an appointment with the doctor. He prescribed a diuretic tablet, which he warned would make me wee like a horse. That night I slept soundly for the first time since the rattle developed and I was triumphant when I returned to the surgery a few days later.

Friend and fellow folkie Pete Davies checks Vin's pulse during a hospital visit in January 2005

'You've cured me, Doctor!' I said. 'I did wee like a horse but that terrible rattle has gone and I slept like a log.'

Unfortunately, the doctor confessed he hadn't cured me at all. Instead he'd confirmed I was suffering from heart failure. He was surprised I wasn't gasping and wheezing as well. The situation was clearly serious and I was taken into hospital later that day. The medication I was given quickly perked me up – but the news that I faced surgery was daunting. There were two options. The first was to open my chest up and give me a replacement valve. There was a less invasive alternative, however, a 'heart-port' procedure using keyhole surgery to repair the faulty valve. It was a scary scenario, but the doctors were confident and I decided to go for it.

I was hallucinating when I came round after the operation – I told Pat to keep an eye on the nurses because they were trying to give me someone else's medication! But once I was home a few days later I felt fantastic. I thought I had fully recovered and was incredibly relieved at the prospect of being able to get on with my life. But a week later I was rushed back into hospital and I was dangerously ill with internal bleeding. The gastroenterologist who repaired the bleeding vessel told me he'd never worked with anybody who had so little blood in their body and was still alive.

I was in a real state. I hated wearing an oxygen mask and dreaded having visitors because I wasn't able to talk to them. The very thought of people coming sent my heart-rate racing. I wanted to be welcoming because they'd taken the trouble to come and see me, but I was gasping for breath. I felt as though I was suffocating or drowning and the sensation terrified me.

I was overwhelmed by the deluge of emails, cards and prayers that flooded in from all over the world, including Australia, Canada and beyond. Every one of them meant so much to me.

My faith also played a major role in helping me come through it. I was profoundly moved when a young priest friend, Father Paul Farrer, gave me the Sacrament of the Sick. Being an old 'left-footer', as Catholics were always called back in the old days, it was without a doubt the best therapy I received. As he anointed me with the holy oils I felt a profound sense of calm and peace come over me. It was an intensely spiritual experience. Eucharistic ministers came into the hospital regularly to distribute Holy Communion and I felt looked after in every respect. It's a mystery to me how people who have no religion manage at times like that. I thanked God for my faith and I also thanked God for the National Health Service. The doctors and nurses were wonderful all the way through my illness. It was comforting to be in safe hands, both medically and spiritually. While I was in hospital I experienced that battle between optimism and pessimism that millions of people have to deal with every day of their lives. I came across the poem *It Couldn't Be Done*, written by Edgar Guest in the 1930s. Reading the words perked me up no end and later I wrote a tune to go with it, which I recorded on *Persona...Grata*.

Somebody said that it couldn't be done
But he with a chuckle replied
That 'maybe it couldn't' but he would be one
Who wouldn't say so till he'd tried
So he buckled right in with the trace of a grin
On his face. If he worried he hid it.
He started to sing as he tackled the thing
That couldn't be done, and he did it!
Edgar Guest (1881-1959), *It Couldn't Be Done*

I was in hospital for about six weeks and when I came out I was weak and listless. The recovery process was long and slow as my poor little stitched-up heart battled to make me better. I just couldn't keep warm and was severely anaemic. I was put on a high dose of iron tablets and even though I would have rather chewed on leaves from the bushes that grow on the Cleveland Hills, I did as I was told and took them. I couldn't do much for myself and my usual walk across the clifftops was out of the question. I previously got all the exercise I needed out in the fresh air and felt uplifted by my surroundings. That daily walk was hard to beat. Before I set off I would check the weather to make sure I had the right clothes on. Then I'd close the front door behind me and continue up the lane alongside a drystone wall, looking over into a field of cows on the other side. I'd then make my way between the sheep and climb up to the highest point on the east coast, 666 feet above sea level. Rain, hail or shine, I walked around 10,000 steps through the most awe-inspiring landscape England has to offer. The circular route was about two miles and I would return home feeling on top of the world. Now, though, I was gasping for breath after the slightest exertion and even having a conversation was an ordeal.

After a few weeks I began suffering from severe palpitations. I became the youngest patient at the cardiac rehabilitation unit at Brotton Hospital near my home. Most of the others had undergone heart bypasses and had zip-shaped scars on their chests. After an hour of exercise I could hardly walk back to the car. I couldn't understand how something that was supposed to help me recover made me feel so bad. My blood pressure was sky-high, which the doctors thought was probably anxiety-related. Eventually, I reached my lowest ebb. I felt sick and extremely low. It's not an easy admission to make, but for the first time in my life I was anxious and depressed. I had always been a relaxed kind of person and it came as a shock. Maybe it's one of the effects of a serious illness – we should be told these things! Perhaps the NHS doesn't have the resources to deal with the after-care of patients as well as it should. One day you're being cared for and everything is done for you and then you step back outside into the world and have to continue your recovery by yourself. For a while I struggled to see a way out of it, but a visit from a doctor friend, Pam Foster, was the start of my mental recovery. Pam sat for three hours and patiently answered my questions and reassured me.

'It's perfectly normal to feel the way you do after what your body has been through,' she said.

The other big turning point came during a family trip to Danby Beacon, a former radar station high on the North York Moors. Pat packed sandwiches and a flask of tea. As soon as we arrived, our youngest son, Louis, climbed out of the car and bounded up to the top of the hill without a care in the world. Watching him sprinting through the heather made me feel incredibly emotional.

'I'd love to walk up there,' I said to Pat.

So we did.

I felt I had a spiritual experience on Danby Beacon that day. I tapped into a rich source of nature's own therapy. It was Sunday and for once I had missed Mass. I normally go to our local parish on a Sunday morning but I was just too ill that day. I felt so low and I couldn't have gone. Up there, though, surrounded by the beauty of God's creation, was fantastic. It did something to me and I didn't feel so bad about not going to church. The whole experience was a prayer anyway. Before long I was able to return to the road again and the repaired valve worked flawlessly for a decade.

Then one night I was playing the Kitchen Garden Cafe in Kings Heath, Birmingham. It was a cracking gig and the red wine flowed freely because I was about to enjoy a week's break. I was in an upbeat mood, the audience were brilliant and the wine was delicious. Instead of doing two sets of forty-five minutes, I did seventy-five minutes and then got completely carried away and did ninety for the second half. I felt on top form as I chatted with fans and signed CDs afterwards. Then I went to speak but found I couldn't talk and was struggling for breath. I silently mouthed my excuses and sat down to try to steady myself, before departing the venue as quickly as I could. The next day I was still a little breathless, although I wasn't in any pain and I began to forget about it. Pat drove me home from Birmingham and I even went for my regular walk over the hills near home. But I made an appointment to see the doctor and the story clearly alarmed him. He thought I might have suffered a minor heart attack, but tests showed it was something called atrial fibrillation, or AF, an irregular heartbeat as a result of the valve repair. I felt fine by now and was relieved to hear it was just a wobbly heart. My GP and my consultant were slightly more concerned, however. They agreed I should go on warfarin. I'd avoided warfarin for ten years. I knew it was originally used as rat poison but was now widely used to thin the blood. I went in there feeling fairly cheerful and by the time I left I was worried. I was told I was seriously ill and my GP said I should go home, lie down and do nothing whatsoever. To make matters worse, it was my friend and former Fettlers bandmate Ron Angel's funeral later that day and I wasn't able to be there.

The bouts of AF made me feel weak and tired. I could just to say detect that my heart rhythm wasn't as it should be, but when Pat put her head on my chest she could tell it was all over the place. I had one during our daughter Katie's wedding and again at my mate Pete Betts' funeral. I was given a change of medication but I went downhill rapidly after that. As well as warfarin they also put me on water tablets. I was left feeling exhausted and breathless and my taste buds were affected too. I wanted to cover everything with salt and ate more sugary foods because at least I could taste them – chips without salt tasted like cardboard. It was only in the minutes immediately after a gig that I could taste everything properly. I kept telling the doctors that I was sure I didn't need all this medication. I was at the end of my tether.

One of the few activities that made me feel better was performing. I could arrive for a gig feeling terrible but as soon as I took to the stage and started singing I was back on top form. Caffeine and alcohol are potential triggers for AF and I cut down on the booze after October 2016. Hundreds of people in the music industry fell by the wayside because of alcohol, and fans buying them drinks didn't help. (Not that I ever objected. I used to ask for a round of applause when someone brought me a drink up to the stage during a show – and then say, 'You too could have an applause like that!') But I'd still enjoy a few pints of shandy and I drank the odd glass of wine when I finished gigs, with no ill effects.

Early in 2016 I went on tour to Australia, after six weeks of my heart beating normally. By the time I arrived I was in AF and for the first five days my heart was out of kilter. My GP would have cancelled all my gigs, just as I'd been forced to do the previous year, but I knew I could sing without any problems.

The first gig was just north of Melbourne. I had a seventy-five-minute slot and I sang like a bird, although I'm told I looked like death warmed up. I felt comfortable and was able to reach loud and long notes with no breathlessness at all. I came off stage feeling fine and when I woke the next day my heart was back to normal. It was exactly the opposite of what the doctors had told me would happen. The medical profession sometimes focus too much on what's written in the textbooks and don't look at the individual as closely as they might – they advised me not to sing, but the adrenaline from my performances made me well again.

Playing the whistle on the Eston Hills

Vin shows off his produce

MAN OF THE EARTH

'All the views that I've cherished,
Those stark purple moors
A stranger's eye could nowt but please
And the contrasting beauty is free to behold
Where those hills meet the Valley of Tees.'

Vin Garbutt, *Valley of Tees*

I was born in South Bank, Middlesbrough, Yorkshire. It was easier to just say I was from Yorkshire to people who didn't know where it was. Then in 1968 they invented 'Teesside'. I was happy enough with that name because it says where we live – after all, the location of the river never moves. But in 1974, just as we got used to being in Teesside, they ripped up the map again. For at least a thousand years we'd been in Yorkshire and in the space of a decade we were dumped into the county borough of Teesside and then the non-metropolitan county of Cleveland. I'm not a fan of the name, even though it has some historical basis. But people on the other side of the river in Stockton and Hartlepool never had anything to do with Cleveland, and one day they woke up to be told that's where they now lived. (There's nothing new about Hartlepool being messed about, mind. In 1139 a peace treaty made the River Tees the border, so it was in Scotland once!)

Back in 1800 this area was partly in Yorkshire and partly in South Durham. There were only a couple of villages here and the accent wasn't much different to what was spoken in the rest of Yorkshire and Durham. It is now though – I have a Teesside accent, and it's unique. But our civic fathers in the little corner of the North East I come from, who should have helped us blossom, have never given proper credit to who we are and where we belong. Everybody needs an identity, but we've never been allowed to have one of our own. And it wasn't just us, the same happened all over the country. Boundaries were changed and the people who lived in these places weren't even asked.

In recent years the bureaucrats have been at it again, carving up Cleveland into four smaller council areas. Then, when nobody had any idea where we were any more, they decided they'd call us the 'Tees Valley'. I'm not even sure what that is – perhaps it was dreamed up by a fan who was inspired by my first album, *Valley of Tees*.

Preparing Christmas Eve paella in 2013 – a family tradition, started by Vin

Making elderflower wine

At Hummersea with pal Pete Davies

People don't believe me when I tell them that we're not actually in a county at all now. Middlesbrough's just in, well, Middlesbrough. Having been in Cleveland, North Yorkshire, South Durham, Teesside, Cleveland and the Tees Valley, us Teessiders don't know where the hell we are. I've lived in half a dozen different places without moving house! I don't think the politicians have a clue where we are either.

I've lived out here in Loftus for thirty years and I still feel like an outsider. It takes a long time for us immigrants to be accepted here. But all Teessiders are sons and daughters of immigrants, even though some people may not realise or want to admit it. Teessiders are young.

The official name now for the borough where I live is 'Redcar and Cleveland' – I hope you're keeping up with this. There was a road sign near me that summed it all up and is featured in the *Teesside Troubadour* film. It says, 'Welcome to Redcar and Cleveland, in the Tees Valley, part of the historic North Riding of Yorkshire, twinned with Troisdorf, Germany.' They have to include all those extra details because nobody knows where we are otherwise. We just chuck everything we can in, and hope some of it sticks.

When I'm abroad, I'm a Pan-Northumbrian. I'm definitely not a Geordie, but exiled Geordies take me in as one of their own and I become almost an honorary one of them. Teessiders don't usually feel much affinity with Tyneside, but when you're far away from home you find that there is a bond after all. When I first went to Australia I played to audiences of just folkies but over the last thirty years numbers have grown, partly by people saying to other North Easterners, 'You have to come and see this fella from Middlesbrough.'

I think the reason Teessiders are less likely to accept the connection with Geordies is that they're the senior partner and we're their inferior little brother. We have this identity crisis to deal with, you see. We may not be much, but we'll be not much on our own, thank you very much – not some satellite of you lot. If we're honest, we Teessiders are slightly envious of the Geordie identity. We should really get over it – after all, there's only us Geordies and Teessiders who understand the difference between the two of us anyway!

Whether we like it or not, there's a definite connection down through Northumberland to Teesside. We had iron mines, they had coal mines. There would have been no Teesside without the steelworks, and there would have been no steelworks without the coal from Durham and the shipyards on the banks of the Tyne, Wear and the Tees, which I sang about in *The Land of Three Rivers*.

Vin and Pat's wedding at St Andrew's, Teesville, on November 5 1977

Vin gives a helping hand at Seaview House

HOME ROOTS

'I'll remember kind faces, fine places I'll see,
The cliffs of Boulby and Hummersea
Where the lobsters live, and the North Sea
Gives up her bounty to the likes of me.'

Vin Garbutt, *The Loftus Emigrant*

I'm many things. I'm a South Banker, I'm a Teessider and I'm a Yorkshireman, and I now live in the most beautiful place on earth. I didn't want our kids breathing in the Teesside smoke all day, as I did when I was growing up. I preferred the natural smells of the East Cleveland countryside to the industrial pollution of South Bank.

Pat and I married in St Andrew's Church in 1977. I was living with Mam and Dad, although I already owned my own house, a modern bungalow. I wanted to buy an old terraced street house but the building society said that because of my precarious occupation I had to buy a newer house that would be easier to sell if it was repossessed – which was a fine vote of confidence in me. We moved in after the wedding and three years later, in 1979, our first child, Emma, was born.

As our family grew, we started looking for somewhere special for them to grow up. I'd always wanted to live in an old stone house and we drove all over Teesside searching for the right place, before settling on 49 High Street, Loftus, in 1980. We bought it from our friends Roy and Sue Enticknap, who lived in another house across the road. Roy was a singer with an *a cappella* folk group, Willard's Leap, who released the album *Adieu John Barleycorn* in 1975. Number 49 was a strange old place. Some of the painted letters revealing that it had once been a fever hospital were still visible on the walls. It was full of character but didn't have a garden, so I bought an allotment where I grew potatoes, cabbages and swedes.

It was marvellous to be out in the sticks and at the same time to be still in Teesside and close enough to my family and everything else in my life. By then I was used to travelling, so they were just short distances to me. I'm fortunate that in my job I can live anywhere because I'm always travelling in any case. Pat did all the driving to ferry the family around, of course, but Loftus was handy enough for Saltburn railway station, so I could jump on the train and soon be on my way to wherever I needed to be in the world. Conveniently for me, the house was also next door to my new parish church, St Joseph's.

Pat and Vin with their first baby, Emma

With Emma and Tim at a folk festival

In about 1983 our neighbour Vin Tabner told us about a derelict farm for sale at Hummersea, on the clifftop about a mile from Loftus. Vin was a fellow South Banker and the brother of the artist Len Tabner. The farm was up for sale with 170 acres of land but there had been no offers, so they were selling the land off to farmers in small parcels. Even though it wasn't far from the High Street we had no idea it existed until Vin took us there. We never would have found it because of the way it's concealed by the rolling landscape. When we saw the beautiful location at the clifftop we were blown away. Because it's a double cliff rather than a sheer one, it's known locally as The Doubles. Vin reckoned we could probably snap up the two dwellings that were joined together in an L-shape, plus an acre of land for each, at a reasonable price. He knew I was interested in gardening and only had the allotment. Pat and I talked it over and decided to take the plunge. We put in an offer and it was accepted.

The old place had been wrecked by vandals and was in a right state. Its most recent owner had been farmer Tommy Hart and his sister, but it had been empty for some time. Every stick of wood from every window frame and even the staircase had been used for making bonfires. The lead from the roof was long gone and the few remaining beams were rotten. It was just a shell. Vin Tabner was a builder and the plan was that he would provide the skills and know-how to help us restore it to a habitable state. As soon as the sale was completed he came and lived in a tent so he could guard the place and prevent any further damage. His family moved in with us for a few months and his wife had their first baby while they were living in our house.

We worked solidly for two years. The kids were sometimes left to their own devices and had to rough it, but overall it was an enjoyable experience for all the family. It helped that Vin Tabner was confident that he could rebuild the place and we had complete faith in him. He knew all about his woods and sourced the right materials from anywhere he could get his hands on them. He bought timbers from the huge Head Wrightson site at Thornaby, bringing a little bit of Teesside industrial history to the project, and parquet flooring from the old Welford's Bakery off the Trunk Road in Middlesbrough. We handed over some cash to the foreman and ran crowbars along the floor to lift it. We drafted in everyone we could to help us to gut the building, even inviting our friends from the Physically Handicapped and Able-Bodied group from Eston and Grangetown for a bring-your-overalls day. We provided the tea and sandwiches and they helped us pull down all the plaster from the walls and ceilings. It was a filthy job and we all looked like ghosts at the end of the day, covered in chalky white dust.

In the spring of 1985 we sold the house on the High Street and moved into a fifteen-quid caravan in the garden at Hummersea. The scale of the task would have been daunting for most people, but Pat doesn't do daunted. Back then she wasn't running Home Roots, so she could focus on looking after the kids and helping with the rebuild while I went off touring and earning the money we needed to pay for it. She put in endless hours of labouring and mixed countless tons of cement. When a huge delivery of reclaimed wood was dumped outside it was Pat's job to move it all round to the back of the property. It might have taken her all day but she loved it. I helped out with my basic DIY skills and did all the pointing in the lounge and up the staircase. I sometimes wonder how long my handiwork will be on show – maybe for many years after we have gone.

Eventually the first couple of rooms were ready to move into, although reaching them was far from straightforward. They were on the first floor and had to be accessed by ladder – there still weren't any stairs. The kids slept in bunk beds in a little room behind our bedroom, which was also used as our sitting room and had a little stove to keep us warm. Outside the door the roof was still exposed and water would gush down like a waterfall when it rained.

One evening at about nine o'clock there was a knock on the door and Pat went down the ladder to answer it.

'I've come to see Mr Garbutt,' said a well-dressed lady.

She had the look of a social worker and Pat panicked. She thought someone had tipped them off that we were all living rough and she'd been sent round to check the conditions were safe for the kids. Pat knew she couldn't possibly take her upstairs, so she just stared back blankly.

'Can I see Mr Garbutt?' the woman insisted. 'I've come to put him to bed!'

After overcoming the shock of these words, Pat realised the woman had the wrong house. She was the district nurse and had come to care for Betty Garbutt's father just over the hill from us.

Hummersea is a truly stunning location. We're on the scenic Cleveland Way, the 110-mile circular walk from Helmsley, up to Saltburn and down along the coast to Filey.

Vin with his youngest, Louis, in 1989

Vin carrying his friend's son, Patrick Jenkinson, with Tim and Emma, and the stunning view from the family home at Hummersea behind them

Cleveland is a Viking word, meaning 'cliff-land'. The Vikings came across from relative flatness and when they arrived here they probably couldn't believe the sight of the hills all around them. Hummersea itself comes from the Viking word for lobster, *hummer*.

I sometimes sit on my compost heap at night and contemplate the stars. Living out here on a clifftop where there's no light pollution is fantastic. I can gaze at the heavens and endless space going on forever and ever. Looking out at the peace and stillness you might think nothing had ever happened here, but that couldn't be further from the truth. This place has a rich and fascinating history. There have been frequent archaeological digs over the years (though they always put the topsoil back on afterwards to let the farmer grow another crop before they came back the following autumn for another go). A few years back they discovered the grave of a seventh-century Saxon princess in Street House Anglo-Saxon Cemetery on top of Boulby Cliff. Some of the jewels found in her grave are believed to have come from Kent, so maybe this princess made the same journey to Hummersea that Pat did.

Wind the clock forward a millennium and we find the fascinating story of the alum quarries on Boulby Cliff. The alum works were started by the Conyers family of Boulby Manor in the 1650s and the hamlet of Boulby was built to house the workers. Roger Osborne's book *The Floating Egg* tells the story of how the secret of making alum was unlocked. Alum is an important fixative that played an essential part in the dying process. Without a fixative, dye would wash out of the cloth and the process just wouldn't work. Alum had to be mashed and boiled and brought to exactly the right temperature – if it was too cold or had been boiled for too long it was no use. Craftsmen from the Ottoman Empire held the secret of making alum and a delegation was sent to find out from Turkish workers in Italy how it was done. The solution was brilliantly simple. They dropped a hen's egg into the liquor as they were heating it. It sank to the bottom, and then floated back to the surface when it reached exactly the right temperature.

As time went by, advances in the industry elsewhere made the mining of alum at Boulby uneconomic and the works closed. Where have we heard that one before? But the old alum workings are still visible up on the cliff. On some of the old maps you can see ponds on the cliff-edge called Snilah ponds that were connected to the alum industry. Sadly, the ponds were filled in by Boulby Potash during the 1960s or 1970s, even though they were probably important to migratory birds and newts and other amphibians.

'Snilah' was actually the original name for our house in Hummersea. We're not sure exactly when it was built, but we do know the renowned geologist Lewis Hunton was born here in 1814. His father was a manager at the alum quarries and Lewis became interested in fossil collecting from an early age. He was the first person to discover that you can tell the age of rock from the way ammonites in the strata change gradually over millions of years. This is still known by geologists as the Hunton Theory. Poor Lewis died of consumption at the age of just twenty-five, but he managed to leave a lasting impression on the world. He's buried where he died in France, but the rest of his family are in St Leonard's Churchyard in Loftus. To think that Lewis sat in the very room where I eat my tea! He changed his name to the French spelling and pronunciation, 'Louis'. By coincidence, we also christened our youngest son Louis, although we knew nothing about the Lewis Hunton connection when he was born.

We are visited by a huge variety of migratory birds here and it's a paradise for twitchers. In the winter, bramblings arrive from Russia and later on fieldfares and redwings come over from Scandinavia. I've had four yellow-browed warblers in my garden at one time. I wouldn't say I'm an expert, but I can tell my willow warbler from my chiff-chaff.

Most of my information comes from one of the birders called Don, who really knows his onions. I've never asked him what his second name is, I've just become friendly with him over the years when he's come to Hummersea to look at the birds. As soon as he arrives with his telescope I know we have interesting feathered visitors, and I go out to join him. Dozens of twitchers descend on us when a rare one turns up. The message flashes through the birdwatching community on the internet and they'll all stand out there for days, just waiting to catch a glimpse. They're a friendly lot and I enjoy talking to them.

One day there was a huge fuss and I found out they'd spotted a red-flanked bluetail from Siberia, which made the papers when it was seen in Hartlepool in 2016. Another time I saw them arrive with their binoculars and I went out and asked what they'd come for. Don pointed to some bushes and in a hushed tone said there was a white-breasted flycatcher on the cliff edge, a visitor from the Turkey area. It's brilliant to think that these rare birds are just passing through and stop off at my place.

We planted most of the trees here ourselves. There were a couple of elms when we first moved in, but they succumbed to Dutch elm disease and there are none left in the whole area now. We have sycamores, ashes and elderberry bushes – *sambucus nigra*.

I saw my first slow-worms down south in Kent but didn't see another for thirty-five years. Then, to my amazement, a whole colony was discovered opposite the Station pub in Loftus. Slow-worms are legless lizards and are a protected species. Environmentalists brought the colony down here to Hummersea and I often find them slithering around my garden. We regularly have puffballs out on the lawn too. They're enormous football-sized fungi that grow incredibly quickly. You wake up one morning and there they are. If you jump on one, it will puff out billions of spores. We've eaten them three times this year and they're delicious. You dip slices in egg and fry them with a bit of salt and pepper – gorgeous. You can't guarantee they're going to turn up the next year, but I hope they do.

I pick the mushrooms I'm familiar with and I'm happy with the puffballs, but there are some others I don't trust myself with, such as the inkcaps that sometimes grow in the back garden. I know there are edible and inedible types of inkcap, and unless you're sure which is which, they're best left alone. When the poisonous ones reach a certain point they start to melt and ooze black liquid onto the grass. They used the ink for the old parchment manuscripts of the Book of Kells and St Bede's Gospels because the poisonous sap is indelible as well as being inedible. It's already lasted for a thousand years and was ideal for the job, as long as you didn't suck your pen while you were writing!

ꕥ

Home Roots Music *is* Pat. We would have preferred to do things the easy way, but when the music industry didn't work out for us we became our own cottage industry instead. Our successful use of the internet has created so much interest that unfortunately Pat has ended up working all the hours God sends. It's become a full-time job, and more. I lack business acumen, so most of the hard work falls on Pat's shoulders - answering emails, sending off CDs, comparing quotes for albums and just dealing with the whole operation. Even though we've cut down on some work I reckon she's grafting harder than ever. She's so capable and she's a 120-per-center. While I've been unwell she's been doing my work as well as her own. I'll have a burst of energy and cut a tree down with a chainsaw, and then have to sit down while Pat lops the branches off and takes it to the dump – it's not good. She's marvellous, a real coper, but I don't want her to burn herself out. I'd love Pat's workload to be reduced and I'd love to take it easier myself. The thing is, when I slow down everything slows down. Without a continued commitment to gigging, fewer people will hear me play and CD sales will plummet – but I know I can't go on doing that forever.

Over the years I covered thousands of miles on public transport but Pat's been driving me to most of my gigs since my health troubles in 2005. We're thinking about moving house so I can be nearer the bus or train and I'm not so reliant on Pat giving me lifts to wherever I need to be. One alternative to moving is me learning to drive after all these years. But I sit in the passenger seat when Pat's driving and I'm amazed at the brilliance of the human brain – all this coordination, overtaking, speeding up, reading signs and dodging obstructions, and I think, how does anybody do that?

I hope I live to be a hundred, but if I died tomorrow, my biggest sadness would be for the family I would leave behind me. I've had a wonderful time and I've never been scared of dying. It happens to everybody and there's nothing unusual about popping your clogs. So many people die so very young and I feel incredibly lucky and privileged to have led such a full and rich life.

'Death is as much a part of life as living.'

Vin Garbutt

EULOGY FOR DAD

Our Dad was born with little warning, in a bucket. My Grandad Alf ran over to my Nana Tess, patted her on the shoulder and said, lovingly, 'You're all right, pet,' then immediately ran out of the house. Apparently, she laughed. That was Dad's introduction to the world, his first experience, and he absorbed it… love and laughter.

He grew into a boy, alongside his brother Michael, and his two sisters, Mary and Ellen, in a house filled with childish noise, humorous tales from his dad, and traditional Irish songs constantly being hummed or sung by his mam. Family celebrations saw those traditions delivered by a clan of entertainers.

Dad took it all in. Always curious, always eager to learn. He never stopped. As a child, his thoughtfulness and intelligence had relief in mischievous pranks. He would stick his head round the kitchen door, suddenly shouting 'catch', throwing an egg, and running away, or balancing bowls of water on top of the door, having identified his sibling victim. Dad's most enduring prank was making his brother Mike wait outside the toilet door, slowly pouring bottles of water into the loo until he cracked up laughing.

Dad made lifelong friends at St Peter's in South Bank, some of whom are here today, and some who'll be glad they're not, because their wait to see him is over. He loved the company he kept, as much as his solitude. He found that isolated freedom in the Eston Hills, spending days growing his love and appreciation of nature and the Teesside countryside, a feeling he later captured in his greenhouse, sharing it with his favourite tomato plants.

He had by this time already discovered music and a discarded guitar in his brother's wardrobe. In that, he found a talent that affected all of our lives, nurtured through playing and singing the songs his mother sang, the songs of his Irish and English heritage.

He studied the roots of folk songs he heard at local clubs, which continued when he eventually followed his school friends to ICI Wilton. Dad found the best of everything and enjoyed his time as an apprentice turner. He always felt he was one of the men of the industry that defines Teesside.

He immersed himself in the local music scene, harking at his true calling like the birds he'd spent so much time admiring. He regularly played at the Rifle Folk Club, using the funds he earned to travel, watching other musicians, visiting people and places, particularly Ireland, in search of his roots.

Then, in 1968, he, and a group of close friends (Speedy John Bryden, Kevin McLean, Alan Brewer, Joe Jones and Pete Betts), left their jobs to busk along the Mediterranean coast in a VW Caravette Dad called 'Sybil Klondike'. That was life-changing for most of them, no more so than for Dad. In Spain and Gibraltar, with his friends, he developed a belief in his ability as a musician and songwriter and came back to England with the conviction that he would become a professional folk singer. From that point, his guitar and penny whistle never left his side – his whistle never will.

For forty-eight more years he travelled and sang professionally, playing sell-out shows to thousands of people from Canada to Australia, Holland to Hong Kong, and crafted sixteen albums along the way. He won a BBC Folk Award for Best Live Act, received an honorary Masters degree from our very own Teesside University, and perhaps most significantly to him, a papal blessing, bestowed upon him by Pope Francis for his services to the charity, Life.

A lot has been written about Dad's career and achievements, and more will be said. It seemed an impossible task to summarise in these words today, so we haven't really. We would say though, the ambition in Dad's life wasn't the pursuit of fame or glory, but to communicate and have a relationship with as many people as possible, with a sincere purpose.

Vin Garbutt was also a husband, dad and grandad. As kids, he'd tell us stories of Murgatroyd Mouse and take us on magical treasure hunts around his beloved Hummersea. Reading from an invisible book, he would take us up to the magic canyon to find the golden fern, where he'd have secretly planted 'treasure'. And his grandchildren loved him for the fun he brought to them, giving a personal song to each.

A few people this week have mentioned how he was like a father figure to them, and some might find that an odd thing to say to his children, but I think he genuinely loved every person he met, and he made people feel that.

He'd watch the news every day and would grieve and worry for every victim, every tragedy, no matter where in the world it was happening. He felt duty-bound to be informed and not to turn a blind eye to the plight of anyone. Even though he couldn't help practically he prayed for every one of them and tried to throw light on them.

Dad was a student of life, who shared his learning and his laughter. With that in mind, we thought it important to share with you a few of his lessons, comments and one-liners:

'Being silly isn't stupid.'
'To bear intelligence isn't sombre, but it can be.'
'Think, be philosophical, question yourself.'
'Love can be said in a word, but there should be no doubt of it in your actions.'
'The best relief is an organic wee in the garden.'
'Don't judge a book by its cover.'
'There are two ends to every stick.'
'Words are important, don't waste or fail to use them.'
'Perspectives are always relevant.'

'Two wrongs don't make a right.'
'Fashion does not dictate.'
'Believe in God, have faith.'
'Life should be verdant and green.'
'Everyone's called Colin.'
'Don't believe what you read or hear, nor assume it's not true.'
'Life has the right to exist.'
'The Ten Commandments are relevant, irrespective of belief.'
'Marriage supports a family.'
'Love, share and practice folk music.'
'Death is as much a part of life as living.'
'Believe the bypass syndrome.'
'There is power in prayer.'
'The capital of Bolivia is La Paz.' – it's actually Sucre
'Comedy and tragedy live side by side.'
'A person will never feel older than twenty-eight.'
'You can never have enough torches, penknives, glasses or daft caps.'
'Avoid the hungry gap.'
'It couldn't be done, but he did it.'
'The punchline lives in those people not yet laughing.'
'Reuse, recycle.' – he'd have had a secondhand coffin!
'Laugh your cap off.'
'Look after the pennies and the pounds look after themselves.'
'Money isn't everything.'
'There are more things 'twixt heaven and earth.'
'Don't talk too proud, nor talk too wise.'
'Honesty is the best policy.'
'Beware the fear of imperfection.'
'Think of others before yourself.'
'The cultivation and expansion of needs is the antithesis of wisdom.'
'Time and tide wait for no man.'

And finally…
'An axolotl is a Central American amphibious salamander.'

Nobody is perfect, and Dad proves that you don't have to be. We're not sure that he approved of pride, but with Dad, having said our piece, it's overwhelming and undeniable and justifiable.

We could never do justice to Dad's life, and it's a formidable task to live up to him – he's a big act to follow. But we have tried to leave just a taste of the beauty of his existence. Dad was loaned to us filled with love, compassion and passion, and now he's been called back home.

Our amazing Mam – she truly is the love of Dad's life. A true companion. Dad was an artist, a free spirit, but she was his rock, the foundation that allowed him to follow, and even occasionally live his dreams. You are forever the most important person in his life. Like he said, you're the bee's knees. A love like that, for a lifetime and longer, it knows no bounds.

Our final words are these from our wonderful Mam:

'I would say to him, 'How come you never have a down day? When you don't feel like giving that smile to the man on the street, when you don't feel like chatting?'

He would say, 'I never feel like that. All I want to do in life is make the world a better place, just a smile is all it takes.'

He would say to me every single day, 'Have I told you that I love you today?' And without fail, the answer would be, 'Yes.'

He was trying to give that message of love to all of you through his music and laughter. Did Vin make the world a better place? I think we all know the answer to that. Now it is our responsibility to carry that love away with us and hand it on.'

Thank you for making the world a better place, Dad.

All the very best!

God Bless.

We love you.

Emma, Tim, Katie and Louis

OUR ABSENT FRIEND

Vin Garbutt: The hardest obituary I have ever had to write

Colossus With a Heart of Gold

I've penned a few one-liners, I wrote a few good songs,
I've met a few good people and some that did me wrong
But once-a-while there comes a smile that holds you in its grasp,
That shakes you to your boots and forces you to ask
If you are lucky, once in life, you'll meet this kind of man
The type of guy that made me ask exactly who I am
I met that man so long ago, when we were young and daft
We laughed and laughed, oh how we laughed, we laughed and laughed and laughed
Some beliefs were miles apart and yet we never fought
Just recognised our differences in answers that we sought
But values bound and stayed with us; will be forgotten never
Like family and love of life and songs we'll sing forever
That voice, those words, that cutting wit, the messages prevail
The fun, absurd, the joy of it, the devil in the detail
The stumblings and the mumblings, as big as any song,
Even tuning his guitar would pull the audience along
So generous of spirit, an open-hearted guy
And when I met his family I instantly knew why
He shared his house, his home, his food, his everything, his kin
*But before I stayed the night I had to put the windows in**
Farewell my friend I'm broken now, but heal I must, and will
Forget you, Vin, I never could, and though your heart lies still
It beats within the ones you've touched, and they are not a few
But thousands all around the world; they're better because of you.

*This line needs a little explaining. I stayed with Vin, Pat and family along with my then-wife Janet and our two sons when we played the Redcar Festival together. Vin, in his inimitable manner, had been pondering the fact that there was no ventilation in the spare bedroom. He'd had sash windows made and decided the perfect day to fit them was the day we arrived. He had been 'working' for hours getting it ready when we turned up. Drinks in the back garden were taken and the stories began. Vin was completely forgetting the time and Pat repeatedly reminded him there was no window in the spare room. He resumed his task and after a further hour or so had managed to glaze two of the sixteen panels in the sashes. In the end I finished the job for him and we went upstairs and fitted them, together. I ribbed him for years about the fact that I had to finish the bedroom before we could go to bed. As always, we laughed and laughed…

The first time I met Vin, we hit it off immediately. I did a floor spot at his gig and he complimented me on my songs, one of which, *Absent Friends*, he went on to record. The day after the gig we met up for lunch and went for a walk along the canal near my home. There was a fair bit of rubbish in the canal and a huge block of polystyrene floated past. Quick as a flash, Vin looked at me and said, 'You know, three-quarters of that is beneath the surface.'
He didn't think like any other person I have ever met. He was constantly playing with words in his head, even my name became Kee Thanh Kok, and he would joke on gigs that I was from Thailand or Vietnam, ironic now considering where I live. Another story I remember was when somebody mentioned Princess Anne. I could see the cogs start to tick. He suddenly said, 'She was a chiropodist, you know, but that was a long time ago.' We all waited with bated breath until eventually someone in the group could stand it no longer. 'Go on, explain.' 'Oh yes,' Vin carried on. 'She worked in the Middle East. There's a very famous song about it.' Silence. 'It's called Jerusalem.' I was so in tune with his humour that I immediately got it and was in fits of laughter as the others looked on, baffled. Vin eventually summed up, 'Anne did those feet in ancient times.'
Once in our house he phoned a mate who had been down on his luck. 'Great news,' said Vin. 'You've got a job? Wow, Selfridges! Have you sold any yet?'
The strange thing was, I was funnier when I was in his company. For days after we spent time together my wife would comment that I was really funny and should use more humour in my act. But it wasn't easy for me, whereas for Vin, it was simply who he was. I don't use this term often, but Vin Garbutt was a genius. There is no other word for it. He could hold an audience in his thrall, have them helpless with laughter one minute and in tears the next. A Vin Garbutt gig was an event, you went home tired. Emotionally drained with your ribs hurting; but ultimately better for having spent two hours in his company. I was lucky for I have spent weeks and months in his company. He was the greatest friend I've ever had and the greatest man I've ever met. I will miss him until I join him – though we still won't agree on where that will be. I love you, mate.
Keith Hancock

I was so sorry to hear of Vin's passing. The ranks are thinning! His songs were direct and honest and moving. I miss him already.
Tom Paxton

I didn't know Vin well, despite the fact that every conversation I had with him invariably ended with his earnest invitation for me to come and stay with him and Pat if ever I was anywhere in the North-East of England. I always found his singing, playing, and songwriting to be stirring, hilarious and honest.
My fondest memory of Vin had to do with seeing him in a small folk club in Australia way back in the early 1980s. I was touring, and my father was travelling with me. It was a night off for me, and Dad and I took a cab out to Vin's gig, which was somewhere in suburban Sydney.
Of course, we loved the show and in particular, Garbutt's in between-song patter, which had us reduced to tears of laughter. The Teesside accent made much of what Vin was actually saying indecipherable to us and in the taxi back to our hotel we both agreed subtitles might have helped. Still, it was a great night.
Pound for pound, one man and a guitar, I would rate Vin Garbutt right up there with the late, great Steve Goodman. And Goodman couldn't play the penny whistle.
Loudon Wainwright III

I met Vin way back in 1980, I think at the Cambridge Folk Festival. Either that or it was in 2015 on Copacabana beach. More likely to be Cambridge, though. I do have a fragmented memory, though, of a concert in a large, hot, crowded marquee in a muddy field somewhere in England in the early 1980s. This marquee was full of well-oiled and mostly bearded individuals who were giving the solo musician on the stage, a tall skinny bloke with a big nose and long, stringy hair, a bit of a hard time. However, Vin – for yes, it was he – was giving back as good as he was getting. Away back then, when Vin's vocal cords were in their Teesside prime, he had a voice that could cut through a four-inch stainless steel plate with ease and so he soon had that noisy bunch stunned into a cowed, submissive silence. It was an impressive performance and I thought to myself, 'Once my hearing returns to normal, I must meet this bloke.' And so I did. I think that's what happened. Anyway, whatever did or did not happen, and however, wherever, or whenever we met is immaterial. What is important is that we became friends, even though Vin lives in the Disunited Kingdom and I live in the Land of Oz, which somewhat limits our opportunities to share the occasional pint together. But of course, both being acknowledged musical geniuses, we tour around the world a fair bit to keep our legions of fans happy, and Vin invariably stays with my wife Carmel and myself when he performs in our home town of Adelaide because we are all good friends and because we offer very attractive B&B rates and I've stayed with Vin and Pat when I've toured the UK. It's all about mutual friendship, with the added bonus of a small but welcome financial advantage – we are both professional folk musicians, after all. This cosy arrangement was threatened once when Vin tried to poison me, he claims accidentally. We were living in Brisbane and Vin, who was bludging* off Carmel and me as usual while he did a concert in town, offered to cook us curry for dinner. Half an hour after we'd finished the curry I was carted off to hospital by ambulance to get, among other treatments, pethidine injections to counter serious abdominal pains. Vin always claimed it was all because I'd had three helpings of the curry, and he may have

had a point, but I can't forget seeing the strange little smile on his face as they lifted my stretcher into the ambulance.
Vin Garbutt is a seriously talented musician. He writes powerful, moving and compassionate songs, sings with passion, honesty, and conviction, with not one manufactured or false note in any of the songs he presents. He plays the guitar in a singularly unique style, but one which always complements his songs and vocal delivery. He is also one of the funniest and most perceptive people you could meet. Given his musical accomplishments it's no surprise that he is blessed with perfect comedic timing, and his introductions to his songs are minor quirky comedic masterpieces. At times they threaten to overpower his musical performance, which is not easily done! They don't, though. Somehow, they dovetail with everything else that's happening on stage, invariably morphing into the unfailingly unique, strikingly original presentation that is a Vin Garbutt concert.
Eric Bogle
*Informal Australian for scrounge

Vin was one of the most naturally funny men I've ever met, not just a super talented musician and songwriter, but a gifted and surreal comedian. Who can ever forget, once heard, his introduction to the *Chemical Worker's Song,* when he told them that because the chorus ended with the words 'but you go', the song was about a butcher called Charlie Go?
Great musicianship married to a love of words and, more importantly, a love of mankind, he was never afraid of sticking his head above the parapet, even though at times he got more flak than he deserved.
There was a time when I was on the road and seemed to be following Vin into places like the USA and Australia, and everywhere I went people were still buzzing from the great gigs he had there.
The Irish have a phrase, 'We'll never see his like again.' It could have been coined for Vin.
Mike Harding

Vin was not only my brother, he was my friend, whose family, music and hometown were the most important things in his life. He put these loves before any other. I was the eldest of the Garbutt children, brought up in a loving, caring family. Being the eldest I had the authority to keep a check on my younger siblings. In particular I felt I had a duty to toughen my kid brother up to help him to become streetwise as we played in the streets of South Bank. Vin was the thinker and daydreamer who had many gifts, but he lacked ability in almost every sport. I was passionate about football and couldn't understand this lack of interest!
As in every family we had arguments and bouts of temper, but I honestly cannot recall any occasion when Vin lost his temper with any of us. He had the knack of turning everything into a joke and any confrontation would end in laughter.
My new girlfriend, now my wife Mary, said as she got off the bus from Middlesbrough

and started to walk up towards our house that she could hear the screams and laughter coming from number 32 Ambrose Road. Our home was a place where everyone was made welcome. The kettle was always on. I often said Vin owed a lot to me, as it was my guitar he first started strumming. I had quickly lost interest in it when I discovered it wasn't as easy to play as it looked. His love of music was his way of getting his thoughts and beliefs across in the many songs he composed that we all came to know and love. My kid brother Vin, his music and his songs will never be forgotten.
Mike Garbutt

We were a close family, brought up in a happy, loving home. As we were growing up he was just always quietly there in the background. Kind, loving and gentle natured. I don't remember him ever being in any kind of bother. He was always happy, never grumpy. I remember one morning when we were all still at home, getting up for work and our Michael saying, 'There's something wrong with that idiot – who wakes up on a morning singing and whistling like that?' Vin was always playfully winding Michael up. I would hear him from outside the bathroom chuckling to himself, laughing at his own thoughts while sitting in the bath. Always a pleasure to be around. In our adult years I had an amazing adventure with him, Pat and Craig Hornby touring Australia. We just had a fabulous time – we laughed all the way around the country. I was so incredibly proud of him performing on stage in front of hundreds of people. I thank him for that adventure so very much. I thank him so very much for being my brother. I miss him so much. My beautiful, kind, thoughtful and loving brother.
Mary Cook

So many wonderful memories of my most beautiful, gentle, big brother Vin. They all begin with the six of us – Mam, Dad, Michael, Mary, Vin and me (the baby) – in an incredibly happy and most secure home. A home filled with love, laughter and music within a nurturing atmosphere of honesty, trust, respect and openness. A dynamic fostered and promoted by our wonderful parents, Alf and Tess. This is the place from where Vin emerged, developed and flourished to touch the hearts and minds of anyone lucky enough to cross his path.
There was our oldest brother Michael, affectionately referred to as 'The Nark', as he was at the top of the pecking order. He loved to wind us younger siblings up at any opportunity. And he did because he could! His wind-ups invariably ended up with him chasing one of us around the house and often out of the door and down the street to shrieks of laughter. But Vin would often get his revenge, even if inadvertently. One time our Mam asked Vin and our cousin Ian Casserley to paint the living room ceiling while she was out. They both dutifully engaged with the task using two-inch paintbrushes as Michael was sleeping on the sofa after his shift at Smith's Dock. When Michael woke up he was covered head to toe in white paint spots – there was hell on! The usual chase around the house and down the street ensued. It was hilarious, even more so when Mam returned to discover paintbrush streaks across the whole ceiling!
Then there were his practical jokes, such as popping his head around the kitchen door,

shouting, 'Catch, Ellen!' as he threw a fresh egg into the living room, which of course I would miss, watching horrified as the egg smashed and splattered on the carpet!
He was such a gentle natured and generous brother to his kid sister. He was always there in the background at home. Gentle, sensitive and loving. I remember coming downstairs on the morning of my birthday to find a £5 note rolled up and pushed inside a balloon he'd blown up and tied to the mirror. He had written 'Happy Birthday Ellen' on it. Imagine receiving a fiver as an eleven-year-old back in the sixties! He introduced me to the big wide world as a teenager, proffering his words of wisdom on the way, such as never buy egg, seafood or chicken sandwiches when you're on the road and don't keep all your money in one place. He was hilarious too. I think he inherited our Dad's wit and sense of humour. Practically every interaction with him was loaded with pun as he constantly played with words such as, 'Do you think I look like a twin, Ellen?' He was just the same off stage as on it. He taught me to play the tin whistle as a child and would often call me up on stage to join him to play a couple of tunes when I was with him on gigs as a young adult. We harmonised well together, on stage and off, in more ways than one. He also had his serious, thoughtful side, of course. I didn't agree with many of his religious principles and we would often have in-depth philosophical discussions on certain subjects. It didn't matter if our views clashed. We never fell out about anything, always agreeing to disagree. We'd often end up laughing anyway.
As we grew older we enjoyed many family holidays together with our children. Pat and I would sit on the beaches with the kids while Vin went walkabout looking for bargains in the pound shops and one-euro shops. We'd all benefit from his retail therapy when he returned. There would always be a torch, chocolates, paper cups and plastic knives, forks and spoons in his swag bag. He would, however, drive us around the bend when it was time to dine. He would have us all traipsing around the town for hours looking for 'rough cafes' as they were better value 'off the beaten track'. He was invariably right, but we did on occasion have to put our foot down and gang up on him when the hunger pangs got the better of us. I often used to wonder how Pat put up with him. She was, of course, perfect for him. The wind beneath his wings. In Vin's words, 'the bee's knees'. One of his affectionate nicknames for her was 'Trumps,' as she always came up trumps with her practical suggestions, caring and loving ways and sound advice, amongst other things. They were always so very much in love. Each other's soulmate.
Wherever he was in the world he would keep in touch with me. He once sent me a little card, 'For no particular reason Ellen, love Vin xxx' written inside. I still have that cherished card. He was so incredibly thoughtful. I would regularly pick the phone up to his voice bellowing, 'Sister!' from the other end. I miss those phone calls so much. I miss him so much. He was full of grace and goodness. He was such a special person who made everyone around him feel special. He was truly gifted in every sense of the word. I remember when our Dad died in 2000. I was talking to Vin about how awful it was to lose him. Vin said to me, 'Aw Ellen, we all have to move along the bench you know.' I so, so wish my beautiful big brother Vin hadn't moved along the bench so soon.
Ellen Forrest

Me, Vin and Pete Betts were all born in November 1947 but I was born on November 4th so I'm the oldest, which gave me an air of authority, as you can imagine! We all got on well and the folk clubs then were a great place where everybody knew everybody and the three of us would swap songs and new guitar chords. We started at the same level as musicians, but by the time we were twenty-one Vin's ability on the guitar and his whistle playing were a cut above anything we could do and he was also far more dedicated to his art. I joined the merchant navy and went to sea, but we kept in touch and when Vin was in Darlington he'd always come to our house and if I was away my mum and dad loved to see him. Underneath Vin's humour he was an earnest, honest, serious man with strong principles that never deviated for life and he believed in the right to say what he believed.
Mick Sheehan

We were to appear in a double-header at the Leeds City of Varieties Theatre. I was thrilled to be appearing at such a wonderful old venue and agreed to do the first half, with Vin doing the second. When I arrived in Leeds after having been held up on the motorway, I found it a terrible job finding a parking place anywhere near the theatre. Eventually I rushed into the dressing room five minutes before curtain up. Vin was tuned and waiting in the wings to go on in my place. I told him I could be ready in ten minutes at the outside but he said he was happy to let me get my breath back. He opened with a brilliant spot and I did the second half, which went down equally as well. Every year in the village I then lived in I put on a concert in the village hall as a fundraiser. The village turned up and we were always full. They were not a folk audience so I always opened the show, had a good middle act that could engage the audience, like Marie Little or Dave Cartwright, and then a final act that used humour and song. Tony Capstick, Jake Thackray and Jasper Carrott had all done a stint. Eventually I thought the audience would accept a more musically based artist, so I booked Vin. I explained to him how the concerts had gone before, and that the audience was not a folk one and suggested they would love his humour and he maybe could select more of his lighter songs. Well, who was I to tell Vin what was best? I finally introduced him and sat at the back of the room hoping for the best. Vin immediately began with a song about someone committing suicide and followed that up with *Sarajevo*. When he came onstage, three teenage girls sitting in front of me had a fit of the giggles at his appearance, but after fifteen minutes both they and the rest of the audience were captivated by Vin's charm, by his humour and by his songs. It was a masterclass in performance and showed me I had underestimated the village audience and certainly underestimated Vin's ability to be true to himself and yet give us all a fantastic night. He was a unique man with a unique talent who will be greatly missed.
Harvey Andrews

Having known Vin since 1973, when we first met at Reading University Folk Club, there are many memories – all good times and never a cross word spoken. Vin asked me to bring my ceilidh band Whittakers Patent Remedy to Middlesbrough for his wedding.

We were billeted in and around Redcar with various folkies, my wife Julie and I with a member of Redcar Sword Dancers who were also performing at the wedding. The day was an enormous success, but a standout highlight was Vin singing *We May or Might Never All Meet Here Again*. Not a dry eye in the house. I learned the song from Vin and it's become a fixture in my repertoire. I've sung it at weddings, funerals and in pub sessions with a crowd of rugby supporters. It's always requested by my own home team of vets when we're on tour. The song made a big impression on me, as it also did on all the wedding guests.
Hugh Crabtree

In August 1975 I was in Pennsylvania in the USA at the Philadelphia Folk Festival performing with Boys of the Lough. In the evening there were parties after all the onstage performing was done. Not having met Vin in the USA before and thinking this was perhaps his first trip over there, I wanted to introduce him to some friends among the American musicians. So I beckoned him across the crowded hotel room where this particular gathering was taking place to have him meet Bruce Philips, the self-styled Utah Phillips, the Golden Voice of the Great Southwest. Getting Bruce's attention I said, 'Utah, this is my good friend from back home in England, Vin Garbutt.' Turning to Vin I said, 'Vin, this is a great friend and songwriter, Utah Phillips.' 'Great to meet you Utah!' said Vin. 'And where are you from?'
Dave Richardson

I saw and met Vin several times and always enjoyed his music and entertaining chat. I've been tempted to nick it a few times but resisted. I also enjoyed his independence, his morals and his passion for those less fortunate. He was a troubadour of exceptional quality and I've always admired him.
Jasper Carrott

I first saw Vin in 1972 or 1973 at our college folk club, MacFolk in Bradford, at the height of the folk boom. Full houses were always guaranteed for the singer/comedians such as Mike Harding, Tony Capstick, and Derek Brimstone. The organiser told me this newcomer was as funny as any of the comedy stars. How true this proved to be – but he was different, he was so much more than a comedian. Vin appeared on the stage looking like a cross between a rock star and Worzel Gummidge. He didn't tell jokes as such, but he held the audience in thrall with his bizarre and hilarious rambling introductions to his songs, many about his native North East, performed and sung with passion. For me, a new star was born. When Vin was hospitalised just down the road from us following complications from his heart surgery, we got a call from him at tea-time.
'Hiya, Pete. Have you had yer tea yet? I'd love a curry if you haven't – I'm sick of being in here – do you fancy picking me up?'
As we'd already eaten, we compromised by sneaking him from the hospital ward, with the connivance of the sister, who said we could take him out as long as we had him

back by eight o'clockish. So, a pint and a half of Guinness and a bar meal later, he was surreptitiously returned to the ward.
Pete Davies

Vin touched the hearts of so many people, fellow-performers and audiences alike, both with the power of his performance and with his outgoing, friendly and vivacious personality. I was still a schoolboy when I first saw him, and he himself wasn't much older, and yet he seemed fully formed in style and in attitude, unique, as well as uncompromising and totally sincere in everything he did. You could perhaps trace his Irish ancestry in his words and in his songs, but the onstage delivery of what he did must surely have come from within him, because there was no-one else to compare him to on that score. When we talked about it once he told me how the humour, the zany use of language and comic phrasing came from his own family, and moreover from Teesside itself. His pride in his background was well known, and he unflinchingly expressed it to the whole world. It was as if the essence of James Joyce, John Lennon, Spike Milligan and Ronnie Drew of the Dubliners had been forged into one whole being in an ICI workshop in South Bank in 1947, and then let loose into the world, armed with a guitar and a tin whistle.
His mastery of the zany tale and comic timing was part of his everyday persona, as well as his professional one, and his deeply caring nature was no surprise to anyone who heard his own songs, and the songs of others that he chose to lend that voice of his to. His home on the cliffs overlooking the North Sea near Loftus was a cherished respite from the rigours of touring, and here he welcomed fellow-musicians and travellers from all over the world across his doorstep, much the same as many of them had done to him, and the rest of us wayward folkies, over the years.
Jez Lowe (reproduced courtesy of the *Northern Echo*)

I remember when Vin was playing locally to us when we lived near Louth in Lincolnshire. This must have been the late 1990s and Vin came to stay with us. My children, who were young boys aged about nine, seven and five, all met him in the kitchen of our house. They'd gone to bed on a Saturday night and in the morning this strange Catweazle character appeared among them. They were certain he was enchanted and from another world. With his glorious Teesside accent, he was a strange apparition. To cap it all, he played some tunes on his whistle for them and henceforth they called him the Pied Piper!
Barbara Dickson OBE

In 2002 Vin had one of his many Australian tours organised and I was doing a round-the-world tour finishing in Australia. During a telephone conversation we discovered we had both independently contacted the Hong Kong Folk Society to arrange a gig on the way back, but they were reluctant to book either of us because their annual festival was taking place the week after we wanted to be there. However, we both got calls from them to say that if we would be their international performers at the Hong Kong Folk

Festival they would move the whole thing forward a week to accommodate us!
Vin had Pat with him and I had my wife Marilyn with me and we had a fabulous weekend in Hong Kong before flying home. I didn't see much of Vin after that because of our work commitments. I think I met him more often in Australia than anywhere else and there are several archetypal anecdotes from his visits there, much celebrated by his Aussie mates.
Perhaps a book of anecdotes and song introductions should be collated. There isn't a day that passes without something reminding me of Vin – he was the bee's knees. All the very best – or should I say *stoelen*!
Bob Fox

I knew Vin for more than fifty years and it was the greatest privilege of my life to count him as a very close friend. Of course, I also got to know Pat, Vin's girlfriend way, way back, and when in 1977 they got married, I was immensely honoured when Vin asked me to be his best man. In the succeeding years, Vin and Pat made me part of their family. By the time I was in my early thirties both my parents had passed away and, being an only child, I no longer had any close family. In the forty or so years since then, almost all my Christmases have been spent with the Garbutt family.
I've often heard it said that after they made Vin, they broke the mould. I don't think anything could be more true. He was a one-off and there was no-one else like him. We are all, of course, unique, but Vin's uniqueness was sprinkled with stardust. He was certainly the greatest and most impressive person I ever met, and the same view is held by many people whose lives Vin touched. No-one who ever met him or saw him perform on stage or spent any time in his company went away untouched or, indeed, unsmitten.
Vin was truly a force of nature – his brain never seemed to switch off. He was endlessly curious about the world and all it had to offer. To walk with him along the cliff-top near his home was an education, as he was so knowledgeable about birds, flowers, trees and all kinds of wildlife. I'm not sure how much I learned in terms of hard facts, but I never failed to be impressed by his engagement with the world and his infectious enthusiasm. He was a gardener – no, that's not right, sorry Vin – he was an *organic* gardener. I was often at his house when Pat, starting to prepare dinner, has said, 'Will you get me a cabbage, Vin?', and Vin's gone out and returned with a lovely big cabbage freshly pulled from the earth.
Many years ago Vin put music to Rudyard Kipling's poem *If*, and the song regularly featured in his set. He first recorded it on his 1983 record *Little Innocents* and then again on his last album, *Synthetic Hues*. The first two lines of the last verse are:
If you can talk with crowds and keep your virtue
Or walk with kings – nor lose the common touch
Whenever I hear the song I think of Vin and how applicable to him those lines are. Vin could interact with an audience like nobody else I ever saw perform. He certainly could talk with crowds, and even if you were seeing him on stage for the first time, it would soon come across what a lovely man and decent human being he was. Although

he didn't walk with kings, he was universally loved and fêted in the folk world. And yet despite all the love and acclaim that he quite justly received, he never had any airs and graces – he remained as down to earth and straightforward as ever. He never lost the common touch. Whether you were prince or pauper, Vin treated you with the same respect and kindness he showed to everyone.

Vin's headstone describes him as a humanitarian, and that is certainly true. He had great compassion for his fellow man and was moved by the conflicts and injustices that are sadly ever-present on our television news, and he also addressed issues closer to home. But Vin's concern for his neighbour wasn't just a vehicle that inspired him to write wonderful songs. Anyone who ever talked to Vin soon discovered how he listened and connected with them with a genuine interest and empathy. He had many friends and for some of them friends, myself included, he was also a mentor. Throughout my own life I have struggled with mental health issues and, when I was younger, with a serious alcohol problem. Truly, without Vin, I wouldn't be here today. I owe him more than I can say. But Vin was there for anybody who was struggling, and I wouldn't be able to count his many acts of kindness, both small and large, that I witnessed or came to know of. But that was Vin, that was his nature.

Vin was the funniest man I ever knew, not only on stage but also in everyday life. I was lucky enough to drive him to hundreds of gigs. I would often hear some of his stage patter repeated, but I never tired of it. The same stories told in the way that only Vin could tell them would still reduce me to helpless laughter, along with that night's audience. But his patter was never exactly the same. He excelled in off the cuff, ad-libbed humour and his speed and wit was amazing. A little bird somehow got into a gig in Guisborough and began flying around the audience and crisscrossing where Vin was on stage.

'There it is Vin, grab it!' someone shouted.

Without missing a beat Vin said, 'You know what? I've been performing for nearly forty years, and people are still calling me Vin Grabit!'

When Vin's daughter, Emma, got married, he was making the traditional speech with a glass of wine in his hand. He had his specs on and a crib sheet.

'Hang on, I'll have to change me glasses,' he said. At which point he put down his glass of wine and picked up his pint of beer. Brilliant!

Vin was a truly wonderful person. I count myself immensely privileged and lucky to have been his friend and I miss him more than I could ever put into words. Thank you, Vin, for everything you did for me and for everything you did to make the world that much sunnier and brighter for everybody.

John Bryden

Vin's fundraising kept us going in Redcar for years and we have many letters of thanks and photographs of the babies whose lives he helped to save because Life was there to help. We will always be grateful that Vin was such an inspiration to us.

Margaret Barron, Life

I first met Vin at York Street Entry School, South Bank, in around 1952 and we were classmates through St Peter's Primary and for two years at the senior school. Two observations from our schooldays…
The budding etymologist: I was puzzling over how to correctly spell 'friend' and the i before e except after c rule was causing me some grief at the age of ten. On asking Vin, he spelt it correctly and observed that the word 'ends with end'. Not much, you may think, but it shows a mind able to see words within other words and an interest in how they are structured and how these patterns could be useful. A lifelong interest in the origin of words and the peculiarities of the English language had already begun.
The budding stage performer: Each secondary school class put on a stage performance at the end of the year and our class teacher, Miss Brown, was especially keen. In the first year virtually the whole class performed by being a circus crowd, describing what we could see and calling out observations to one another. As we rehearsed, some parts were altered so that 'star performers' were given more to do and it was very noticeable that Vin became one of the central characters quite quickly. Also, while most of us were sitting and fixed in position, Vin was moving around and acting as well as declaiming lines. We won, as we did in the second year, although I was not part of the performers in that year – Vin, however, had a major role. Miss Brown was quick to see his potential as a performer.
Chris Sandrawich

My mother Audrey Robinson, now in her eighties, first took me and my brother to see Vin with The Fettlers at Middlesbrough Little Theatre back in the 1960s. She has followed him ever since. She joined a folk club in the 1990s and became good friends with Vin's pal John Bryden, a lovely bloke. Due to Mam's friendship with John she attended many of Vin's gigs. In the 1990s I moved to Norwich, where Mam now lives, and I took her to see Vin in Suffolk. He came on stage, sang a few songs, told a few stories and spotted her in the audience. He suddenly stopped and asked had she got on the wrong bus because she was a long way from home! It's a memory she has treasured.
Kate Witcher

I first saw Vin at Eston Folk Club, upstairs in the Cleveland Bay, in about 1970. My friends and I were in L6 at Eston Grammar and we went every week, always dead excited if Vin was going to be on! We all fancied him, with his wild curls, big personality and a voice that stopped you in your tracks. He was our own Bob Dylan. I vividly remember his banter with the immensely likeable Pete Betts. What a pair of mates they were. One comment by Vin had me in stitches. His sister Ellen was at the folk club one night. She had to leave early and when she went, Vin came out with, 'I can have a good swear now – shit, shit, bugger, bugger!" It was very Monty Python and, like all Vin's banter, done with affection and good humour.
Ruth Watkin

Vin's lyrics made a big impression on me. I wrote to him to request some of his lyrics and he very kindly sent me handwritten sheets. I made regular use of these when teaching General Studies at a local college. A few years ago Vin kindly gave permission for the lyrics of *Fell Off The Back Of A Boat* to be used by Skinningrove History Group for a publication and as part of a presentation at Cleveland Ironstone Mining Museum. This event ended with the audience singing the song to round off a show about how Skinningrove has been represented in the arts.
John Roberts, Loftus

I was involved with Eston Folk Club and the Redcar Folk Festival in the early seventies and Vin was a regular act on both events. I applied for him to be auditioned for Opportunity Knocks, the talent show with Hughie Green. Sadly, Vin was not successful. I suspect he didn't show them his trick of playing two pennywhistles at the same time, one up each nostril.
Ken Scott

A mate of mine from Leeds came to Middlesbrough to see Vin for the very first time. Towards the end of a great night's entertainment and in a brief pause between songs, my mate shouted out in his broad Leeds accent, 'Never mind the singing, give us another introduction!'
Steve and Birgit Glasper, Great Ayton

I saw Vin at the Castle Folk Club at Richmond, North Yorkshire, in about 1972, when the place was full of Green Howards who had just got back from a tour of Northern Ireland. He sang *Welcome Home Howard Green* and they nearly raised the roof of the place. He made quite a few fans that night.
Marjorie Stirk, Mickleton, County Durham

I remember being in a group with Vin among us in Middlesbrough Town Hall crypt during the Eisteddfod. Groups had been competing from many parts of Europe and it was a time to relax, imbibe and socialise. Vin was at that pivotal point in his life when it was time to decide whether to make the giant leap away from industry and into the world of music. He produced a penny whistle and entertained an appreciative audience. An official suddenly appeared and ordered Vin to stop as he wasn't a participant in the Eisteddfod. It's ironic that if Vin was in concert at the town hall now we would all be scrambling for tickets to see him perform.
Paddy Mackin

I first saw Vin in 1981 at the Redcar Folk Festival. I remember going along to an early morning penny whistle workshop in the Swan when Vin asked the packed audience if they'd brought their whistles along. Everyone said 'No' apart from one bloke (which annoyed Vin as he stressed he was there to teach, not perform) and then my father-

in-law piped up that I had my whistle in my jacket pocket. I was encouraged by Vin to get it out and he then asked if me and the other guy knew *The South Wind*. We did and Vin told us to play the main tune while he played harmony on his whistle and a guitarist accompanied the makeshift threesome. It was one of the most nerve-wracking moments of my life yet totally exhilarating to play along in front of a packed crowd with your idol. Another time myself and my father-in-law arrived late to a workshop Vin was hosting at the Redcar festival. The room was filled to capacity with no spare seats and we just stood watching from the doorway. After a few minutes Vin noticed us and asked if we wanted to come and join them. He saw there were no spare seats, so he and his fellow musicians shuffled up and made room for us at their table – truly magical.
Graham Hall

A few years ago we were having a chat with Vin after a gig and Sue said, 'I first saw you back in 1976.'
Quick as a flash came the reply.
'Ah, so you've come for your money back!'
Rob and Sue Nicholson

Once at the Cambridge Folk Festival I shouted out a request to Vin to sing Lynda for me, which he did, despite, I believe, being asked not to by the organisers. Vin was not invited to as many festivals as he should have been, given his status and popularity, because of his outspoken opinions. However, he never shied away from talking about issues he saw as important and where injustice had occurred. The organisers who acted in this way should hang their heads and in my opinion have no place in the folk music world.
John Jas and Helen Smith, Scottish Highlands

The first time I ever saw Vin was in the late 1970s at Sidmouth Folk Festival in the Drill Hall. He ended his spot with *They Don't Write 'em Like That Any More* and turned the last chorus into an endless repeat of, 'When it comes to an end, it's let's sing it again, they don't write 'em like that any more…' until a couple of blokes came and picked him up by the legs and carried him, still playing and singing, out onto the fire escape.
Irene Marshall, Derby

In the early 1970s Vin was presenting the prizes at a songwriting competition at the Guild Hall in Newcastle. When asked up by the compère, Vin took the trophy and launched into a thank you speech!
Chris Tearney

Every year my family would have a week's holiday in York. Lots of us went, including my mother, who was in her late eighties. At some point during one trip my mother and I were sitting in the car waiting for everyone to join us. I had Vin's live CD Plugged on

the stereo and *Believe Me, If All Those Endearing Young Charms* started to play. My mother's eyes filled with tears and she said she could remember her father singing that song to her mother. My mother was born in December 1910 and yet the years slipped away and she was once more back in her childhood. Vin's wonderful rendition of that song shows how timeless and poignant songs can be.
Chris Jordan

At the Ripley Folk Festival in 1970, Vin launched into a long tale about worrying that the Flintstones cartoon video wouldn't be allowed everywhere in the Gulf. The patter ended: 'Kuwait won't allow it, but Abu Dhabi do.'
Gerry Gough

I once pulled up next to Vin at Bingham Leisure Centre and offered to help with his guitar, as he was carrying all his merchandise. He accepted and when we got to the door the person there allowed me to enter (as I had a guitar) and asked Vin for his ticket!
Martin Clarke, Kettering

I first saw Vin in Leeds some thirty years ago and have followed him all over the place ever since. In September 2014, my husband and I booked to go to Australia for our ruby wedding, but I got cancer and had to cancel the trip. We had a garden party instead and to our surprise, Vin came and sang for us at our house. He sang for three hours.
Jacqui Wright

I will never forget when Vin found a loose plank in the stage floor at Cambridge Folk Festival in the early seventies and used it thereafter as percussion in sync with his guitar. It was so funny, but also effective.
Jools Emerson

I was standing quite upset at a funeral. Vin came up to me and said, 'Look at that.' He pointed to some flowers growing out of the ground. Bless you, Vin. Effectively, you said life goes on.
Clare Wakefield

In about 2009 there was a reunion in a village hall in Dunoon, Scotland for singer-songwriters who had attended the week-long songwriting courses at Martyn Wyndham-Read's home in France, where Vin was a tutor in the early 2000s. Paula Ryan, a singer-songwriter from York, was all set to perform, with Vin in the audience. In front of Paula was her marimba, her percussion instrument, her version being an enclosed wooden box resembling a small coffin. The hall went silent and just as Paula was about to speak, Vin stood up and said: 'Before Paula starts, can we have a minute's silence for the dead ferret?' Timing immaculate, humour spontaneous and hilarious.
John Storey

Nick Fenwick and I were at the Campbells' folk club in Birmingham. Vin was the guest and he and Pete Betts were staying with Nick. At the end of Vin's performance there was a thunderous chorus of approval from the audience. Ian Campbell, in Old Testament mode, raised his arms and eyes imploringly to the ceiling as if expecting divine intervention and said, 'What is it that this man has?' From the back of the room a voice cried out, 'Talent!'
Ed Pickford

I'm a friend of Vin's daughter Emma, known to all her friends as Gabby. We spent a year in Hertfordshire during a musical theatre degree, where it was clear to all that Gabby has inherited Vin's wonderful talent for songwriting, being a natural lyricist and playing the tin whistle to a master standard. Gabby and I later joined forces to work in a touring singing group and write a musical together as a composer and lyricist. Along with Gabby and my partner, Davyd, we had the amazing experience of seeing Vin live in concert at Hitchin Folk Club in Hertfordshire. We were mesmerised by his set, cried at his wonderful song *John You Have Gone*, about his late friend. We also experienced Gabby joining him on stage in a tin whistle duet, with a mesmerising rapport of playing in harmony, improvising and stunning the audience with a captivating dad-daughter musical connection that could not be matched elsewhere. One of my greatest honours was being chosen to sing at Vin's daughter's wedding accompanied by Vin's son, Tim, on the guitar.
Wesley Strahan-Hughes

At one charity concert at Farnsfield, Notts, Vin was asked to draw the raffle. He took the bucket full of tickets, thrust in his hand, withdrew a large bunch of tickets and threw them in the air, before declaring, 'They're not winners!' Then he did the same thing twice more. He did eventually draw the raffle properly, but by this time the floor was covered with tickets and the audience were rolling with laughter.
Diana and Shaun Power

I first saw Vin at the Woodman Folk Club in Kingswinford around 1995. I remember his often-stated aversion to 'Chris Peters' in the audience. One time at Burntwood Folk Festival some glasses were dropped behind the bar, making a very loud crash. Vin asked, 'Could that chap put his glass eye back in?' Another time at the Woodman he was taking some time to tune his guitar and was asked, 'Do you want a tuner?' Vin replied, 'No thanks, I hate fish.'
Paul Bedingfield

Vin's songs, with such meaning, will always be there
His voice reaching out, showing his love and care,
A theme hit hard and rested in his mind
And with pen in hand, the words he would find
Then the tune, sometimes haunting, would reach the heart

Enough very often, for the tears to start;
So many fans and friends have stories to tell
He was always kind and knew them well,
He travelled the world, made good friends there too
Relaxed in anyone's home and glad to do
Something special for some folk, the joy he would bring
Like for our ill son, he came to sing...
Our memories of that day will never go,
There must be many others too, who will also know
Of his love and generosity, as he travelled around
Then finding quality time for his family, love so sound;
So many songs over the years
So many stories, the laughter and beers,
We thank you, Vin, for bringing us much pleasure
Your music and banter, we will always treasure,
We raise a glass as we listen once again
And with sadness say, 'All the Very Best', the old refrain.
Chris Key

After a concert in the Yarra Valley of Victoria, Australia, on St Patrick's Day in 2013, we took Vin and Pat for a short drive to a secluded and beautiful small section of rainforest named Wirrawilla, up in Toolangi. The myrtle beeches are host to many ferns and mosses and the bubbling creek beneath the boardwalk constructed to protect the forest floor is home to platypus and other creatures. The forest is always filled with the sound of birds and each visit shows something new, depending on the way the sunlight filters through the canopy overhead. After walking slowly through this exquisite rain forest, Vin asked if we'd mind if he played his whistle. He pulled it out and began to play. The magic of that tune, played in just this spot, will remain with me for the rest of my life.
Cecilia Sharpley, Healesville, Victoria, Australia

We were involved with organising the Hong Kong Folk Society and Festival and Vin came out many times. About ten of us went to a restaurant with Vin in Sai Kung, a fishing village where we lived. On seeing the Chinese writing on the noticeboard at the back of the restaurant, Vin said, 'Oh look – it says, 'Sorry, all Vin Garbutt CDs sold out!''
Patty and Jim O'Boyle, Durham City

As well as Vin writing *Lynda* about my Auntie Joan, here's another coincidence. I met Vin's mam and dad before I met Vin. It was in late 1999 and I was making my film *A Century in Stone,* about Teesside's iron and steel origins. I was interviewing the very last of Eston's ironstone miners. They were all well into their eighties and nineties and one of them told me to go and see a bloke just down the road called Alf Garbutt, as he had also worked in the pit. So I walked straight down and knocked on the door of 32 Ambrose. This little old lady answered. I explained what I was doing and she invited me in and Alf was sitting there in his chair. He told me he was suffering with his back from a pit accident when he was a young man. It turned out he was a horse driver in Eston pit back in the 1930s. Now these weren't ponies like in coal mines but Clydesdales and Cleveland Bays, big heavy horses capable of pulling tons and tons of ironstone. Alf told me he decided one day to ride one of them in the pit to save time. It wasn't allowed and it geed up and bashed his back against a low ceiling. I'd been listening to his tale for quite a while before I caught a glimpse of a picture frame on the wall. It was of the two of them with that folk singer, Vin Garbutt. Then the penny dropped, it was Vin's mam and dad! So Vin and me really did seem destined to cross paths eventually and when we did, it seemed virtually from the off that we'd known each other for years.

I made the film about Vin because he and his story were uniquely precious. I'm so glad I did because I didn't expect it to become so precious so soon. And the same goes for this book. In the nick of time. Nice one, Mick!

Craig Hornby

Valley of Tees
VIN GARBUTT

THE YOUNG
TIN WHISTLE
PEST
VIN GARBUTT

KING GOODEN
VIN GARBUTT

ESTON AND CALIFORNIA
SOCIAL CLUB
Vin Garbutt
Eston California

VIN GARBUTT

VIN GARBUTT
LITTLE INNOCENTS

VIN GARBUTT
LIVE IN AUSSIE
SHY TOT POMMY

VIN GARBUTT
WHEN THE TIDE TURNS

VIN GARBUTT
BY-PASS SYNDROME

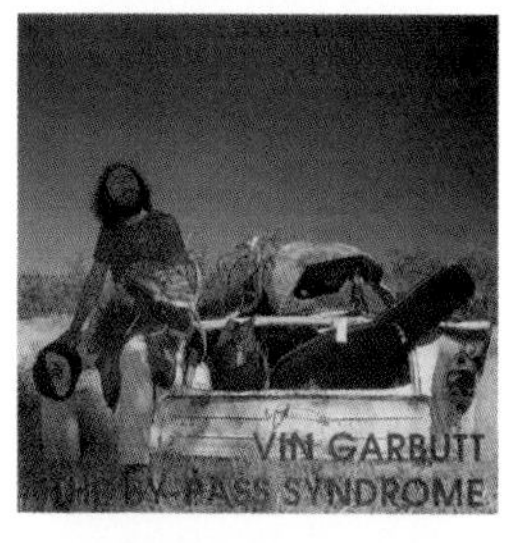
VIN GARBUTT
BY-PASS SYNDROME

Plugged!

the
Vin Garbutt
SongBook
volume one

VIN GARBUTT
PERSONA...GRATA

Synthetic
Hues
Vin
Garbutt

CATALOGUE

The Valley of Tees	1972
The Young Tin Whistle Pest	1974
King Gooden	1976
Eston California	1977
Tossin' a Wobbler	1978
Little Innocents	1983
Shy Tot Pommy	1985
When the Tide Turns	1989
The By-Pass Syndrome	1991
Bandalised	1994
Plugged!	1995
When the Tide Turns Again	1998 (reissue of 1989 album)
Word of Mouth	1999
The Vin Garbutt Songbook: Vol 1	2003
Persona ... Grata	2005
Teesside Troubadour	2010 (documentary feature film)
Synthetic Hues	2014
All the Very Best!	2021 (autobiography)

www.vingarbutt.com

Keep up to date with new editions and releases from McGeary Media by visiting themem oirman.com or emailing thememoirman@gmail.com.

With thanks to all who supported this special limited edition in Vin's memory

Ian Abell
Shaun Able
Billy Adamson
Derek Agar
Steve Agar
David Aiken
Gill and John Akers
Keith Albans
Graeme Aldous
Dave Allan
John Allcoat
Frank Allen
Ken Allinson
Patrick Ambrose
Bill Angus
Paul Appleton
Paul Archer
Ian W Armstrong
Marilyn Ashton, née Dawson
Stuart and Karen Askham
Linda and Malcolm Atkins
Assie Aukes
George Bacon
Anne and Alan Bailey
Howard Bailey
Leigh and Sarah Baker
Justine Balfour
Ed Bancroft
Jenny Bancroft
Martin Banks
Jenny Bannister
Andrew Barber
Lara Barnes
Stevie and Joan Barnes
John Barry
Peter Barry
Alan Bartlett
Marc Bartram
Adrian Bass
Nigel Bassett
David Batchelor
Pete Bateman
Chris Bates
Kate Battersby
Arthur Beadle
Stuart and Gill Beadle
Paul Beales
June Beasley
Daz Beatson
Jacey Bedford
Chris and Dave Beeby
Craig Beeby
John Beeching
Paul Wise
Jon Benns
Faith Betts
Fran Biggs
Barry Bilclough
Paul Billings
Michael Billington
Jack Robert Birch
Marian Bird
Jane Birkitt
Kevin 'Poppy' Birkitt
Peter Bishop
Mick Bisiker
Peter and Kath Biswell
Iain Black
Black Pebble Media
Mike Blackburn
Cecilia Blaney
John Blanks
Paul Blaylock
Dave Blenkinsop
Stephen Bloundele
Evie Bluel
Penni Blythe
Adrian Boddy
Ian Bolton
AJ Booth
David Booth
Paul Boshell
Richard and Kim Bouchier
John Bowe
Chrissy Boxall
Russell and Deirdre Boyd
Geoffrey Boyle
Elaine and Sam Bracken
Bob Bradbury
Keith Bradbury
John Bradley
Ada Brass
Sandy Brechin
Thomas Martin Brennan
Gill Brice
Jenny Brooker
Dave Brookes
Andrew Brotherston
Dave Brown
Malcolm Brown
Ron Brown
Peter J Browne
Shaun Browne
Ian H Bruce
Marian Bruce
David Bryan
John Bryden
Roger and Moira Bucknall
Adrian Budd
Peter and Annie Bugden
Lorraine Bullman
Adam Burke
Michael Burns
John Burrell
Chris Burrows
Anthony Butler
James Callaghan
Dave Callicott
Mik Calvert
John D Campbell
Alan Carder
Herbert Carman
Jeffery Carman
Laura Marie Carman
Robert Carman
Ronald Richard Carman
Pete and Jenny Carpenter
Tricia Carr
Phil Carter
Rachel Cartwright
Ian and Jan Casserly
Clare and Allan Castro
Mike Chapman
Trevor, Audra, Ryan and Natalie Chapman
Trevor Charnock
Josie Childs
John S Christie
Janet Clark, née Tansley
John and Sue Clasper
John Clasper

Wendy and Peter Clayton
Glenn and Yvonne Coggin
Kev Collier
Chris Collins
Mike Collins
Rita Collins
Brendan Conway
Mary and Richard Cook
Bridie, Joel, Jessie and Rowan Coombes
Neil Cooper
Richard Coopey
John Cordey
Ann and Danny Corey
Len Corns
Mike and Rita Corrigan
Steve Coverdale
Eric Cox
Roger Cox (1947–2016)
Hugh and Julie Crabtree and family
John Scott Cree
Martyn Cresswell
Marcus and Margaret Croft
Philip Croft
Marcus Crompton (aka Marcus Atan)
Martyn and Gini Crompton
Tom Culpin
Jean Cusic
Tom Cusic
Heather Dale
Denis Dales
Tom Daley
Carole Dally
Dawn Dalrymple
Meg Daly
Maura Ann Dasey
Joe and Ann Davidson
Margaret Davidson
John Howell Davies
Pat Davies
Pete and Doreen Davies
Father Pat Day
Michael Day
Ron Day
Elaine De Gregorio
The De Souza family
John Dent
Bernard Dermott
David Derricott
Malcolm Devereux
Kerry Devine
Will and Maggie Devine
Martin Dewick
Frank Dewings
Michael Dewison
Hugh Diamond
Lisa Didier-Carter
John and Edith Diggles
David Dixon
Ian Dixon
Raylton Dixon
Barbara Dobby
Denis Docherty
Denis Patrick Docherty
Ed Lawrence and Sam Dodds
Kate Dodds
Dogfinger Steve
Mike Doran
Annie Dorgan
Maggie and Paul Dorsman
Doug
Sandra Duffy
Sue Duffy
Chris Duggan
Nick Duggan
Tony Duggan
Tony Dunbar
Pete Dunk
John Dunleavy
George Dunn
Marlene Dunn
Denis Dunning
Margaret Dunsire
Susan Durkin
Alison Dyer
Tom Easterling
Eddie
Steve Edge and Margaret Whale
Ian Edwards
Paul Edwards
True Family Edwards
Val and Trev Edwards
Elaine
Martin Eldon
Lynda Rose Elliott
David Elrick
Kathy Elvin
Beryl Anderson
Joseph Esme
Bill Evans
Clem Evans
Clement Evans
David Evans
Martin Evans
Mick and Jenny Evans
Mike Evans
Margaret and Bob Fagan
John and Sally Faisandier
Paul Farrer
Micheal Farrow
George Featherston
Anne Feeney and Malcolm Heyes
Jim and Isabelle Fell
Mick Fellows
Mary Felton
Vin Felton
Denise Fenwick
Captain Iain Ferguson Gilmour
Jim Ferguson
Duncan and Bridget Ferns
Felicity Finch
Peter Finch
David Finn
Dom Finn
Paul and Melanie Fisher
Tony and Sarah Fisher
Dave Fitches
Fritz Fitton
Edmund Flach
John Flattley
Doreen Fleming
Ged Fleming
Tony Fleming
Craig Fletcher
Henk and Sjaan Fontaine
Eric Ford
David Forden
Dave, Jean and Matthew Foreman
Linda Fornal
Ellen and Mike Forrest
Maureen Forrest
Alex Fowler
Sandie Fowler
Jim Fox
Joyce Fox
Tony Fox
Ian and Elaine Francis
Eric Freeman
Ray Freeman
Allan Frewin
Pauline Friend
Dave Frost
Alex Gallacher
Dean Gallacher
Denis Gallilee
Louis Garbutt
Mike and Mary Garbutt
Ralph Garbutt

Theodore Garbutt
Tim and Sarah-Jo Garbutt
Indigo Garbutt-Price
Katie and Alex Garbutt-Price
Luna Garbutt-Price
David Gawthrope
Keith Gays
Maggie Gee
Stevie Geoghegan
Angela and Ray Georgeson
Ian Gerrard
Alan Gibson
Janet Gibson
Derek (Giff) Gifford
Sue Gill (Nana)
Herman Gilligan
Andy and Jane Gilliland
Peter and Kathleen Gilliland
Jackie Gitsham
Chris Gledhill
Chris Gleed-Owen
Ian Gobbi
Ged Golden
Steve Goldsack
Steve Goodchild
Albert David Gordon
Jody and Damian Gough
Julie and John Graham
Matt Grant
Carolyn Gray
Stewart Green
Paul Griffiths
Sue Griffiths
Dennis and Lorraine Grogan
David Guest
The Guillorys
Jane Guinery
John Guy
Lyn Guy
Ian and Pat Haley
Mick Hall
Peter Hall
Tim Halliday
Michael Hamilton
James Hammill
Gerard Hampson
Jack Hancock
Keith Hancock
Sam Hancock
Rachel Hand
Stu and Debs Hanna
Gerald Hannon
Martin and Annette Harold
David Harris
Keith Harris
Mike Harrison
Scott Harrow
Paul Hart
Paul M Hart
Michael Harvey
Jon Harvison
Gill and John Haveron
Carol Haynes and Liz Sowter
George Hegarty
Alan Helm
Alan Henderson
Colin Henderson
Dave Henderson
Jack Henderson
Mike Henderson (Stowsler)
Nick Henderson
James and Sarah Hennessey
Neil Hewitt
Pete and Heather Heywood
Terry Higgins
Brian Highley
Christine Hill
Peter George Hill
Graham and Lesley Hodge
Bob and Gina Hodges
Judi Hodgson
Tony Holden
Howard Holdsworth
Ellie Homer
Dave and Jill Hood
Pat Hood
Caroline Hopkins
Craig Hornby
Tony and Jo Hornby
Tony Hornby
Ashley Horsfall
The Howard Family
Tony and Jane Howard
Emma Howells
Evie Howells
Fleur Howells
Zachariah Howells
Andy Howes
Ian Hoy
Nic Hoy
Keith Hudson
Joanne Hughes
Marshall Hughes
Keith Humphreys
Glenn Hunter
Kevin and Carole Hunter
Rob and Liz Huntley
Marina Hurley
Clive Hutchison
Ian and Wendy
David Illingworth
Trevor Ingham
Alan Ingledew
Keith Irwin
Julia Ismay
Brian Jackson
David James
Jane Jarratt
Pete Jennings
Joe and Sam
Eric Johansen
Steve Johns
Bernadette Johnson
Jane Johnson
Rob Johnson
Graham Johnston
Gavin Joines
Jon The Trucker
Clive and Moira Jones
David Paul Jones
Dianne Jones
Ian Jones
Mark Jones
Sheila and Stephen Jones
Sue Jones
Roger Joseph
James Christopher Joyce
Marisa Kaleem
Jill and Gavin Kane
Kate and Ando
Father Tony Keefe
Graeme Keenan
Jimmy Kelly
Paul Kelly
Roy Kelly
Steven Kelly
Chris Kendall
Cecilia Kennedy
Glenys Kennedy
Barbara King
Brenda and Brian King
Julia King
Simon RJ King
Stephen King
William King
Tony Kingsbury
Linda Kirtley
Cheryth Knight
Sue and Adam Kruczynski
Dave and Sue Lawrence
Martin Lawrence
Chris Laydon

George Layfield
Kevin and Hazel Leavesley
Caroline Lee
Ken Lee
Brendan Leeson
Jeremy Leigh
Brian Leng
Barb Leonard
Tony Leonard
Harry and Kath Levey
Edward Le-Vine
Geoff Lewis
Iain Lewis
Mike Lewis
Derek Leyland
Lenny Liddell
Graham Liggitt
Lindsay and Greg
Barbara Lister
Dave Littlehales
Gordon and Jackie Littlejohn
Joanne and Ian Littler
Andrew Lombard
Mary Lombard
Chris Loughran
Jez Lowe
Alan Lowey
Gill and Peter Ludlam
Dave MacEachern
Peter MacFarlane
Ed and Laura-Jane Macholc
Eddie Mack
Alex Mackie
David Mackin and Family
Paddy Mackin
Ken and Gill Maggs
Tony Maher
Jack and Maggie Major
Ellen Malin
Tony Malone
Colin Marchment
Ken and Sue Marr
Geoff Marron
Alice Martin
Michael J Martin
Kevin Matthews
Lester and Harold Matthews
Anne Maxwell
Bob May
Brian May
Barbra Mayer
Paul and Marie-Therese Mayne
Pete McCarthy
Trev McCarthy
Michael McDonagh
Eddie McDonnell
Eugene "Macca" McElvaney
Paddy McEvoy
Duncan (Isbiscuits) McFarlane
Anne McGeary Carvell
Barbara McGeary
Benedict McGeary
Brendan McGeary
Damian McGeary
Eila McGeary
Lyndsey McGeary
Pat McGeary
Patrick McGeary
Judy Mcgloin
Phil McGloin
Malcolm McGregor
Mike McGrother
Anne McGurn
Pamela McIvor
Simon McKeown
Gillian McKillop
Jim McLaren
Kevin and Laura McLean
Martin McLeman
Allan McMillan
Stuart and Ellen McNeill
Edwardo Mcnulty
Gill McPhee
Jim McPhee (1936–2014)
Neil McRitchie
Blind Willie McThomson
Joe Meagher
David Medcalf
Graham Metcalfe
Miggs
John Miller
Margaret Miller
Mike Miller
Phil Millichip
Paul Millington
Chris Milner
Marion Milton
Andy Mitchell
Colin and Jill Mitchell
Mike and Carole Mitchell
Pat Mock
David Monks
Judy Moody
Liz and Alan Moody
Brian Moore
Craig Moore
Barry J Moorhouse
David Morgan
Frank Morley
Joan Morley
Laura Morley
Kevin and Wendy Morris
David Morrison
Margaret Morrison
Sue Moyers
Margaret Munro
Paul Munster
Peter Murphy
Rosemary Murphy
Vincent Murphy
Chris Murray
Phil Murray
Steve Murrell
Ken Myddelton
Luke Myer
Phil Myers
Ruth Myers
Andy Nagy
Gerald Napier
Tom Napper
Jan Nary and Gary Rankin
Andrew Nash
Gloria and Jim Neale
Margaret Nertney
Sheila Nesbitt (Gallagher)
John and Diane Nichol
Lynne Nicholls
Paul, Jenny, Sam and Toby Nicholson
Bob Nielsen
Tania Nolan
David Normanton
Michael Noteyoung
Anne Nuttall
Angela O'Brien
Bill O'Brien
Dougie Ollett
Mark O'Neill Revie
Paul O'Neill
Vicky Openshaw
Chris Osborne
Edward Owen
Tom Owens
Jim Oyston
Liz Padgett
Chris and Emma Padmore
Jacky Paffard
Alan Paling
Anne Pallett
Vilma and Steve Parmley
Kim Parnaby
Barry Parnell

Annie Parsons
Geoff Paterson
Pat Patrick
Maggie Pattinson
Andrew and Heather Pattison
Sue Pattison
Lis Payne
David Pear
Mick Pearce
Kevin Pegden
Laurie Pelmear
Margeret Perkins
Bryn Phillips
Pete Philp
Chris Piercy
Chris Pinkney
Peter Pinkney
Bob Pitt
Barbara Ann Pixton
Dave Plimmer
Stephen Podger
Mike Clayton and Emma Porter
Stephen Powney
Phil Preston
Steve Price
Jane Hendey Pritchett
Karin Pronk
Sue and Ken Punshon
Dave Purvis
Mark Quinn
Jeremiah Randall
Tony Ransom
Carl Reader
John and Alison Reader
Geoff and Anne Readman
John Reed
Reeniola
Hans Reusen
Glenda Reynolds
Steve Reynolds
Larisa and Tony Rice
John and Fiona Richardson
Alan Richens
John Richens
Michael and Sheila Richens
Simon Rinaldi
Duncan Rippon
Richard Rivett
Rob and Josee
John and Joan Roberts
John Roberts
Martin and Penny Robertson
Audrey M Robinson
Diane Robinson
Ken Robinson
The Robinson Family
Deborah Robson
Stephen Robson
Geoff Rodgers
Jonathan Rogers
Elizabeth Rolley
Jim and Becky Rolley
Sue Rotheram
Doc Rowe and Jill Pidd
Eddie Russell
Mollie Russell
Sue and Tony Ryder
Peter Rynn
Bill Sables
Annette Sandrawich
Chris Sandrawich
Pete and Brenda Sargieson
Garry Savage
Ron Sawyer
Leigh Sayers
Derek Schofield
Antony Brian Scott
Michael Selby
Jeni Sandercott
Robin Sermon
Ian Sanderson
Matthew Setchfield
Bob Sharp
Marion and Richard Shaw
The Shea Family
Andy and Jacquie Shearman
Peter J Shearon
John Shiels
Dave Shorten (1953–2018)
Mike Simmons
Wendy Ann Simon
Harry Simpson
Margaret Simpson
Rob Skidmore
Isaac Christopher Skilbeck
Danny Skipper
John and Christine Slattery
Howard Smeeton
Andrew Smith
Gerry Smith
Ian D Smith
Jimmy Smith
Kris and Gerry Smith
Rosie Smith
Sandy Smith
Tony Smyth
Sue and Jim Soutar
South Bank Girl x
Tony Spackman
Alan Spence
Canon Robert Spence
Norman Springthorpe
Diane Stack and Peter Hawksworth
Alfred George Stallard (age five)
Frank Stamp
Bob Stanton
Gordon and Glenda Steel
Paul Steiner
Ann Stephenson
Anna Stewardson
Kristen Stewart
Alexandra Stickels
Peter Stickels
Marjorie Stirk
Ray Stirling
Syd, Rick and Scott Stirling
Neil Stobbart
Brian Stockton
Peter Stockton
John Stockwell
Peter Stoddart
George N Stoker
Maureen and Peter Sugden
Kev and Joyce Suggitt
Barry Swan
Joy Bachman Swift
Becky Taylor
David Taylor
Gordon Taylor
Hugh Taylor
Julie Taylor
Mau Taylor
Philip John Taylor
Ricky Taylor
Chris Tearney
Dave Tearney
Ronnie and Julia Templeman
Ian Tewson
Bob and Liz Thomas
Ian (Tich) Thomas
Michael Thomas
Andrew Thompson
Graeme Thompson
Terry and Liz Thompson
Tommy Thompson
Nils Thorlund
Patrick Tiernan
Sylvia Tiffney
Robert Till
Eileen and John Tilley
Keith Tillotson